BLACK SHEEP
AND
KISSING COUSINS

BLACK SHEEP
AND
KISSING COUSINS

HOW OUR FAMILY STORIES SHAPE US

ELIZABETH STONE

Times
BOOKS

Design by Blackpool Design

Library of Congress Cataloging-in-Publication Data
Stone, Elizabeth, 1946–
Black sheep and kissing cousins.
Bibliography: p.
1. Family.   2. Storytelling.   I. Title.
HQ503.S76   1988   306.8′5   87-40582
ISBN 0-812-91255-1

Manufactured in the United States of America

9 8 7 6 5 4 3 2

First Edition

For my mother, Aurora B. Stone,
and in memory of my grandmother—
in Sicily, Annunziata Bongiorno, here, Nancy Bonney

ACKNOWLEDGMENTS

I could not have done this book alone. First and foremost, I want to thank the hundred or so people who agreed to be interviewed for it. I am grateful to them for their time, their insight, their generosity, and their reflectiveness. For some people, telling their family stories was pleasurable, for others painful. For all of them, it seemed significant, persuading me that a book on the subject of family stories should be written. Because those who shared their stories appear pseudonymously in the following pages, I cannot thank them by name, but I can—and do—thank them deeply.

Second, I want to thank those who took valuable time from their own lives to scout for people for me to interview in their part of the country and took care of me while I was there. In Houston, it was Cynthia Macdonald; in Chicago, Lois Baum and Christine Vogel; in West Virginia and Pennsylvania, Maggie Anderson, Anna French, and Devon McNamara; in Boston, Ellen Cantarow.

Others were also very generous in helping me connect with people I would never otherwise have gotten to. My thanks, therefore, to Louise Bernikow, Paula Clendenin, Tom Collins, Helen Epstein, Sherry Huber, Margo Jefferson, Anne Kostick, Freda Bein Muldoon, and Judith Stitzel.

I also want to thank the members of my own family with whom I compared notes about the stories we knew in common, though the versions were not always identical: my mother, Aurora Stone; my sister, Virginia Jerome; and my cousins, Marion

Castellucci, Larry Olivo, and Christine Vogel. My thanks, too, to those who read sections of this book, sometimes many times over, and were generous and helpful in their suggestions. I am especially grateful to Tom Anselmo, Ann Banks, Louise Bernikow, Ellen Cantarow, David Finkle, Joy Harris, Margaret Lamb, Cynthia Macdonald, Alan Mandell, Devon McNamara, Carol Sternhell, Aurora Stone, Deborah Tannen, and Christine Vogel. For enormous help in research, I thank Anne Finnan of Fordham University's College at Lincoln Center Library. My deep and affectionate thanks go to my editor, Elisabeth Scharlatt, who championed this book from the very beginning.

A special and separate thanks to my husband, Reamy Jansen, who generously read this book in various drafts many many times over, who made valuable suggestions, who was unfailingly encouraging, and who took over far more than his fair share of our joint responsibilities so that I could get this book done. He is the subject of some especially flattering family stories I tell to our children, Paul and Gabriel.

CONTENTS

INTRODUCTION   3

PART I · FAMILY STORIES AND THE FAMILY

CHAPTER 1 · FAMILY GROUND RULES   15
CHAPTER 2 · FAMILY DEFINITIONS   32
CHAPTER 3 · FAMILY MONUMENTS   48
CHAPTER 4 · UNDERGROUND RULES   75
CHAPTER 5 · FAMILY MYTHS   96

PART II · FAMILY STORIES AND THE WORLD

CHAPTER 6 · THE PECKING ORDER AND
            HOW TO SURVIVE IT   111
CHAPTER 7 · OF MONEY, SELF-WORTH,
            AND LOST FORTUNES   146

PART III · FAMILY STORIES AND THE INDIVIDUAL

CHAPTER 8 · LEGACIES   165
CHAPTER 9 · FAIRY GODMOTHERS AND PATRON SAINTS   196
CHAPTER 10 · IN PURSUIT OF FREEDOM   220

NOTES   245

BLACK SHEEP
AND
KISSING COUSINS

INTRODUCTION

The storyteller takes what he tells from experience—his own or that reported by others. And he in turn makes it the experience of those who are listening to his tale.
                                        —WALTER BENJAMIN,
                                        "THE STORYTELLER,"
                                        IN *Illuminations*

I n the beginning, as far back in my family as anyone could go, was my great-grandmother, and her name was Annunziata. In the next generation, it would be my grandmother's first name. In the generation after that, in its anglicized form, Nancy, it would be my aunt's first name and my mother's middle name, and in the generation after that, my sister's middle name as well. I never met that first Annunziata, but my mother often told me a family story about her which, as a child, I knew as well as I knew the story of Cinderella and loved better.

Annunziata was the daughter of a rich landowner in Messina, Sicily, so the story went, and she fell in love with the town postman, a poor but talented man, able to play any musical instrument he laid eyes on. Her father heard about this romance and forbade them to see each other. So in the middle of one night—and then came the line I always waited for with a thrill of pleasure—she ran off with him in her shift.

I didn't know what a shift was and didn't want my settled version of the story disrupted by any new information. I loved the scene as I saw it: in the background was a house with a telltale ladder leaning against the second-story window. In the foreground was my great-grandmother, like some pre-Raphaelite

3

maiden, dressed in a garment white and diaphanous and flowing, holding the hand of her beloved as she ran through a field at dawn, toward her future, toward me.

As a child, I was on very close terms with that story. I loved and admired my family—my grandmother especially—and as I saw it, her mother had been the start of us all. I never thought about any of my other great-grandparents or who they were. My grandfather, my mother's father, had died long before I was born; so I didn't think about him in any way that would bring him or his parents to life for me. As for my father, his parents had come from Austria, but he wasn't close to them, so I certainly wasn't. Nothing to build on there.

As a further refinement, I have to add that I paid absolutely no attention to the framed picture of my great-grandmother hanging over my grandmother's bed. That was just an old woman who, despite the fact that she happened to look like Sitting Bull, was of no interest to me. It was years before I realized that the person in the frame and the one in the story were the same. For me, it was always the stories that held the spirit and meaning of our family.

The first appeal of that story, then, was that it seemed to be the story of our genesis as a family. But there was a second appeal as well, and it was that my great-grandmother was everything I would have made her if I were inventing her. She was spunky, dazzlingly defiant, and, I was sure, beautiful. Later, when I understood more about class and money, I admired her for having chosen my poor but talented great-grandfather in the first place. She was principled and egalitarian, someone I wanted to be like, hoped maybe I already was a little like, and most important, felt I *could* be like. She wasn't distant like a film star or imaginary like a fairy-tale heroine. She was real. And she was my relative.

Other family stories stayed with me, too. Some were old and ancestral but some were new, about my mother's generation or mine. None was elaborately plotted; some relied only on a well-developed scene—like the one in which my great-grandfather and his half-dozen sons were playing music after dinner in the courtyard as people came "from miles around" to listen. And still others were simply characterizations of people—"you had one ancestor who was a court musician" or "you had another ancestor who was an aide to Garibaldi." These qualified as stories in the way haiku qualify as poems. Almost any bit of lore about a family member, living or dead, qualifies as a family story—as long as it's significant, as long as it has worked its way into the family canon to be told and retold.

These stories last not because they're entertaining, though they may be; they last because in ways large and small they matter. They provide the family with esteem because they often show family members in an attractive light or define the family in a flattering way. They also give messages and instructions; they offer blueprints and ideals; they issue warnings and prohibitions. And when they no longer serve, they disappear.

I first began to realize how much these stories mattered in my own family when I was doing an article on growing up Italian-American for *The New York Times Magazine*. My grandparents had both been immigrants who came here from Sicily near the turn of the century—my grandfather in the late 1880s, my grandmother in 1905. They could both read—my grandmother was eager to learn English and get a library card—but other than that there was nothing to distinguish them from the millions of Southern Italians who had come when they did. But their six children and their children's children hadn't turned out at all the way, demographically speaking, they might have been expected to.

It wasn't at all "typical" that one uncle would want to become a writer and would succeed at getting several of his novels published, nor that my mother would go on to Hunter College or end up playing in a Strindberg production on Broadway. All six of my grandparents' children read too much poetry, listened to too much opera, cared too much about getting rid of their Brooklyn accents and too little (with one exception) about improving their finances. My generation wasn't typical either—too many people with artistic inclinations, advanced degrees, and galloping exogamy.

When I tried to understand what had lured us off the demographic tack, the only thing I could find were our family stories. In the canon were the proud or inspirational or defiant stories my grandmother had told to her children (including the one about going to night school at the age of fifteen to learn English). Added to them were the stories that the children themselves, my aunts and uncles, had contributed over their lives. School stories, friendship stories, Sacco and Vanzetti stories, Depression stories, at-home stories, love stories, almost all of them nudging and pushing us in the direction of assimilation. A single surviving story about a long-dead pair of family cats named Abraham Lincoln and George Washington wouldn't have meant anything if it had not been surrounded (as it was) by a host of other stories that, all together, gave the big picture.

These stories seemed at once to sponsor and mirror our aspirations as a family. Taken in aggregate, they had a number of clear additional messages, discernible to us as members of the family. But I also noticed that our most idiosyncratic family conviction—that the arts are supremely important and certainly more important than money—was there even in that very first story, when my great-grandmother chose as her true love that talented but poor postman.

What struck me about my own family stories was first, how much under my skin they were; second, once my childhood was over, how little deliberate attention I ever paid to them; and third, how thoroughly invisible they were to anyone else. Going about my daily life, I certainly never told them aloud and never even alluded to them. Based on all visible signs, those who talk of weakening family ties could have concluded that family was not one of my major concerns and that wherever it was I had come from, I had left it far behind. But they would have been wrong, as wrong about me as they may be about others. Those who say that America is a land of rootless nomads who travel light, uninstructed by memory and family ties, have missed part of the evidence.

The family storytelling that has always gone on in my family goes on in families everywhere. Like me, people grow up and walk around with their stories under their skin, sometimes as weightless pleasures but sometimes painfully tattooed with them, as Maxine Hong Kingston felt she was in *The Woman Warrior*. This is what I've learned after interviewing more than a hundred people from a variety of regions, races, ethnicities, ages, and classes. Loosely, their experiences have been the same as mine. Though family storytelling happens casually and unreflectively, the realms family stories invariably enter into are predictable. The family is our first culture, and, like all cultures, it wants to make known its norms and mores. It does so through daily life, but it also does so through family stories which underscore, in a way invariably clear to its members, the essentials, like the unspoken and unadmitted family policy on marriage or illness. Or suicide. Or who the family saints and sinners are, or how much anger can be expressed and by whom.

Like all cultures, one of the family's first jobs is to persuade its members they're special, more wonderful than the neighboring barbarians. The persuasion consists of stories showing family members demonstrating admirable traits, which it claims are family traits. Attention to the stories' actual truth is never the family's most compelling consideration. Encouraging belief is. The family's survival depends on the shared sensibility of its members.

The family's first concern is itself, but its second realm of concern is its relation to the world. Family stories about the world are usually teaching stories, telling members still at home the ways of the world according to the experiences its elders have had. Often the news is not good—money is too important in the world, in all sorts of ways, and the family, almost any family, seems to have too little of it. They don't measure up. Or the family's racial or ethnic group doesn't afford them a comfortable place on the social ladder. Family stories convey the bad news, but they also offer coping strategies as well as stories that make everyone feel better.

Family stories seem to persist in importance even when people think of themselves individually, without regard to their familial roles. The particular human chain we're part of is central to our individual identity. Even if we loathe our families, in order to know ourselves, we seem to need to know about them, just as prologue. Not to know is to live with some of the disorientation and anxiety of the amnesiac.

How else can one explain the persistent need of many adopted children to know more about where they "really" come from? Something intangible and crucial is missing. To know themselves, they seem to need to know more of the collective family experience that predates their birth. They need their family stories.

All of us, long after we've left our original families, keep at least some of these stories with us, and they continue to matter, but sometimes in new ways. At moments of major life transitions, we may claim certain of our stories, take them over, shape them, reshape them, put our own stamp on them, make them part of us instead of making ourselves part of them. We are always in conversation with them, one way or another. The ancestral figures in them—especially grandparents or great-grandparents of the same sex as us—often become a major part of our imaginative life. They can, along with other powerful cultural archetypes, maybe from fiction or film, serve as our role models and guides.

I stumbled into the realm of family stories through my own fascination, but once I'd entered into it, I found that many others were already there. Writers, novelists, and playwrights have always known the power of family stories, how they stay with us, whether pointing out a course or functioning as a curse. Thomas Hardy's Jude Fawley knew through family stories that "the Fawleys were not made for wedlock." Charles Dickens's Mrs. Pocket, in *Great Expectations*, took to heart family stories she'd heard about her noble lineage, not to her family's advantage. More recent testimony to the power of family stories has been given by William Faulkner, Tennessee Williams, Toni Morrison, and Alice Walker.

As for nonfiction, one almost never reads a biography or autobiography without finding the writer relying on family stories to explain things. They're in Russell Baker's *Growing Up* and in Susan Cheever's *Home Before Dark*, in Lillian Hellman's *An*

Unfinished Woman and in Eudora Welty's *One Writer's Beginnings*, in Kate Simon's *Bronx Primitive* and in Peter Collier and David Horowitz's *The Kennedys: An American Drama*. And of course in Maxine Hong Kingston's *The Woman Warrior*. Family stories are revealing in ways that genealogies can never be.

My fascination with family stories is also shared by those in a variety of academic disciplines. Folklorists have long recognized them as a genre, part of the oral tradition, and have identified certain recurring themes, among them love stories and stories about lost fortunes. I have profited from their probing into the functions such stories might serve.

Among psychologists, Erik Erikson and Bruno Bettelheim looked at narratives in illuminating ways. And Carl Jung's awareness of what in our most ordinary midst is archetypal and part of collective memory enabled me to see more than I might have otherwise, particularly in terms of how we use our ancestral relatives as guides and models.

Among family therapists, who examine the family not as a collection of individuals but as a dynamic system, family stories are getting more notice. Clinicians don't call them family stories—they call them "myths" more often—and by dint of who comes their way, they most often find them notable for their pathological qualities. But family therapists are also aware how profoundly these swarms of narratives can affect what we see and therefore how we live.

Sociologists, too, have noticed family stories, at least in passing. Robert N. Bellah and his colleagues, in *Habits of the Heart: Individualism and Commitment in American Life*, posited the existence of what they called "a second language," the language and implied morality that comes from groups such as the family. Though it is, in public life, an inaudible language, it speaks deeply and persistently to us all, and so I would call the language of family stories a first language, a private language.

How early in a child's life does family storytelling start? Children love stories, so it's as early as a child understands language. How early do these stories make an impression? The youngest person to volunteer a family story to me was a three-year-old

friend of my older son's who had been told a story about his
mother when she was a little girl. I later checked with his mother:
his details were slightly off—her parents hadn't boarded the train
and left her behind in the train station, as her son had said;
she'd walked off the subway train, the doors closing before they
could stop her—but he'd gotten her sense of their neglect of her
entirely right.

This single instance corroborates what I believe is more widely
true: our families begin to tell us their stories early in our child-
hoods when we're as blank and unresisting as we're ever going
to be. Forever after, even when we repudiate, we're among the
devout believers, just as Voltaire surmised.

I didn't interview my son's friend. My one attempt at interviewing a child, an eight-year-old, was a failure; assessing the
impact of family stories doesn't happen till much later. But this
is the place to say how I proceeded with my interviews and why.

The assumption on which this book is based is that a family
has a shared sense of what its stories mean, or at the very least,
are supposed to mean. That collective understanding is exactly
what allows these stories to serve purposes other than enter-
tainment. My assumption was based on my experience with the
nuclear family of my birth, my extended family, and the family
I live in now with my husband and children. But in the course
of doing this book, I saw over and over that family stories have
collective meanings. I checked meanings with other members
of my own family; in other families as well I spoke to sets of
siblings, or parents and adult children. People's versions of things
weren't always identical but they were always compatible.

I might have done this book by getting myself invited to other
people's family gatherings and then just waiting for the stories
to come out. But even more than I wanted to hear family stories,
I wanted to know what they meant to the people who knew
them, and so one-to-one talks (and occasionally one-to-two)
worked best. I wanted the chance to compare notes and probe
and ask questions, and with this approach I could.

I interviewed friends, and friends of friends, and even friends
of friends of friends. An ad I placed in *The New York Times Book*

Review brought me many more people, as did notices placed on college and community center bulletin boards. While I welcomed all the people who came my way, I also made a deliberate effort to find as wide a cross section of Americans as I could: people as young as twenty-two and as old as ninety-two. I also wanted regional diversity, so in the course of my interviews I traveled to Chicago and Houston, to Boston and Appalachia. (Actually, traveling turned out to be relatively unnecessary since very few people seem to stay put. In Texas, I met a New Yorker; in New York, a West Virginian; in West Virginia, a Bostonian; in Boston, an Iowan; and in Chicago, a Texan.)

I also wanted as much ethnic and racial diversity as I could get. I interviewed Blacks and whites, Asian-Americans of Chinese and Japanese ancestry, and those with Native American antecedents. I tried to include as many ethnicities as I could: German, Italian, Puerto Rican, Spanish, WASP, Mexican, Danish, Swedish, Norwegian, German Jewish, Eastern European Jewish, Dutch, Hungarian, Irish, and Greek among them.

As for a correlation between the kinds of stories I heard and the home region or ethnicity of my teller: neither was as telling a factor as a family's tenure and status in this country. Those whose families had been here longest and had been the most prosperous tended toward a sunny worldview—the world was generous and individual initiative mattered deeply. Eastern European Jews, southern Europeans, and Blacks tended to posit a world which was less giving, even dangerous, and where individual initiative could be, and was, undermined by chance, oppressive authority, and even the weather.

But what distinguishes families from one another is not as remarkable as what makes them all alike—happy ones, of course, but unhappy ones, too. Families everywhere have their stories, many of them entertaining, all of them meaningful, pertinent, and binding.

01292 8112

PART·I

FAMILY STORIES AND THE FAMILY

Something nourishing starts going on as I'm telling you this story. I start to see a picture. Immediately I feel—and it's important for me to say this—I'm not just Dan Vernale who is here. I'm Dan Vernale who has this history. Even though I don't know the whole story, even though it's confusing, I know that I'm bigger than I am by having this background. I have many more people, I have a gang, I have a group, I have a family.

—DAN VERNALE,
NEW YORKER, 53

Conversations between family members are allegorical. Talking across stories, other things are being laid down. The facts of the story are just the vehicle.

—BEN RINDT,
CHICAGOAN, 53

We're extremely independent, all four of us—my mom from my dad, me from my parents, and my sister from my parents and me. I think that these stories, when we got together—I'm sure of this—were a way of reassuring ourselves that we were a family unit. In their telling, only people in the family would appreciate and laugh and carry on because they knew the staples involved. The experience of telling and listening was something only our family could do, so it was very important that we do it. Once they were told outside, they would just be kind of cute stories.

—B. C. HEINZ,
INDIANAN, 26

CHAPTER 1

FAMILY GROUND RULES

In 1890, my grandfather, Gaetano Bongiorno, came to New York from the Lipari Islands off the coast of Sicily. He was a young man of eighteen, serious and somewhat stolid, but also big and hardworking. Like many Southern Italian men of the time, he was a "bird of passage," a man who had come here to work so he could earn money for his family back home, rather than to settle down here. Over the years, he had a variety of jobs, among them piloting a barge and working as a longshoreman loading and unloading the ships that came into Brooklyn harbor. After work, he would go home to Union Street, where he lived with the two married sisters who had preceded him here. It was even cozier than that; Gaetano's two sisters had married two brothers and those brothers also happened to be their first cousins.

The years went by, and Gaetano showed no sign of returning to Italy or marrying and settling down here, either. By 1905 he was already thirty-three. One day in the mail, however, a letter came. Along with it was a photograph of his cousin Annunziata, the youngest sister of Gaetano's sisters' husbands.

Gaetano was taken with the photograph of this young woman, and as his sisters had been badgering him to marry, he decided

to try to arrange a marriage with her. And so Gaetano sailed to
Sicily, went to his uncle, Annunziata's father, and asked for
permission to marry her. My grandmother was agreeable to marrying Gaetano. She was fifteen. The idea of marriage seemed
very grown-up to her, and the prospect of coming to live in
America was exciting. Besides, my grandfather was tall and
redheaded, and his looks appealed to my grandmother. So the
betrothal was arranged and the marriage soon followed.

In 1905 my grandfather and his bride returned to Union Street
and his two sisters and two brothers-in-law, and there they *all*
lived until Gaetano and Annunziata could find a place on Union
Street of their own. And thus it was that two sisters and a brother
married two brothers and a sister and all lived right on top of
each other on Union Street in Brooklyn.

The story of how my grandparents had come to marry was
often told in my family, and what it said to me was that family
was so important that one should even try to marry within the
family. I remember at four or five having already decided which
of my male first cousins I would eventually marry. The whole
story, including my grandfather's Union Street living arrangements, also told me that the essential unit was the extended
family. The nuclear family—a couple and their children—tucked
itself into the larger unit.

While my conclusions about whom I ought to marry were
unwarranted, there was no doubt that the story implicitly laid
down other rules about what family members should do for each
other. The fact that my grandfather had lived with his two sisters
and their families for years on end was expressed without comment. There was nothing extraordinary about it, nothing even
especially laudatory. That was what family members did for each
other.

And yet this story could so easily have been told another way,
with another meaning. My grandmother was the youngest of
twelve children, almost all of whom had left Sicily in the hopes
of better prospects elsewhere. A few had come here, a few had
gone to Australia, and still others to South America. The story,
with a twist in tone, could have become a lament about the

Bongiorno diaspora, the disintegration of family. Perhaps the insistence on family unity and the belief in Bongiorno closeness was an implicit defense against—and emotional denial of—the fragmentation which had left my great-grandparents alone in one place while their children were scattered elsewhere around the world. But the facts of a family's past can be selectively fashioned into a story that can mean almost anything, whatever they most need it to mean. Homage to family unity was apparently what my family needed, and so that's the story the Brooklyn Bongiornos made for themselves out of selected bits of their collective experience.

By the time I was four or five I was convinced that the bulwark of family could protect me from death itself. There was a little boy my age named Vincent who lived next door to my East Fifth Street cousins. One hot August day, he had come to a family birthday party. Within a week of the birthday party, Vincent was dead of spinal meningitis. I remember that my aunts thereafter decided that only cousins could come to our birthday parties. Though everyone I asked remembered Vincent's death, no one else remembered my aunts' decision to close the birthday party ranks. Perhaps I invented it. Just a few weeks after Vincent died, I was hospitalized myself with polio and certainly needed to think that I could find in my family a magical protection. I was also sure that my full recovery was due to my aunt's novenas. In fact my gratitude went entirely to her and not at all to the doctors or to whomever she addressed in her prayers.

There is no doubt that we learn about the idea of family and how to be a member of a family from our families. Much of our instruction is mute: the experience of living in a family tells us what we can expect from relatives and what we owe them. But family stories are one of the cornerstones of family culture; they throw what may be mute and habitual into sharp relief. By their presence, they say what issues—from the most public and predictable to the most private and idiosyncratic—*really* concern a given family.

Family stories in fact are not just secondhand accounts of

someone else's experience. To the listeners, the stories can be experiences in themselves, and as such they exert a force and influence of their own, sometimes so that the listeners are quite conscious of what's going on, but usually more subliminally. But one thing is certain: given that a story is told in the context of family life, its meaning is circumscribed; when there are clusters of stories gnawing on a given theme, the meaning is more limited, even if no explicit gloss is ever given.

The family, of course, doesn't invent itself or its concerns but is sculpted by class, by the times, and by ethnicity as well as by the combination of individual personalities that comprise it. My family's conviction that the collective welfare of the family is more important than the goals of any one individual—which is the subtext of the story of my grandfather in America—may be unusual in American culture but is, or was, typical of Italian-American culture. There was once a study, done among schoolchildren of varying ethnic backgrounds, that asked whom they would share with if they were given a million dollars. The children named friends as well as charitable organizations as beneficiaries. It was only the Italian-Americans who distributed their hypothetical gift entirely within the family.

Family stories reach into even more private realms of experience to warn and instruct, however subliminally. They tell us about the decorum and protocol of family life—what we owe and to whom, what we can expect and from whom, in time or money or emotion. From the stories we hear, we learn matters of both substance and style.

HOME IS WHERE
WHEN YOU HAVE TO GO . . .

I want right at the outset to talk about an imbalance in family stories about the family. There is no lack of men in family stories at all. They appear plentifully—as returning soldiers or prosperous lens grinders or guileless immigrants, as errant schoolboys or black sheep or heroes who save the townspeople from drowning in the flood. But men do not feature prominently as family members acting in their familial role. And they often do not tell their own stories. Instead, their stories come down the generational pike riding sidesaddle, via their sisters, mothers, wives, or daughters.

Family stories—telling them and listening to them—belong more to the women's sphere. When I interviewed married couples, it was not unusual for the woman to know more of her husband's family stories than he did, usually because she'd heard them through her mother-in-law. In this way, despite the convention of patrilineality, the family is essentially a female institution: the lore of family and family culture itself—stories, rituals, traditions, icons, sayings—are preserved and promulgated primarily by women.

On a statistical level, women's prominence in the family is apparent. The number of female-headed families has grown dramatically in our time. In 1983, 5.7 million families were headed by women, which meant that 22 percent of all children were growing up with just one parent, usually the mother. The increase in such families is usually attributed to the increase in divorce, the American inclination to self-fulfillment at the price of commitment and self-sacrifice, and the greater number of women in the work force.

But it seems to me that men's hold on the family and the family's hold on men first began to be challenged with the beginning of the Industrial Revolution. Industrialization was responsible for creating the first widespread division between the public world and the world of home.

Men inherited the world, and when they came home they told stories of work and identified themselves essentially in that fashion, while women were left to keep the family going. Family stories, telling them and listening to them, grew out of the way people lived and to some extent still live. Family stories are often told in an almost ritual fashion, for instance at holiday family dinners, but they are also told incidentally, because someone says something that sparks someone else's memory in the course of daily living, while both are making the beds, cooking the meal, or folding the laundry, and these tasks remain essentially although not exclusively women's work. As a result, through the universe of family stories, we glimpse a world in which women play a more substantial role than men and come through far more untarnished. Thus family stories are the obverse of more public and codified cultural genres in which men invariably play the more dominant and flattering roles.

I didn't begin this research by thinking of family stories as a women's genre, but the men I interviewed first alerted me. Says twenty-six-year-old B. C. Heinz, who grew up in Indiana, "From everything I've studied or seen, I would expect the men to be the storytellers. In tribes, the *griots* who tell the family genealogy are always men, but that's not my experience. If I want family history, I go to the women. If I want to hear about the men, I still go to the women. It's my aunts who tell stories about my father. Never my father himself."

Ben Rindt, an Illinois businessman in his fifties, observed that in his family the storyteller was his great-uncle and almost all his stories were about men and their adventures—on the prairies, in the farmyard, in the stock market. After telling me a particularly dramatic story about his great-grandfather's experience in a wagon train attacked by Indians, he concluded that these were not really *family* stories at all. "If you only see men on a wagon train, that's an expedition, an adventure," Rindt mused. "But women are necessary to represent us as people. If women are there, it means families are there, and it means people are really suffering."

The first and cardinal rule of family life, as embodied in family stories, is that when people are *really* suffering, you can count on the family. Family stories about the Depression that exist in every American family survive not because they're dramatic (they're usually not) but because they're exemplary—the family's celebration of itself for coming through.

Then there's the matter of sickness, affliction, and death. As a nation, no matter how mobile we are and no matter how often we've heard that the family is defunct, we do seem to live with the legacy of the stories we've heard—that it's the responsibility of family to come to the aid of those in trouble.

In family stories, as in practice, the responsibility falls more heavily on the women, who probably are listening more closely anyhow. Whatever the details, the flavor of our narrative legacies is not very different now from what it was fifty years ago when Ma Joad in John Steinbeck's *Grapes of Wrath* took her aging mother on the road westward to California, ministering to her as she grew weaker and frailer and finally died.

The ideal of caring for aging parents is sufficiently strong that even the most undeserving aging parents can ride its coattails. Rowena Court, born and raised in Texas, tells a story about her grandmother and her great-grandfather that makes the point. "My great-grandfather," she begins, "abandoned his family when his kids were still young. He disappeared, and the family thought he was dead. One day when Nanny was about thirty years old, her father showed up at her front door. She was married and had kids of her own by then. She said, 'Who are you?' And he said, 'I'm your father, and I need some place to stay. I'm dying and I need someone to take care of me.' And she did. First she nursed him, and when he died, she buried him." Home is where, when you have to go there, they have to take you in.

Family stories such as this continue to exert a force on the way we live now. They establish the ideal that we depart from only at the price of our own guilt. Only 5 percent of the nation's elderly are in nursing homes. Even among the very old—eighty-five and over—77 percent remain outside institutions. For aging family members who live on their own, family bonds do seem to hold up. According to the National Institute on Aging, 80 percent of the elderly see "a close relative" every week. Equally consistent with the family stories, the emotional responsibility continues to fall on the women in the family, usually the daughters, but occasionally the daughters-in-law as well.

Such loyalty is by no means automatic or the inevitable consequence of propinquity. It's based on a deep stratum of belief which the family works unceasingly to instill. After all, it is rarely the case that unrelated people who spend enormous amounts of time together at work or in the neighborhood will continue the connection if their circumstances change.

Family members may have no more in common with each other than they do with neighbors or coworkers, so the fact that family members almost always keep their connections no matter what, means somebody's been doing something to make sure that these connections survive. It is a relationship supported by an idea that kinship matters profoundly.

Of all the family bonds that we expect to hold up under duress—mother or father to child, child to mother or father, sibling to sibling—the mother-child bond is, for reasons of both biology and social practice, the most invincible, the most mythic. Anthropologist Robin Fox believes the essential irreducible family unit is neither extended nor nuclear but just the pair of a mother and her child.

Indeed there is a "Pietà" genre of family stories involving a suffering child (usually a son) and a ministering mother that appears in family after family. In Irene Goldstein's story, the most striking motif is maternal sacrifice, and indeed a whole family's sacrifice, at a very very high cost. The mother is Irene's grandmother Irena, and the son is Kurtzie, her father's younger and slightly retarded brother.

> This is a big story, and it's about how my grandmother was basically the reason that my father's whole family didn't get out of Austria at the start of World War II. The story was that the whole family had gotten visas to go to Palestine in 1935—everyone, that is, except Kurtzie. They wouldn't give one to Kurtzie because he was retarded. My grandmother said if Kurtzie didn't go, she wasn't going, and as a result the entire family said that they weren't going. And so the whole family died. That's seven people—my grandmother, my grandfather, my father's oldest brother, his wife, my father's oldest brother's son, my father's fiancée, and Kurtzie. Only my father survived.

That story is certainly about loyalty, *blind* loyalty. I know that one of the things that was told to me was that my grandmother loved her retarded youngest son most of all and could not bear to leave him behind. In this story, my grandmother Irena also seems a totally mythical character, at least in the sense that she didn't seem to be in touch with the kinds of things that other mothers were in touch with like cooking or dirty diapers. What comes through is a totally idealized notion of the maternal, the maternal perhaps as envisaged by a Victorian. Loving, sacrificing. For my father, she was an ideal, and I think he tried to integrate some of what he imagined her qualities to be into himself.

What is so striking about Irene Goldstein's story is that it makes clear how willing family members are to sacrifice—or repress—their own point of view in favor of the collective familial point of view. Irene's father lost an entire family, a fiancée, and almost his own life because his mother was steadfastly loyal to her young retarded son. Somewhere he must have questioned whether it was worth it, somewhere he must have felt enraged at his own losses. It is inconceivable that this same scenario could have played itself out as it did with a group of unrelated individuals. But day by day and story by story, the family teaches us that such extremes of altruism and self-sacrifice are, if not customary, at least not astounding.

If the mutual bonds between mothers and children are the hardiest, then perhaps the most fragile are the ones between siblings, especially brothers, since they are often beset with both emotional reserve and rivalry. If there is any twosome in a family likely to drift apart, it is a pair of brothers.

And so the family stories that are meant to emphasize the extreme importance of family connections and coming through for one another often focus on brothers. The most common celebrates the ideal, those occasions when brothers under siege act as they ought to. From her mother, Jane Gilbert often heard the story of a long-dead ancestor who fought for the South during the Civil War.

His name was Hubert and he was a prisoner of war, or maybe he was just in a hospital, with his brother. Both of them were soldiers and both were wounded and put in the same bed. The brother died and Hubert spent two days lying in bed with the corpse of his brother. On the surface this is a horrible story, but it was never told as something to make you shudder or go ugh. To me it had something to do with closeness and sticking with your family, even if they're not alive anymore. They told this story with a kind of pride, or strength—that they lay there in that bed and one of them was dead and one was alive. The way I always envisioned it was that the live one, Hubert, even though he was feverish, he didn't want anyone to know his brother was dead. He wanted to keep his brother with him.

The chafing part of family loyalty, of course, is that it often involves delaying or forsaking one's own individual wishes. In fact the tension between individual desire and collective weal is present in almost all realms of human life. The family, as an inherent partisan of the good-of-the-many, mostly offers stories in support of its own interest, though paradoxically these stories are told by the very individuals who may have had to subordinate themselves.

PROXIMITY

All families agree that when someone's life is on the line, the family has to do something, but in other realms there are more differences between one family and the next. What about how close to one another grown family members should live? As one man I interviewed put it, "One of the messages was 'Don't go too far.' "

What rules, however veiled, do other families have about such matters? Erik Erikson, in *Childhood and Society*, believes that in nineteenth-century American frontier families, the young, sons especially, had to be raised in a way that wouldn't keep them from pursuing their manifest destiny. Better, then, to have rather elastic family ties that wouldn't bind, because one way or another, the value of exploring, getting up and going, had to be instilled and take precedence over staying huddled together on the same acreage.

Margo Henson, a poet in her forties, is a New Yorker born and bred, but her interior life and her poetry are filled with her maternal ancestors, the Lugers, a prairie family such as Erikson had in mind. Small and pale, with thick, loosely plaited red hair and green eyes, she sits with me over lunch one day and talks these ancestors back to life. She speaks of their bombazine dresses and their fascinators so intimately that one could almost imagine she herself had worn them just yesterday.

The issue of sons moving on is very much a theme in her stories, and its urgency, especially as it relates to the economic survival of the nuclear family, comes through strongly in the first story she tells.

My mother's family were the Lugers. A bunch of the Luger boys came from somewhere outside Vienna, where they already had a furniture store, to Minneapolis to start another one. The other brothers all had boys but my great-grandmother proceeded to produce six girls—Anne, Olivia, Clare, Julia, Amelia, and Elizabeth—before she got to the two boys, Peter and Ferd. So then my great-grandmother said to her husband, "What is going to happen to our girls? When we die, what is going to happen? Your brothers have nothing but boys. Are they going to take care of our girls, because our girls can't work in the store. We have to do something!"

What they did was to pack the whole family into the back of the Conestoga wagon, leaving the other Luger boys and their families behind, and to head across the Northwest Territory to Fargo, which was just a beginning town at the time. And they set up their own store. Somewhere along the line, they also lived in Wabash and in Reed's Settlement on the Mississippi.

It's clear that in the Henson scheme of things, family proximity, for the sons at least, is not a major value, and even more, that the nuclear family must take precedence over the extended family.

What about the daughters? Are they free to get up and go? The beginnings of an answer lie in two other "traveling" stories Margo Henson tells.

> These are both traveling stories. One is that my great-aunt, when she was three or four, decided to leave home. She made up her mind to run away and she just packed herself up and left. When she got to the edge of town, she found a little boy who was wandering around, not knowing what he wanted to do that day. So my aunt picked him up and the two of them went off across the prairie together. They weren't picked up till about five or six hours later. There's a newspaper photograph of the two of them that I have which is entitled "The Runaways."
>
> The other story is about another one of my great-aunts. This is when they were living on the Mississippi and my aunt was about ten. She had read about New Orleans and had been fascinated by it. And there she was living on the Mississippi River and knowing that New Orleans was at the end of it! It was winter and the Mississippi was frozen. So my aunt talked three friends into skating down the Mississippi to New Orleans. They took off and weren't discovered until rather late that night, very cold and extremely frightened on the banks of the Mississippi.

Are these just "cute" stories of failed and foiled runaway daughters? Margo Henson thinks not. "This is the matriarchy telling its own story. There were a lot of women in that family, and they all lived very constricted lives, especially because only two of my great-aunts married. They were better than middle class. My great-grandfather made quite a bit of money and raised his young women very well. They were all given artistic educations.

"Great-aunt Anne was the painter in the family and, so the story goes, wanted to go to Paris but was not allowed to.

She was quite a good painter, too. Maybe not brilliant, but well above the maidenly average in the 1800s. My great-aunt Clare played the harp. She was a redhead, too. She had a little harp, a traveling harp, and she always wanted to go to Ireland and travel around on the back of a cart and play in villages.

"Instead, they spent their lives working at the family store—Olivia was bookkeeper for near fifty goddamn years. The others did various things—taking stock, selling in the store. I felt they had these little cameo lives, but there was all of this enormous energy that never got used, that was waiting for some kind of release. I feel that very strongly."

So the initial family ground rule, which gave sons permission to move on but kept the daughters at home, thwarted, with nothing to look back on but childhood runaway foibles, became transformed so that the succeeding generations—Margo and her mother—would receive a very different instruction.

As Margo says, "I have a very strong feeling of imperative. My opportunities in life have this push behind me from these women who never had the chance. In fact I feel a responsibility to go and do what they had not done." And Margo Henson has acted on that "imperative" persistently. Every summer she sets off for somewhere, sending postcards the way Hansel scattered bread crumbs.

She has also drawn on the ground rule that one *must* get up and go when the issue is the economic well-being of the family. She married in her twenties and had one son. But when he was eight or nine, Margo and her husband divorced. For a while she taught writing in various New York City colleges, but in the late 1970s, when colleges were tightening their belts and reducing their faculty, the jobs dried up.

Since she had primary financial responsibility for her son, by then a senior in high school, she found a solution—an unconventional one, but one her great-aunts would probably have approved of. She found a live-in tenant to stay with her son in their brownstone in Brooklyn, and for herself she found a series of artist-in-residence positions at colleges around the country, six weeks here, six weeks there, a weekend at home in Brooklyn whenever possible.

In Rachel Kalber's family, the issue of how near family members must stay or how far they can go is also a vital one, and so the family has a small cluster of stories that huddle around the theme, worrying it and examining it.

The first story has to do with her father, a Russian Jew by birth, who, says Rachel, came from a long line of rabbinical scholars and teachers. Like his male antecedents before him, he was as a young child sent by his family to a distant village to study Talmud. In the context, the importance of becoming a Talmudic scholar is so great that it supersedes the value of staying geographically close to the family.

At the time that this story takes place, Chaim Kalber had been away from his family studying Talmud for eight or nine years. Says Rachel Kalber:

> My father left his home in the Ukraine when he was nine years old. He was the child chosen to be sent away to study. So he went and studied at the yeshiva and slept in the synagogue on the floor and ate meals on charity.
>
> Then when my father was seventeen or eighteen, he was conscripted into the czar's army. This was World War I, and he was a corporal or a sergeant. At one point he was told there were a bunch of soldiers that had run away— AWOL—and that he had to take them back to be jailed. Walking along with the group, he realized that one of them was a Jew. He began talking to this man, asking what had happened, why he had run away. The man said that his father was sick and close to death and that since he had not been granted a leave, he had to run away. My father started to ask him where he came from, and it turned out that the man was my father's brother!
>
> What I felt when I heard this story was "Oh, the things I take for granted—the family closeness, knowing what's happened in the family." These things were denied my father. To be so far away that you couldn't recognize your own brother and would have to find out in this horrible way that your own father was dying—it was a

very brutal world that my father was telling me about, and it made me feel my good fortune: the fact that I was secure and nested, that I'd always know who my father and mother were, that I'd always know how my brother looked.

While on the face of it, the story seems to underscore the fragmentation of the family, it is to the Kalbers a cautionary tale, describing how dreadful—but not how forbidden—it is to be so separated from family. As Rachel hears the story, it has a mystical cast to it, demonstrating that, miraculously, family members will somehow find each other, no matter what.

The subtlety of the Kalber family instruction is that it insists that family members be closely involved—telepathic becomes the ideal—but it does not insist that they live geographically in one another's midst. The additional point is that Judaism and, by extension, education are so important that it is permissible to sacrifice immediate family closeness for undertakings related to either.

A second Kalber family story reiterates the instruction that its members share in an almost telepathic intimacy. Again, this is a story that Rachel first heard from her father.

> The year was 1918 or 1919, the year of a terrible pogrom in the Ukraine. My father, by then working for the Central Jewish Organization, had been sent to collect all the children orphaned by the pogrom and to bring them to a central place.
>
> He came back to his home village to discover that the cossacks had tried to hang his mother and sister, but that they had been cut down in time to save their lives. [After an episode in which Rachel's father was almost killed by the cossacks, he collected the orphans and traveled with them to a town about one hundred miles away.]
>
> An aunt of his was living there. She said, "How is your mother? Is your mother all right?" She said she'd had a dream two weeks before in which she saw my father's father running. [He had in fact died at the start of World War I.] In the dream, my father's aunt said to him, "Yakov, why are you running?" And he said, "I'm running to

save my wife. I have to save her. And the children."
My father then told his aunt the story about how his
mother and sister had been hung and then cut down. My
father always cried when he told this story. He was very
moved.

This story was a staple in the Kalber repertoire. "I first heard
this story as a child," says Rachel Kalber, "and have heard it
often since then. What I got from it was that the Jews were
always in danger, and that there was some way in which our
family would rescue us. Even my father's run-in with his brother
was a miraculous reunion. There was no way you could really
lose the family, even if they died. Family was all, and you
couldn't break that connection."

The constellation of values that these stories promulgate has
guided the family for several generations now. When Rachel's
parents came to this country, they settled in Florida for a while,
where Rachel and her brother were born. When Rachel was
fourteen, she was allowed to go to New York to attend a school
superior to those in Florida. "Like my father, I was the child
chosen to study," she says. Now Rachel Kalber is the mother
of a daughter of her own, who is on the verge of entering college.
Though Rachel is divorced and has full responsibility for child
support, there is no question in her mind that her daughter will
go away to college. For an education, even a secular one, she
knows that her parents will contribute.

In *Habits of the Heart*, sociologist Robert N. Bellah and his
colleagues coined the phrase "communities of memory" to characterize those groups whose members' affiliation was based not
only on current similarities but on a more rooted historical affiliation. Among these "communities of memory" they included
the family. "Families," they wrote, "can be communities, re-
membering their past, telling the children the stories of parents'
and grandparents' lives, and sustaining hope for the future. . . ."
Family stories certainly do this. In fact the implication of what
Bellah and his colleagues had to say is that the mere existence
of family stories—whether happy or unhappy—exerts a binding
cohesive force.

But family stories do even more. For good and for ill, they delineate the rules and the mores that govern family life, rules that succor and support as well as rules that chafe uncomfortably; rules that are out in the open as well as those that operate only by stealth. Indeed, family stories go a step further and define the family, saying not only what members should do, but who they are or should be.

CHAPTER 2

FAMILY DEFINITIONS

My father was estranged from his family and not much of a storyteller anyhow, so I grew up feeling that my real cousins, aunts, and uncles were the Bongiornos. In fact the extended family was more compelling to me as both an idea and an entity than my immediate family, which seemed in comparison rather meager in both number and spirit. My sister and I were our parents' only children. In real families—the family my mother grew up in—there were lots of children.

Stone was my last name, opaque to me in meaning. But being a Bongiorno was rich in connotation. It meant being spirited and bright, it meant having artistic talents, it meant not caring about money, and it also meant having a quick temper. This volatility was by no means a negative quality. In fact when my aunts, uncles, or cousins told stories about the Bongiorno temper, they told them with great zest and much laughter.

My grandfather, despite his surname, was not a true Bongiorno. He died when my mother was twelve, and was reputed to have been a rather phlegmatic, laconic man who sat, like Alice's caterpillar, enveloped in great clouds of cigar smoke. The true Bongiorno was my grandmother, the first Annunziata's youngest child.

My grandmother lived till I was sixteen, and she was the hub of the family's life. She lived in the upstairs of a two-family house on East Fifth Street in Brooklyn, with one of my aunts and her family; downstairs lived one of my uncles and his family. The rest of us, like spokes on a wheel, lived nearby in Brooklyn or on Long Island. My mother and her sisters went to see their mother once or twice a week, and on holidays we all went there.

When I think of my grandmother now, I still think of her in the way I've reserved for those I knew intimately when I was very young. It is all physical and sensuous: the elderly smoothness of her fleshy arms, the soft feel of her dark flowered print dresses, the hazy aura of Old Spice that always enveloped her, the way she had of nervously rubbing her thumb against her index finger. I never saw any signs of her temper, though. Everyone said she had "mellowed."

One story still told over and over, even in my generation, is about the time my grandmother was serving soup to her six children. As she circled the big round dining room table, ladling the soup out to each child in turn, a quarrel broke out between two of them, Nancy and Bart. My grandmother tried to stop the squabbling but with no success. Exasperated, she took the soup tureen and upended it over Bart's head.

A related story also focused on Bart, my grandmother, and the same dining room table. My uncle had in some way incurred her wrath. So she took her shoe off and proceeded to chase him around the table. In that story there is no dénouement, just the relish in the fray itself. But in a related story (which is perhaps only a variation of the same story), the shoe is replaced by my grandmother's favorite Galli-Curci record, which regrettably came to the end of its serviceability in the vicinity of my uncle's head.

The primary heir to the Bongiorno temper in the next generation was my aunt Nancy, the one who did *not* get soup spilled over her head—and there is at least one story to prove it. My aunt had a mauve hat (some say puce) which she wore every day to work, rain or shine. Some days she had good days, and other days she had bad days. And when she'd had a bad day, she came home ill-tempered and out of sorts. She didn't want to be further crossed. As a warning to her brothers and sisters, she'd put her hat on backwards, and word would go around, "Nancy's got her hat on backwards. You'd better leave her alone."

A number of us in the third generation, including me, are said to have inherited the Bongiorno temper. In my case the signs were apparently unmistakable even in my early infancy. My mother frequently tells a story contrasting me with my younger sister. When my sister was upset, she would cry and great piteous tears would roll from her eyes. But, says my mother, I didn't weep so much as scream out of impatience or frustration. No tears at all.

As stories go, this one certainly isn't interesting, nor is it particularly compelling. But the longevity of this extremely unpersuasive story was what first made me wonder why certain family stories survive while others do not. Clearly the criterion for survival has little to do with narrative verve alone.

The answer lies in how families work. Just as every individual has a sense of his or her own identity, so every family has a sense of its own identity. Usually this familial identity is not articulated or often said out loud, although the fact is that just about any given family member will, if questioned, define what it means to be a member of the family in ways that are at least roughly consistent with what other family members would say.

Almost always, too, there are family stories to fasten the identity in place and keep it from floating off, slithering away, or losing its shape. When family members talk about the nature of their family identity, they will usually illustrate the "truth" of their assertions by telling one or another of these designated family stories. Family definition stories express a belief about the family, although to an outsider, the belief may not be entirely substantiated by the family's facts.

Invariably, these family definitions, whatever their content, are construed as positive by those that subscribe to them. While they're meant to bolster the family's esteem, and are therefore benign in purpose, they have their unpleasant uses. They may, for instance, be used to ostracize or exclude those who don't measure up. The late David Kennedy, one of the sons of Robert

F. Kennedy, was not perceived as a "true" Kennedy because he was said to lack the punch and aggressiveness defined as essential Kennedy traits. Similarly, my grandfather was said not to be a true Bongiorno because he had none of the volatility the family prided itself on. But more usually, family definitions and the stories that serve them are benign in purpose, meant less to fix family members in arbitrary or rigid roles than to provide co-hesiveness and a sense of belonging.

There is no way of predicting what the specific content of a family definition will be, although there are a few generalizations that consistently hold up. First, the family definition will usually include a number of attributes, as in my family it included not just volatility, but artistic inclinations, intelligence, and indif-ference to money as well. The breadth of definition is to ensure that there's something for everybody in it.

Second, to an outsider, the attributes that a family member claims as family traits may seem humdrum or inconsequential or even unattractive, but to the family member the presence of these traits will almost always demonstrate that the family is indeed "special" and in some way superior to all other families. In this way the family identity corresponds to the sense of generic specialness that most of us privately believe ourselves to have, even if we know better. Thus the family definition is in some way an *ideal*, whether obvious or covert, that the family as a group has for itself. Third and related, in some cases you might say that the family definition also serves as the family's most important instruction to, and perhaps covert ground rule for, its members—what they *ought* to be like.

And finally, the nature of the family definition and the in-dividual stories used to buttress it give clues as to the family's organization and its power center. It's customary for the standard-bearer to be a member of the most senior generation. But it has to be a generation of recent enough vintage so that individual members can still be recollected and characterized. Usually it's a particularly beloved grandparent or great-grandparent who may now be dead but who is still a distinct and palpable family presence, as my great-grandmother and my grandmother were.

The implied fantasy is that this elder is the founder of the tribe and the creator of its ethos, rather than just a member of the generational rank and file, as in fact we all are. The elder's attributes, real or imagined, now become the family's.

Many people feel they participate in at least two family traditions and thus have two family definitions to draw from. In the best of circumstances, the two sets of family definitions are complementary. Second best, one family definition will be more appealing than the other, and the individual will rely on one as if to rescue himself or herself from the other. In the worst cases, the two family definitions will be in conflict, and the individuals will have to negotiate the conflict as best they can.

Anyone can understand why the Bongiornos of my mother's generation would have wanted to think of themselves as especially spunky and artistically talented. Talent is inherently attractive, not to mention "special," plus it gave them a kind of blood entitlement for their own aspirations in the world, given the family's strong determination to assimilate in America. But it takes some deciphering to understand why they would have wanted to see themselves as volatile and quick-tempered, traits one wouldn't immediately seize on as attractive.

The answer lies in their strong desire to be at home in America at a time when, as Italian-Americans, they anticipated rebuff. I think my mother and her brothers and sisters saw their temper as their *élan vital*, their stamina and vitality, their insistence on not being cowed or intimidated or defeated by their status as newcomers in America. From my perspective as an adult, they were rather gentle people, maybe even meek. Except for my aunt with the backwards hat. And some say even she has softened.

As for the family's allegation that my grandfather was not a "true" Bongiorno, this has, I believe, less to do with his temperament than with his values. Unlike his much younger wife and his children, he was conservative, loyal to the ways of the old country. He smoked Di Nobilis and read *Il Progresso*. According to one derisively told family story, he built a garage and painted "No Smok" across its door. When my grandmother enrolled in night school to learn English, my grandfather made her drop out, thinking it unseemly that a married woman should be in school. He never bothered to learn English, and later on insisted that his oldest daughter drop out of high school to help him in the grocery store he eventually owned.

My grandfather died in 1929, when most of his children were still quite young. Had he lived, he never would have allowed my mother to go to college, or later, to go on stage, nor would he have permitted her younger sister to go abroad as a nurse during World War II. And he never would have understood his eldest son's dream of becoming a writer. These are the reasons he wasn't a "true" Bongiorno. That he was laconic was the least of it.

WHEN A LOOK BECOMES A LOGO

I met Laura Holmes, a woman in her late twenties, because I had given a talk in her college writing class about the research I was doing on family stories. She sought me out after class because she had been thinking about her family's stories for a long time and very much wanted to talk about them.

Initially, as we sat down over coffee in a restaurant near her school, Laura Holmes didn't think her family even had a family definition, though she said right away that the family "look" was very important. "We're all little and blond and blue-eyed and good-looking, and that's the way we think of ourselves. When we're all together, we sit in a large circle, and we all face each other—the chairs are around the edges of the room. And then you're allowed to say maybe one sentence about what you're actually actively doing right now—your job, or your career, or your plans for your new house. Then after that one sentence, the conversation turns one of two ways—either to what a family member, usually a child, has done that's cute. Or more usually into 'Remember the time. . . .' The point is to stop outside influences, to keep the family outside of time."

The image of the assembled clan, as if perpetually fixed in their familial roles, reminds Laura of her great-uncle Edgar's living room and how it's set up: "His house is an example of what all our houses are like, though to a lesser degree because we haven't been around as long. He lives in a house that was built in 1730, and he collects photographs of his relatives. He sits them in chairs around the edge of the living room, rather like we all sit when we're together.

"So his entire living room is a ring of chairs with pictures of us on them, but that means he doesn't have anyplace to sit. So he put another ring of chairs inside the first ring and began to put photographs on them, too. By the time I was eight, he had two complete circles of chairs and half of a third one. Now he's completed the third row and is working on his fourth. And there's no room to walk. Photographs everywhere. Everywhere."

The profusion of photographs underscores the importance of "the look," whatever it meant, and on reflection, Laura concluded that she knew what it meant. "We're not that rich or that smart, but we've been around, and there's a feeling that good-looking is related to well-preserved. What I mean is we're *strong* and we *last*." Thus the family saw itself—and prided itself as well—on a kind of plucky durability, one which to them seemed almost chromosomally linked to hair shade and eye color. Their looks were their logo.

Another story, where a single physical feature had come to symbolize the entire family ethos, was told in the Mercutio family. Yolanda Mercutio, a psychologist now in her forties, heard the story frequently from her father and loved it every time.

"My father said that when I was born I had the long thin nose of my mother's family," she recounts. "He said he went into the hospital nursery and he went like that to me"—she presses her index finger to her nose—"and he made it the small round nose of the Mercutios. I *loved* that story! And I believed it until adulthood. Finally one day I thought of that story and I said, 'Wait a minute! There is such a thing as genetics!' I had taken science courses in college, but it never occurred to me that my father's story didn't really explain how I got my nose."

Yolanda Mercutio's pleasure had to do with what it meant to be a Mercutio. "To be a Mercutio was something to live up to. My uncle will tell stories about how great the Mercutios are—not only were they great because they were rich, but because they were amazingly kind and generous. My uncle would tell stories of how it was in Italy—a table would be set for forty or fifty people—with all kinds of food and feasting. To be a Mercutio means you're always there for your friends. When my uncle said, 'He's a Mercutio,' it was a point of high praise." In the context of Yolanda Mercutio's family, it was generally understood that the Mercutios were superior to the Masellos, the family of Yolanda's mother. "And so," concludes Yolanda Mercutio, "that's why I loved the story of how I got my nose. It meant I was more like my father and his family, and that's the way I wanted it to be."

The Holmes family and the Mercutio family could put as much meaning as they did into a merely physical trait because they were building on a myth that every family in the world participates in. I mean the myth of "blood." Now blood itself, as an idea, has always had an awesome power to move us. It's part of the Christian symbolism involved in Communion, part of most puberty rites, and a sign of marital consummation.

In its secular familial context, "blood" means relatedness, though to be scientific about it, the fact is that even a blood test cannot conclusively establish paternity. But never mind, when we think of families, we think of "blood" lines, and the image this summons up in our minds is of a rush of blood coursing down the generations, undiluted and unalloyed. Our collective fantasy is that the same blood that surged through our ancestors surges through us with undiminished power. Thus a certain tilt to our nose or a given hair color is the sign of our ancestors' blood pushing through our skin, proof of blood's undiminished power, and therefore proof of a genetic familial cohesiveness and likeness through the generations as well as within any given generation.

It really isn't that way, of course. Though we may use the

powerful associations we have with blood to promulgate the idea
of the sacred and enduring familial bond, the fact is that the
cohesion and durability of family is an idea—a value—that has
to be rebuilt every single generation. It's just that we use the
myth of blood as a foundation and build the myth of family
definition on top of it.

Really, each one of us is the product of a confluence of strangers.
We come from two families—not one—even if we look only as
far back as our parents. If we look back another generation, it's
four families; another, and it's eight; and just another, and it's
sixteen. Seven generations back, it's 128.

And so the blood that coursed through a great-grandparent
or even a grandparent is but a thin trickle in our own. To put
it another way, as writer Alex Shoumatoff has, "the chances of
inheriting a particular trait from any one ancestor seven generations back are very slim . . . only . . . $\frac{1}{128}$ of the genes of
an ancestor seven generations back will reach you. . . . And
the genetic gap between siblings, only half of whose genes are
'identical by descent' . . . quickly widens along *their* lines of
descent; their children, who are first cousins, share only an
eighth of their genes." The point is that family is always jerry-
built and has to be reconstituted and reimagined every generation.

In this effort, family stories—especially those about family
definitions based on shared physical attributes—are important.
They draw on and, in so doing, recharge the powerful myth of
blood connection, *shared* blood connection. They dramatize blood.
For the Holmeses, blondness meant durability; for the Mercutios,
a round nose meant generosity—as if either durability or generosity was a genetic trait that could be passed along from one
generation to the next.

But in the end it doesn't matter whether Holmeses really are
sturdy and durable, or whether Mercutios truly are kind and
generous. At least a layer of family cohesiveness comes not from
actually *having* these traits, but from *sharing* the belief in having
them. It's a secret belief, too, not widely known and possibly
not shared in by outsiders. Thus knowing the family definition
and the stories that anchor it is like knowing a password or a

secret handshake. And it's all the more binding, as secret knowledge always is.

A FAMILY DEFINITION
AS AN INSTRUCTION
FOR PUBLIC LIFE

It's unlikely that I would have crossed paths with James M. M. Terrell had he not answered an ad I placed calling for family storytellers. A born storyteller with an exquisite sense of timing and irony, he told me in our first phone conversation that he had recently, while traveling in Scotland, regaled an entire pub till dawn with the family stories in his repertoire.

A lawyer and a keenly intelligent man, he grew more cautious when he understood I was after something more than amusement, but he was eventually willing to probe his family stories aloud. More than any representative of any family that I spoke with, James had a family definition that was exceedingly public, outward-looking in its orientation. For well over a century the Terrells have been known by name to many. In the latter half of this century alone, Terrells have been art collectors, novelists, civic leaders, philanthropists, theologians, lawyers, and social scientists. In the city where James Terrell grew up, a city of millions, and even in his home state, the Terrell name is even more widely known.

What fosters the Terrells' sizable contributions to public life is money, old money and vast money. The most recent relative to refill the family coffers was an industrialist two generations back who made several million dollars by patenting a device that is still used around the world in steel production, a device as crucial to steel production as a thumbtack is to a bulletin board. "That's what keeps on pumping money into this crowd," says Terrell.

But having money is not part of the Terrell family's self-definition, nor are any attendant money-making traits. Rather, the family's self-definition is a consequence of its vast wealth, and perhaps, in the face of it, an instruction. "It's more altruism and service that show how little our lives are governed by money. And we're all taught that through all these people in our family who are in public service and who've thought about their responsibilities in life."

And then, with real amusement, Terrell begins to recount family stories, which in aggregate suggest that a certain kind of *noblesse oblige*—his term—is a blood attribute.

The first story Terrell tells is about an ancestor who was a contemporary of Ulysses S. Grant and Robert E. Lee.

> They all went to the same military academy and they were all in the same class. And they all sat up one night deciding who was going to go with which side. Lee went with the South, and Grant and my great-grandfather— although he was from Maryland—went with the North. Grandfather fought with some distinction for the North, and then in the Indian wars that followed the Civil War. If you read *Bury My Heart at Wounded Knee*, you'll find a very long passage about him. He was the only white man in the whole book who treated the Indians correctly.

"What's the point of this apocryphal story?" muses James. "The point is that each of the three made a choice based on patriotic reasons. Of course Lee and Grant were not in the same class, but whatever generals it was that night deciding on their actions, what was important were their own notions of duty. And it also shows where the family was at that crucial moment in our history."

Another war, World War II, leads Terrell to tell another story. One of his great-uncles was passionately interested in codes, anagrams, and cryptograms. It led him to the sorts of linguistic studies which prove that the works of one great author were actually written by another great author, studies that were eventually debunked by academics in literature.

However, his great-uncle's zeal about anagrams turned out to be of interest to the United States government during World War II. "My uncle had in his employ about eight little old ladies who sat there and did these anagrams which were nothing more nor less than code-breaking. The Navy came and sat them down and said, 'This is the Japanese code,' and they said, 'That's a piece of cake,' and broke the code.

"Again, although this story does a disservice to the many individuals who did work in cryptanalysis during World War II, the story makes the point that some good could come from their effort, that their intellectual undertaking was not in vain. At least that's what I take from that story."

The postwar family stories suggest that the family has continued in the same trajectory. A Terrell museum wing was bequeathed and installed in the 1950s. In the same decade, James's grandfather, a liberal lawyer, defended local university faculty in danger of losing their jobs over allegations they were communists. In the 1960s, James's father, also a lawyer, donated his legal expertise to a civil rights group, the Student Nonviolent Coordinating Committee (SNCC), and spent a good deal of time in Mississippi. James began to make his own way as a lawyer in government during the 1970s.

"We don't seem to be giving up," says James. "We haven't peaked or bottomed. Throughout the years service to fellow man and to country keeps reappearing. Where I come from, many people have such incredible gobs of money. We sort of outdo them in class and liberalism and patriotism, by showing how little money means to us."

FAMILY DEFINITIONS, ETHNICITY, AND RELIGION

In all the family definitions so far—Bongiornos, Holmeses, Mercutios, and Terrells alike—the families' sense of their own nature never draws on any affiliation or group beyond the family itself, at least not explicitly. But those attuned to the subject of ethnicity will recognize that families often idealize, and claim as their own, exactly those traits which might be characterized as national traits from their country of origin—and might be used to stereotype them.

The Bongiornos, despite their uneasiness with their Italian heritage, embraced and idealized just the trait which most characterized them as Italian—their volatility. In fact, as social scientists begin to research ethnicity as it relates to social values and practices, it does indeed emerge that Italians as a national group tend to be more accepting of a broader range of emotional expressiveness than many other ethnic groups. By the same token, those of Italian background have traditionally placed more value on interpersonal relations than on workplace success—consonant with the value placed on generosity by the Mercutios.

Meanwhile both the Holmeses and the Terrells idealize an optimism and hopefulness which social scientists say are characteristic of white Anglo-Saxon Protestants. Thus while it's not my intention to focus on the relationship between family and ethnicity per se, it certainly is more than coincidental that families tend to encourage, foster, and indeed idealize some of the very traits they are stereotyped as having, even if occasionally the stereotype is negative. The family, then, is at least temporarily an agent of ethnicity. For most of us, ethnicity, even when reinforced by family definitions, will fade over two or three or four generations because our ethnic background doesn't so much identify who we are as where our ancestors once lived.

But for Jews, ethnicity has nothing to do with region and everything to do with a set of religious and social beliefs, a long history of oppression, and—some would say—a loose blood tie among all its members. Hence in Jewish families, the fact of being Jewish is often an explicit component of the family's identity. But there is a wide range of implicit connotations a Jewish family may have in mind when it includes Jewishness in its family definition.

To Sharon Medlow, who grew up in a working-class Jewish

family in the Midwest, being a Medlow is full of meaning that loosely involves Judaism.

> Being a Medlow means being strong and being tough and being able to survive. Period. It means not having as much as other people. The Medlow family crest, if we had one, would say, "You'll survive." It would certainly have some Jewish symbol on it—the Torah or the menorah. And it would clearly have some image of power on it, like a fist. But the idea of being Jewish in my family was not religious, it was ethnic: being Jewish is like being Black. It's being part of an oppressed people, and having to know how to fight back.

Where did this definition get its start? The most powerful story in the Medlow family repertoire is about Sharon's father's little brother, Louie, who died of pneumonia the snowy night their father was out getting medicine. The earliest articulation of the Medlow family definition, which in fact has nothing to do with Judaism, dates back to the aftermath of this episode, drawing on how the strongest members of the family behaved in the aftermath of the child's death. The weaker members—Louie's mother and one of his older brothers—were presumably not perceived as embodying the family definition.

"It was my great-grandmother who saved the family," says Sharon Medlow. "She was the Rock of Gibraltar during that period. She peddled on the streets of Chicago to keep the family alive. When everybody else—my grandmother and one of my uncles—was falling apart, she was always solid. She also took care of the kids—my father and his two younger brothers. Medlows survive, they're survivors."

The fact, of course, is that Sharon Medlow's great-grandmother was not a Medlow, either by "blood" or by marriage. However, such fine points of genealogical accuracy are never what matter to the family members who tell such stories. What matters is the strength of family identity. In this case, the blending of the Medlow family ethos with the "survivor" ethos of Judaism reinforces and intensifies the Medlows' sense of themselves as survivors.

Rachel Kalber's family definition, and the stories that go with it, also incorporate Jewishness, though in ways having nothing to do with endurance. "Being a Kalber," she says, "is being a special Jew. It's an elite within an elite. A chosen within a chosen." Now a psychotherapist in her mid-forties, Rachel Kalber no longer embraces the definition as fervently as she once did, but she knows it by heart. Her doubts about its truth do not, in equal measure, dislodge her belief.

The essential Kalber in her family was her father's grandfather, himself an "elite within an elite."

> His name was Chaim Gott—which means God—and he was a man so good that the townspeople in his little village in Russia would bring their children to him to be blessed, they felt he was so saintly. He used to, among other things, write letters for the illiterate.
>
> Chaim Gott was a child during the time that the cossacks used to come and kidnap kids, and he, the legend went, hid in the cemetery behind a gravestone one night during a roundup of that sort, and miraculously escaped it. When Chaim Gott died, rich people came to try to buy his tefillin—his phylacteries—because they were thought of as this hallowed object. My father said that he himself was referred to as Chaim Gott's *eynikl*—God's grandchild.

Now while "special" was generic in the Kalber family, it also meant being especially smart, perhaps because part of Chaim Gott's Jewish specialness was his capacity as a Talmudic scholar. At any rate, often enough in Rachel Kalber's own life, she has heard family stories—even one about herself, prenatally—which tied her into the family definition. "My mother tells that when she was pregnant, she sat in a room with several pregnant women. And the first one said, 'I would really like a boy.' And the second one said, 'I don't care what it is, as long as it's healthy.' My mother listened to this, and then she said, 'As long as my kid is *smart*. I don't want a dummy.' I heard that story a hundred times."

Perhaps the message is so loud and clear to Rachel Kalber because both her father and her mother came from families which they privately defined as "an elite within an elite, a chosen within a chosen." And it is a definition still surviving even in branches of the family which Rachel Kalber has no contact with. Last year she met for the first time a distant cousin from California, the granddaughter of Rachel's mother's sister. Rachel and her cousin talked family and discovered they knew many of the same stories and thought about them in the same ways.

"The 'specialness' is being passed down, from generation to generation to generation," says Rachel Kalber. "And it was an instructive conversation for me because the feeling I always got in my family was that we were terribly special, at the same time as we were horribly flawed. My mother used to say to me what her mother had said to her: 'My worst are the world's best.' By that she meant that if she compared her kids to anyone else's, her kids would shine, no matter how terrible they were." And so, down the generations it goes.

In my travels, I heard quite singular family definitions. It turned out that Collinses were "executives," O'Briens were "hooligans," Talbotts were "plucky losers," de Filipis were "fey," Wisnicks were "funny," and diNapolis were "stubborn." It emerged that Danny Ballow had "the famous Weintraub intelligence," Meg Congers was "the last of the crazy Callahan women," Linda Lefkowitz believed she had a dash of "the Lubchansky glamour," and B. C. Heinz changed his life and got himself relocated from Indiana to New York through a combination of "the McBurney sense of fancy and whimsy from my mother's side, and from my father's, the Heinz ability to balance a checkbook." And Heinz was one of many who lived quite comfortably as the point of confluence of two family traditions, each complementing the other harmoniously.

CHAPTER·3
FAMILY MONUMENTS

STORIES OF LOVE, LINEAGE, AND MARRIAGE

For the past several years, Jane Gilbert and her companion, Nicholas, have lived in an airy brownstone apartment on a tree-lined street in Brooklyn's Park Slope. It is a lovely, warm, and urbane apartment, with high ceilings and parquet floors, just a short walk away from the best croissant shop in the neighborhood.

Jane Gilbert, trim, honey-haired, and freckled, is quite at home in this milieu. It is an easy commute to her job giving creative writing workshops to Brooklyn public school children and not far from the hospital where Nicholas is a doctor on staff. But where Jane lives now is worlds away from her childhood.

She grew up in Mannington, West Virginia (pop. 2,747), where her father was a science teacher in the high school. Mannington was also where her mother was born and where her father's family moved when he was ten. All the family stories Jane Gilbert tells bear the imprint of that part of the country. On her father's side, the stories go back to the family's earlier days as mountain Virginians, first as farmers, then as miners. It's the same on her mother's side—generations of farmers, and later miners, in nearby southern Pennsylvania. Some of them are bizarre stories, like the time Uncle Clyde lost a leg to gangrene and insisted on a full-fledged funeral for his departed limb, flowers and all.

Even as a child of four or five, Jane knew and loved the lore of her family—the Gilberts and Proctors on her father's side, and the Picketts and Lawrences on her mother's side. She thought she'd heard just about all the stories, especially about how the older generation got together and sometimes how they came apart, but as it turned out, there were one or two that she never heard at all till she was an adult, and even then her mother told them to her in secret.

This was a legend that I had to get secretly, which is about my grandmother's divorced father. When I was a little girl, we used to get letters in this strange old shaky handwriting from a lady named Lally—Lally Proctor. I knew that my grandmother's name had been Proctor before she married my grandfather Gilbert, so as a child, I thought that maybe Lally Proctor might be my grandmother's mother, even though my grandmother called her 'old Lally.' 'Oh, I got another letter from old Lally.'

It turned out that old Lally had been the hired woman who worked for my beautiful great-grandmother, Millie Proctor, who rode a white horse. Lally worked on the farm and did the chores so that Millie could keep her hands white and ride the horse and read books.

Meanwhile, Millie's husband, Joseph Proctor, my great-grandfather, was apparently put off by Millie's "airs," even though she was his wife and the mother of his children, and so he took up with Lally, and eventually they picked up and went west, all the way to Arkansas. And Millie was able to get a divorce, and of course the daughters, including my grandmother, stayed with her. When they told the story, they said the law—and I still don't believe this is true—was that my great-grandmother could get divorced and remarry (and eventually she did), but that my great-grandfather, who was at fault, could *not* be divorced, and so he and Lally had to live in sin out there in Arkansas. That's the way they told it.

The rest of the story is that my great-grandfather could never really make a go of his life after that. He had had a very good rich farm when they lived as a family, but the story is the farm failed after that. It spoiled his life. And apparently it spoiled my great-grandmother's life, too, even though she was able to get a new husband and everything. He wasn't as handsome, as good, as high in status, as Joseph Proctor. Millie's new husband was rougher, and conceivably he drank a little. It was tragic in another way for my grandmother, who never saw her father again, even though he would write her notes and send her presents. A lot was lost when this divorce happened. After both Millie and Joseph were dead, Lally would write to my grandmother in her shaky old hand.

Such are the sad consequences of being a wife who puts on "airs," and of being a husband who commits adultery, abandons his family, and lives "in sin" forever after. Family stories about love, courtship, and marriage are often helped to survive by a heavy component of drama, but their survival is not explained by this alone.

The fact is that the family, any family, has a major stake in perpetuating itself, and in order to do so it must unrelentingly push the institutions that preserve it—the institution of marriage especially, but also the institution of heterosexual romantic love, which, if all goes the way the family would have it go, culminates in marriage, children, and enhanced family stability. Behavior that threatens family stability or continuity—sexuality that gets out of hand or illegitimacy that brings an unknown bloodline into the family—has to be censured. Even love affairs cannot be *too* passionate in the family version of things because they threaten the collective welfare of the family, pulling one of its members into an entirely private twosome.

And so, although in our time and in our culture we assent to the individual's right to make his or her own personal choices about love and marriage, at bottom it remains family business. And make no mistake, the family works overtime to make its instructions felt.

LOVE AND MONEY . . .
AND RELIGION, CLASS,
AND EDUCATION

One of the clichés of our culture is that it's as easy to fall in love with a rich man as a poor man . . . (or woman, for that matter). But the slogan's triteness doesn't mean we don't take it seriously. In family love and courtship stories, the theme of money—of marrying money or having enough to qualify as a suitable mate—appears just as often as the theme of love.

Traditionally, of course, the man is the breadwinner who enhances his desirability by demonstrating his earning prowess. This value appears in family stories, regardless of the family's class background. Danny Ballow, for example, grew up in the Bronx in a working-class family. His father was a pants cutter who never really earned much money, although he always wanted to. "When I was growing up in the 1950s," recalls Danny Ballow, "my father made $5,000 a year, but by the end of his lifetime, he had saved $100,000, which he thought of as the greatest achievement of his life. It showed what a good person he was."

The idea that money enhanced the elder Ballow's worth—as a potential husband as well as a man—is the point of a courtship story Danny Ballow heard frequently.

> My father met my mother after he had already left England and come to live in the United States. He would go back and forth for visits, and on one of the visits to Liverpool he met my mother. They wrote back and forth over a few years in between his visits. They had an "understanding."
>
> At one point, there was some question on my mother's part about whether he was good enough for her. So he came from America bringing all his bankbooks with him. He went and had a long talk with my mother's brother. This was my Uncle Ben, who was studying to be a rabbi. My

father spread out his bankbooks and showed him how much money he had saved. I think after that they got engaged and when he went back to America, he sent her money to buy an engagement ring. And that's the famous bankbook story.

Love and money often appear in tandem in family stories, as they do in Danny Ballow's case—where in fact money, symbolized by bankbooks and an engagement ring, is a more dominant theme than love. Nor does the Ballow family lament this. To the contrary, moral approval of this state of affairs is evident in the cameo appearance of Uncle Ben, less a character than a religious reference point. In other families, however, love and money may appear mixed in with other more complicated marital instructions.

In the family of Donald Tomlinson IV, money was an important family concern. There were stories in the Tomlinson family about the big family estate his father's family used to have in Cincinnati. "It was a compound right in the city—acres and acres which overlooked the Ohio River," says Donald Tomlinson. "There was a wall which ran around the estate and they had lots of servants. They weren't incredibly wealthy, just pretty wealthy. They didn't have inherited wealth which passed on from generation to generation. My grandfather's generation pretty much ate all of it up by the time they died. They had earned it."

Donald's father grew up with the appetite for wealth but apparently lacked either the drive or the acumen to earn money in quite the way Donald's forebears had. As Donald puts it somewhat vaguely, "My father did all right . . . for a while." But he didn't really have to. "The money that sustains everything," says Donald, "comes from my mother's family. My family really lives off that income to a large extent."

And the Tomlinson family ethos seems to encourage marrying for money. The simplest and most straightforward story is one Donald Tomlinson heard from his father. "He was once in a class with a priest, and the class asked, 'How can we get ahead?'

And the priest thought about it for a minute and said, 'Marry it.' That means marry money. One of the boys asked, 'Father, what about love?' And the priest replied, 'If you meet enough rich girls, you'll find one that you love.' "

It is a cynical story, further complicated by the priest's presence. After all, he was a man for whom marriage was not a value. His presence is not accidental, or perhaps it is merely congruent with another motif in the Tomlinson gestalt about marriage. As Donald Tomlinson points out, he feels he comes from a family that doesn't really know how to marry. "My grandfather and his brothers," he says, "were all very successful, very successful. But except for my grandfather, none of them married, and there is a kind of panic in my own mother that all these Irish bachelors that she's raised—I have five brothers—will just sort of meander on into this kind of vague Celtic twilight of Irish bachelorhood. I'm thirty-three and not even quite sure how to *get* to marriage. I do have one brother who's married," he adds, "so it can be done."

There's one factor in the Tomlinson mélange about marriage that Donald Tomlinson IV feels will ultimately give him the impetus to enter into marriage. He describes a photographic collage that's been a presence in his family for a long time. "It's a picture of the four generations of Donald Tomlinsons. It had been in my aunt's house, but it was hung in my room when I was six or seven. There's a picture of my great-grandfather, the first Donald Tomlinson. He has a beard and looks very nineteenth century. My grandfather, Donald Tomlinson, Jr., is pictured as a man around forty. My father, Donald Tomlinson III, looks how he looked at the time I was born. And then there's me at the end, and in the picture I'm one or two. I guess that had a lot of emotional impact on me. I feel the pressure to provide the next Donald Tomlinson." He is also moved, and obviously so, by what he calls "the sacramental and solemn progress of the generations."

It doesn't escape Donald that the collage excludes the women involved. "My father once said, 'Stay single and raise your kids the same way.' I'm afraid there's not much romance you can pick up within the family. That's because you're talking about a family of Irish sons—I'm one of six sons, my father was one of two sons, and my grandfather was one of three surviving sons—it's an all-male environment. It's like Genesis with the 'begats.' The women just aren't around." Only their money is.

Instructions about marriage and race, rather than money, were important in the family of Ricardo Nuñez. Not only was there a rash of stories about his German antecedents, but the story of his parents' own marriage, told from his father's point of view, made the explicit point that marrying light was advisable.

The scene of his parents' courtship was in Mexico, where his mother grew up and where his father had come after fleeing Franco's Spain.

> My father was the manager of a large ranch, thousands and thousands of acres. And my mother cane there to teach English to the kids of the ranch owner. My mother had been born in New Mexico, but her parents were Mexican-born and came back to Mexico when she was still small; anyhow, she knew English. So the two of them were working on this large ranch.
>
> My mother was very fair skinned, and so they used to call her *La Blanca*, which means the white one. When she went to work on the ranch, my father found out about it, and so he was going around and looking. It seems there were two other men who were after my mother—short dark Mexican-looking types with broad features. My father said, "This won't do," and so he started courting my mother. Then he had to travel with my mother to where her parents were living to ask for my mother's hand in marriage.

What's striking about this story is that there's no personal component: nothing about how Ricardo's father actually felt about Ricardo's mother, and nothing about how she felt about him. But the stark point remains clear: it was better to marry "the white one." That's how Ricardo heard the story, and that's how he told it.

SPECIAL MARRIAGE INSTRUCTIONS

Beware Passionate Love

As Jane Gilbert had learned from her family stories, flyaway passion was a danger to family stability: it led to divorce, abandonment, and agricultural ruin. This was the choric message from the Proctors and the Gilberts, the Lawrences and the Picketts. And yet great passions, or the tendency to them, seemed to run in the family. As Jane put it, "One of my aunts by marriage says, 'Oh those Pickett girls, they just lose control all the time.' "

As an antidote to all these turbulent inclinations, the family often told stories about how slowly and reasonably each set of Jane Gilbert's grandparents had gone about courtship. The point wasn't how they had met—in each case, they had *always* known each other, and that turned out to be a fact of biography that just about everybody approved of. It was part of the point.

I'll start with the Gilberts—Tessa and her husband, Cartwright, who had grown up together in Lee County, Virginia. They had always known each other, and in fact a cousin of Tessa's married one of the Cartwright brothers.

The families grew up together and Tessa and Cartwright were always sweethearts. He finally went away and got a job. Not far by today's standards, but several days away by foot and wagon. It was over the mountains.

Finally he sent word that he was ready for her to come and marry him. And so she went and her family wasn't too happy about it, because even though they knew Cartwright Gilbert, and knew he was a good young man, they didn't like the fact of her just going over there. But she went and took another young woman as a companion. They went on the back of somebody's wagon, and Cartwright picked them up and took them to a boardinghouse, and they all stayed in separate rooms.

Well, just then the circuit preacher was leaving to get to the next town he was preaching in. They saw him and

stopped him and they got married in the road, standing
beside the preacher's wagon. This is not romance. This is
people who've always known each other, and this is just
what they did.

As an untutored listener, I thought the story was rather rich
with urgency and covert sexual excitement, otherwise why wouldn't
Tessa and Cartwright have waited the week or two until the
next time the circuit preacher came around? But this was Jane
Gilbert's story, and she knew its implications.

This was not only because she knew how it had been told to
her, but because she understood the story in its familial context.
She knew the Gilbert codes, patterns, and values that governed
daily family life, and she knew the rest of the stories that un-
ambiguously told her what the story of Tessa and Cartwright
ought to mean.

The story of Tessa and Cartwright, said Jane Gilbert, went
with the story of Opal and Henry.

My grandfather Henry Pickett had also known my grandmother for many, many years, and the story, as my mother
tells it, is that Henry had been going to visit Opal for years
and years, going over to her house and sitting on the porch,
just about every night. He was a tall shy kid, a baseball
pitcher on the local team. And one summer evening, Opal's
mother came out and said, "Henry, don't you think it's
about time you and Opal got married?" And Henry said,
"Well, I guess it is." And so they did.

Taken together, these stories seem a perfect team, but Jane
Gilbert had never explicitly articulated to herself the load they
jointly pulled until I asked her. After mulling silently for a while,
she said, "I haven't really tied all these together before, but
they're all a warning about passionate love in a way. The immediate marriages I come out of are all marriages that lasted.
My grandparents knew each other for a long time. My dad and
mother knew each other from the time they were ten or eleven

and my dad moved to my mother's town. They went through high school together.

"No one ever said this to me in so many words, but there was a message to me: be darn sure about the man you hook up with and don't go for some flash in the pan that attracts you momentarily." She laughs, somewhat abashedly. "I really hadn't thought of it, but this is really very anti-romantic love, isn't it?"

At the time Jane Gilbert told these stories, they were of more than academic interest to her. She was in her early thirties and on the verge of getting married to Nicholas, whom she'd been living with for the previous ten years and had dated for five years prior to that, "on and off." Her previous caution about marriage apparently demonstrated her obedience to her family's unvoiced instructions. Not that a ten-year attraction was a "flash in the pan," but, given her background, it took her quite a while before she began to be sure she wasn't just rushing into something. "It took me a long time to accept the man I live with," she says somewhat sheepishly, "because I *hadn't* known him all my life."

MARRY ORPHANS OR IMMIGRANTS

As Laura Holmes tells it, she comes from a family that has always been close and insular. "I come from a Baptist family that was very matrilineal. The matrilineal line came to this country in about 1630, first to Massachusetts and then to Connecticut. They settled the center of Connecticut and started the Baptist church there. In the Baptist church I was raised in, we're all related, and we all called each other cousin, even though some were only obscurely related—second cousins twice removed, fifth cousins four times removed.

"Our founding mother was Drusilla Peters. She was accused of being a Salem witch for selling her soul to the devil at the strawberry banks. As a result, she was jailed for a year. It was her husband who accused her." Laura Holmes knows all this because several years ago curiosity prompted her to do some genealogical research. It was also an effort on her part to break out of the family insularity by trying to place the family in time and space. In short, in the world. She tells the stories as a rebellious insider, someone who knows the thrust of the family instructions and still feels their power, but who is increasingly trying to get a breath of fresh air.

Her family of this generation is still very close-knit. At its core, says Laura, are her mother and her aunt—two sisters—and their spouses and offspring. When I ask her how many children there are in her family, she says she's the seventh of eight, totaling up the children of both her mother and her aunt and placing herself accordingly. "The two families function as one. We're like a clan. Those are the real terms."

Clearly, then, Laura Holmes's family is tribal, matriarchal, insular. And with herself as a notable exception, it seems to want to stay that way. But how do they do it? Clearly, to perpetuate itself the family members in the current generation—most of them female as it turns out—have to marry someone sometime. The rule, says Laura, is "Don't let any outsiders in." And an "outsider," as the family defines it, is anyone who's not an immigrant or an orphan.

The gist of the instruction seems to be that the women in this cohesive and insular family must marry men only from weak families or absent families, men who can be absorbed into the existing family structure and ethos, and who won't draw the woman into their own familial orbit, thereby threatening the family's tight collective sense.

There's a subsidiary rule, too. "If you do marry outside—someone who isn't an immigrant or an orphan—it won't last. It also helps," Laura adds, "if you marry someone blond and blue-eyed like us. My father is bald now, but we've heard the story a million times of how he was called 'Whitey' as a young man because his hair was so blond. The marriages that don't seem to last involve men who have dark hair and dark beards. It's as if they stand out, they can't be worked in."

Where are the stories that make this instruction clear? The central story, as it turns out, is not a specific anecdote involving particular people at all. Rather it is a keenly subjective look at the "begats" so that they become thematic and instructive rather than descriptive. "The paternal line always seems to sort of fizzle out," says Laura, "and that's because our family is full of male orphans and immigrants without a past of their own. My great-great-great-grandfather was an immigrant, so was my great-great-grandfather. My grandmother's husband was first generation. And my father was two at once—an orphan and an immigrant. He wasn't even sure of his mother's name, whether it was Jeanne or Jane. Turned out it was Jane."

Laura believes that those of her sisters or cousins who defy the instructions are doomed to failed marriages. And she feels it's rather like a family curse. "In my generation the divorce rate is very high. My sister married one of the boys from town. He was Polish Catholic and it just didn't work. He just wasn't accepted. Their marriage failed. My first marriage failed. When I told my mother I was getting divorced, there was a minute of silence. Then she said, 'Well, now you can get your teeth fixed.' And that's all that was ever said. Ever."

Laura Holmes is married for a second time now. Her husband, she says, comes from a very closely knit family and so she continues to feel uneasy. His dark hair and even darker beard do nothing to assuage her discomfort.

Better Not to Marry at All

When it comes to family stories, everything depends more on the uses made of them than on their content alone. The appearance of one blighted marriage or one philandering mate or one illegitimacy in a family story does not mean that the family tradition is opposed to marriage or heatedly engaged in the battle between the sexes. Often such singular appearances are warnings against the aberration, not against marriage. This was certainly the case in Jane Gilbert's family, a family opposed not to marriage but to impulse and perhaps passion.

But families have their traditions, and if marriage is a well-entrenched tradition in some families, in other families it is clearly less well rooted, and sometimes actually prohibited. Sometimes the prohibition or wariness about marriage has nothing to do with marriage itself. It may have to do with a family's desire—usually unconscious, but sometimes quite conscious—to maintain the original family unit. That way, the parents remain the parents, and the children remain the children, despite time and change. The disruptions, realignments, and redefinitions inevitably occasioned by marriage don't occur.

In other cases, there almost seems to be a family curse—highlighted in family stories—that travels down the generational lines, where members of one generation after another will marry unreliable men or promiscuous women. To put the same observation in more contemporary terms, families learn about what marriage means from their experience of marriage. When the adult members of the family have not learned how to choose a partner, or how to be married, because no one in their parents' generation ever did it well enough, they cannot pass this capability on to the next generation, either by example or by commentary. After three generations of repeating the same mistake, a family tradition—or call it a curse—does seem to be at work.

Polly Gardner, born and raised in Kentucky, comes from a long line of women and men who do not think well of marriage, though, as Polly tells it, the blame falls more on the men—perhaps because it is the women who tell the stories. The first story, nonetheless, was told to Polly by her father and it concerned his parents.

My father's mother was a secretary at the local college for the physics professor and the English professor. The physics professor was Gardner, and my grandmother got pregnant by him, which caused a scandal, and they both lost their jobs. Three days after the wedding, Gardner, the physics professor, joined the merchant marines and was never seen again. My father told me that story. He said that he never met his father till he was an adult. Twice a year he would get postcards from all over the world, and once every five years, he would get a phone call. "I'm in

town. Would you like to have dinner?" I never met my
grandfather at all.

As for Polly's mother, her grooming for marriage was not much
better. Polly's mother's mother, so the story goes, grew up in a
one-parent family, since her own mother—Polly's great-grandmother—had died giving birth to her. As for Polly's grandmother, "I think she got married when she was thirteen. She
married the first man who came around. It wasn't even like a
courtship. Anyhow, we never heard about any love part of the
marriage. It was more 'He came around and asked could he
marry me, and I said yes.' And that's all the story my grandmother tells."
But Polly's grandmother's marriage didn't last either.

> In town, they called my grandfather Applejack. Do you
> know what applejack is? It's before moonshine becomes
> moonshine. If you won't wait for it to ferment, it's apple-
> jack. My grandfather just drank a whole lot of applejack.
> And dated other women. Finally my grandmother said,
> "Enough is enough," and she left him, which was pretty
> strange for the 1920s. She raised her six children herself.
> She did people's laundry by night and was a waitress at the
> Greyhound bus station in the day. The one poignant note:
> even though she'd thrown him out, she did his laundry for
> him until the day he died.

So what happened when the daughter of Applejack and the
son of the physics professor met? There's not even much of a
love story to go with their earliest relationship. "My mother
married my father on the rebound," says Polly Gardner. "I think
she was impressed by his courtship—that he would swim the
river to see her. Then there was World War II and he went
away—he joined the army, which was kind of romantic." As
for the rest of the story, there *is* no rest of the story: "My parents
were divorced when I was six months old. My mother came
back home and my grandmother watched me while my mom
worked as a secretary."

Polly is now in her early thirties. What does she make of her legacy? "I've been raised by two divorced women, and I'm a divorced woman myself. There was always an air of 'We can do it without them.' I got some things that maybe weren't positive to build a marriage on. When I got married at twenty-three, I made almost the same choice my mother did. My husband was like my father in hippie clothing, and I married him because I didn't know what else to do with myself. I had to grow up a lot, and I think now I have. Maybe I'll be able to live my life without following the scripts I've always known."

PREDICTABLE MOTIFS IN FAMILY COURTSHIP STORIES . . . AND WHAT THEY'RE DOING THERE

In most families, if there is ambivalence about marriage, it is altogether masked, hidden under the genuine pleasure and excitement families feel in the face of an imminent marriage. The incipient spouses are of course excited by the adventure, the new life, heralded by marriage. The parents feel not only their offspring's pleasure vicariously but also a deep sense of satisfaction, even accomplishment, at having safely and soundly ushered their child into the connubial harbor. Marriage, though not the social imperative it once was, still stands for a major rite of passage into adult life. To have a child marry suitably means that one has done a good job as a parent.

But there are regrets, dissatisfactions, and reluctances that inevitably attend even the most deeply welcomed marriage. The old cliché that "a son is a son till he meets his wife, but a daughter's a daughter for all of her life" hints at one strand of familial unease in the face of marriage—marriage inevitably means an acute rearrangement of the original family balance, loyalties, and alignment.

Patrilineality notwithstanding, this is especially true for men. Because family culture is essentially created and promulgated by women, it is often the case that sons—that is, new husbands— are more usually integrated into their wives' families than the other way around. And so when a son marries, his family may, with reason, mourn the dissolution of the way things were.

The tension between a family's desire to see their offspring married and their simultaneous resistance to it is also hinted at by the lore in our culture surrounding in-laws. The term "family," no matter how troubled and beset the family in our culture may be, still has strong positive connotations. On the other hand, no one sits up nights longing to become an "in-law." Mothers-in-law, at least by reputation, are always bossy, meddlesome, and generally unwelcome. The trouble for the new couple is that they simultaneously have to contend with three families— each spouse's original family, plus the new entity they themselves are trying to establish. They sense, correctly, that while their families are undoubtedly pleased to have them married, their families may nonetheless be resistant to a new configuration in which they will not be central.

As for the couple themselves, they are presented with a problem they never dreamed of. Family means "blood"—it means "blood is thicker than water"; it means living among "blood" relatives; it often also means genealogy, lineage, ancestors, the family plot, the old photographs, and shared memories. It is on these charged images—and not blood or chromosome tests— that the blood-ideology of family is based.

The central paradox and challenge of marriage is that we have to make family out of someone we're not related to; miraculously, we have to thicken water into blood by making an erstwhile lover into a family member. Indeed our kinship nomenclature hints that ideally we ought to turn lovers into brothers or sisters to go with the fact that our spouses are our parents' sons- and daughters-in-law, and our siblings' sisters- and brothers-in-law.

In cultures where arranged marriages were the norm, the task of marrying was probably psychologically simpler. The family arranged it. Therefore in marrying the individual was not, by

any independence of choice, distinguishing himself or herself
from the family. Where tribes, or at least extended families,
were the basic unit, the new couple were not required to form
an entirely new and independent entity. Whether the culture
was patrilocal or matrilineal, the rules were all explicitly established long before the joining of any particular new couple.

Thus while our families may spend decades teaching us, telling
us family stories and thereby trying to assure that we will choose
to marry just whom they would have chosen for us, the fact
remains that we marry people who aren't family members and
must thereafter found a new family and establish a new family
culture replete with all the requisite fables, festivities, and folk
heroes. To some extent, we must ring out the old in order to
ring in the new.

As folklorists have observed, the courtship story tends to be
a staple in any family which tells stories at all. This is because
the courtship story bears the same relation to the new family as
a creation myth does to any larger culture or civilization. The
courtship story is the story of How the Family Began, or this
branch at any rate. It is the first collective memory of the new
family, paradoxically shared even by children who were unborn
at the time. Delmore Schwartz once wrote a short story building
on this theme. The narrator in "In Dreams Begin Responsibilities" has a dream in which he is an onlooker to what seems to
be a movie about his parents' courtship, which he knows will
result in an unhappy marriage. Though the narrator would have
been unborn at this time, he can hardly keep himself from
shouting advice and instructions to the hapless couple onscreen.
He feels "responsible"—and hence the title—for the outcome
of the events before his eyes, though they were of course already
fixed. He even screams out, at one point, "Don't do it. . . .
Nothing good will come of it, only remorse, hatred, scandal,
and two children whose characters are monstrous."

Founding a family and creating an ethos—apparently even an
unhappy one will do—that will hold up for a quarter century or
more, till the next generation is grown, is indeed a major imaginative undertaking, so it helps if the courtship story can really
get the ball rolling. It helps if the founding love story has a

certain imposing quality to it, a sense of inevitable destiny, a feel of grand forces at work.

LOVE AT FIRST SIGHT

Though the content of the courtship story varies from family to family, in the most serviceable of them certain motifs are likely to be present. As a whole, these motifs help make the new family feel real and sanctioned, no matter what the resistance of other family members is or has been. What follows are two family stories about first meetings. Although they are unlike in content, they share certain motifs and purposes. The first, set in Liverpool in the 1930s, is the story Danny Ballow's father told him about how his relationship with Danny's mother began.

> My father had come back to England to visit his mother, and he saw a group photograph including my mother hanging in this club he had belonged to. My father said, "Who is that woman? I want to meet her." My father was thirty-eight by then, and he'd never gotten married.
> He says that six or seven years before that, he was in the same room as my mother, at this woman's house, and he wanted to meet her then, but the story is the woman liked my father herself, and so as soon as my father walked in the door, she pushed my mother out the back door and said, "You leave."
> So anyhow, this time around my father went to the next club dance, and there he saw my mother. He went up to her and said, "I want to dance with you," and after the dance, he said, "I want to marry you." Love at first sight is a typical thing in my father's family.
> But my mother said, "Who is this guy?" She was only twenty-five. So my father just kept pestering her. There was some question in her family about whether he was good enough. Anyhow somewhere along the way, my mother finally accepted my father's proposal.

Sharon Medlow's parents met on a beach in the Midwest during the late 1940s, but there are elements in the story she

tells about that meeting which give it much in common with
Danny Ballow's story.

> My parents' love story is one of mythic proportions—at
> least it's always seemed that way to us kids. My father is
> eight years older than my mother, and the story from his
> side is that he walked onto this beach one day and he saw
> her lying there with her friends—she was wearing a two-
> piece bathing suit.
>
> Right then and there he said to his best friend, "See that
> woman over there? I'm going to marry her," and his friend
> said, "You're crazy, you don't even know who she is." And
> my father said, "I'm going to find out," and he went over
> and introduced himself. According to him, he spent quite
> a bit of time just trying to get her to talk to him, ingratiating
> himself with her. He said he was in love with her from the
> moment he met her, and she was the most beautiful woman
> he'd ever seen, and he's never seen a more beautiful woman
> since or been in love with anyone else since.
>
> Her parents were Romeo-and-Juliet hostile to him. There's
> a distinction between Russian Jews and German Jews, and
> while my father's parents were Russian Jews, my mother's
> mother was a German Jew, which is supposed to be a higher
> class. So right from the beginning there was this hostility
> from my mother's mother to my father. They were sort of
> fighting for her.
>
> My father courted her, and my mother was more reluctant
> than he—younger and more innocent—but she fell in love
> with him, too. Their friends still tell stories about their
> romance. They've been married thirty-five years now, and
> they've certainly had their problems, but there's a great
> amount of love and affection and passion and energy be-
> tween them.

While the stories are not alike in content, they share four
fundamental similarities. First, there is, at least on the man's
part, the conviction that this was "love at first sight," and an
immediate and overwhelming certainty that this would be the
woman he would marry. Second, there is the suggestion of powerful sexual attraction. For Danny's father, the proposal came
right after he'd first danced with his wife, and for Sharon's father,

the decision was made when he saw this woman in a two-piece bathing suit. Third, each story reveals some familial opposition to the match—doubt as to whether Danny's father was "good enough" and a much more frank objection to Sharon's father. Fourth, the women are initially resistant, slower to be smitten than their eventual mates.

One can't ever know what the relationship is between the event as it happened and the event as it's come to be remembered, but one can conjecture that when certain elements seem to be a staple of courtship stories, it is because their presence serves some function.

On the face of it, each story suggests that each man took a second look at the woman in front of him because he was sexually attracted to her. Nothing strange in that; it's just one of myriad ways to intimate to men in this culture that a keen male sexual appetite is inherent. But between the experience itself—on the beach or at the club—and the story of the experience something happened. The experience of sexual attraction became apotheosized into something much grander and more forceful—it became "love at first sight." In short, whatever happened after the original glance or encounter—the developing relationship, the marriage—was made to cast its shadow back to the first encounter, as if it had been there to begin with. Thus in hindsight do we make grand destiny out of a simple quickening of the blood.

There's more to it. It's no accident that family opposition is an integral part of the courtship story. It takes some doing for a couple to counter the opposition of either family. A man's sexual attraction alone lacks the necessary stature. One can't, after all, be self-righteous about lust.

But in our culture, "love at first sight" makes a claim for importance that can't be so easily dismissed. It justifies the suitor's otherwise disrespectful defiance of what the family of his beloved wished for. As for the beloved, since she is more likely than her husband to maintain strong ties to the family, and eventually integrate him into it, it is psychologically appropriate that she not be cast in the role of a blatant defector. Her reluctance, in addition to reinforcing the notion that women are not driven by their sexuality, constitutes her loyalty to her original family.

There is also the fact that in our culture romantic love eludes both rational analysis and individual control. We like it that way, too. In love's mystery lies its power. It is not willful; we do not consciously decide to fall in love. Instead we feel it as a summons, a command from outside ourselves. Hence in honoring it, we may indeed oppose a family's wishes, but only because we are answering a "higher" authority, not because we are merely defiant or disrespectful.

Indeed, historically, as the family's role in choosing a spouse declined, family opposition to individual choice increased, and concomitantly the idea of romantic love became especially persuasive. At the heart of Romeo and Juliet's passion, and inseparable from it, is the opposition of the Capulets and Montagues.

KISSING COUSINS

When Marian Glover's parents decided to marry, there was quite a to-do among the Glovers, the family of Marian's father. The Glovers were a Black North Carolina family, with branches in Atlanta, who traced their ancestry back to a white United States senator. They were "aristocratic" among Blacks, says Marian Glover. In this century the Glovers were educated—at Harvard, Radcliffe, Oberlin—and they were professionals as well, pursuing careers as doctors, ministers, and lawyers. One was a colonel in the Spanish-American War.

But Marian Glover's mother's family wasn't from the same social milieu at all. She had grown up Kansas City, Missouri. Her father's mother was an American Indian. As for her father's father, nobody knew anything about him at all, which makes Marian Glover think he must have been "kind of an embarrassment." Her mother's mother's family were all originally from New Haven.

When Marian's father brought her mother home to North

Carolina to meet his family, Grandmother Glover was rather cool in her reception, aggressively naïve. "Do you ride a horse?" she wanted to know. "Do you carry a gun?" "My grandmother," says Marian, "claimed to think of Kansas City as being the Wild West. She was the kind of person who, if she decided she didn't like you, was going to make you very uncomfortable. She decided my mother was not an appropriate person for my father, because my mother was not from a known Negro family—like the Christ-mases from Washington, D.C., or the Bousfields from Chicago—and so she was going to make my mother feel un-comfortable."

Nonetheless the young couple eventually married, which in the face of so much Glover resistance undoubtedly took some strength and resolve. Says Marian, "My mother and father always felt they might have been related. My grandmother on my moth-er's side had family in North Carolina, and if you look at my parents, they favor one another. Through some third cousin or something or other they felt they had some distant attachment."

The Glovers apparently never made any effort to document their surmised consanguinity, and to this day Marian doesn't know whether or not her parents were blood relatives. On the face of it, it seems most unlikely, especially given that they were from such different geographical and social worlds. What is interesting is that they wished to believe they were at least distant cousins, and held on to the belief, and passed it on to their daughter, despite the lack of evidence and despite the fact that, except among European royalty, intermarriage of any sort is not at all culturally fashionable.

The belief in, if not the fact of, consanguinity has its uses. Founding a family, as I have been suggesting, requires conviction even more than action: one has to believe in the transubstan-tiation. Especially before the advent of shared relatives—I mean children—it is an enormous imaginative undertaking. And it is helped immeasurably if two unrelated people can share in the belief that indeed they are already blood relatives. Their work, then, is already well begun for them, and they need only pick up the bloodline and continue it into the next generation.

In listening to family courtship stories, I was surprised (though only at first) at how frequently my tale-tellers' courtship stories included an assertion, always rather casually slipped in, that the newly married couple were in fact relatives. What blood does not provide, narrative can.

Of course the fact is that intermarriage has, historically speaking, not been unusual, more because of limited mobility than because of especially incestuous inclinations. Anthropologist Robin Fox speculates that "eighty percent of the world's marriages have been with second cousins. In a population of three to five hundred people, after six or so generations, there are only third cousins or closer to marry."

Alex Shoumatoff writes that intermarriage also occurs in non-rural populations. "In 1875, 7.5 per cent of all the marriages among Jews in England, who at that time constituted a closed, endogamous religious isolate, were between first cousins, about three times the rate among gentiles. In most of the world's upper classes, cousins have frequently married to keep wealth and power in the family or because of a dearth of other acceptable mates."

What Fox and Shoumatoff offer might explain a courtship story that circulates in the Wisnick family, an extended family of Russian Jews who settled in Iowa early in the century, and who as Jews were in a very small minority. As Jane Wisnick heard the story, her paternal grandparents were second cousins. Not only that, but, says Jane Wisnick, "We have lots of two-sisters-marrying-two-brothers, and lots of nieces-marrying-uncles."

I think back myself to all the times I heard the story of my grandfather Gaetano, and how he lived with all those sisters and cousins in that hotbed of intermarriage on Union Street. The story of how he came to marry my grandmother was so detailed that I never doubted for a second that they were actually cousins, and I still don't, though perhaps they were not the first cousins they claimed they were.

What was crucial wasn't the verifiability of their relatedness, but the pleasure we took in it. After the story, someone or other would usually add, as a humorous tag line, "Yeah, better to keep it all in the family." And that satisfaction—of belonging to a cozy, intimate, solid, enduring tribe—is the impulse that leads people to imagine kinship, making family out of those who would be family.

REVISED AUTOBIOGRAPHIES

Spouses not only have to create a family feeling with those they marry, but often they also have to find some comfortable place for themselves in their spouse's original family, especially if those they marry come from closely knit families. Most usually, though not always, it is the husband who must make a place for himself in his wife's family, because "a daughter's a daughter for all of her life." There is a third motif in or attending the family courtship story which helps accomplish this, and there's a hint of it in the line Laura Holmes's extended family liked to circulate about the orphan immigrant Laura's mother had married. "Your father's bald now," they used to tell her, "but when he was a boy his hair was so white, they called him Whitey."

On the surface, this is neither much of a story nor obviously meaningful, but it meant something to Laura, her mother, and her mother's entire family. Laura Holmes's extended family, as she noted more than once, were all blond and blue-eyed and had made those physical characteristics a sign of family membership. Hence when they recalled John Lee Holmes's long-departed blond hair, they were not simply being nostalgic or descriptive, but reaffirming their fantasy of his blood-place in their family. It made it seem as if this immigrant orphan from Belfast had always been a Connecticut Yankee in their familial court.

Apparently this was a fantasy that John Lee Holmes himself was eager to share, perhaps because he had no family of his own and was eager for one, but also because he had truly become enough of a member of his wife's family to understand their coded rules. At any rate, says Laura, he established a fantasy genealogy for himself which gave him American roots he didn't have. It was not identical to the lineage in Laura's mother's family, but it was made to weave in and out of the high points of American history, just as Laura's mother's lineage did.

There was one story her father told her in which this imagined genealogy was conveyed to Laura as the truth. "The story was that we were related to Robert E. Lee." The thread that made this claim possible, says Laura, is that her father's name was John Lee Holmes. "It's impossible," says Laura Holmes now. "My father was born in Belfast. And not only that, but my mother's family has always lived in New England, while Robert E. Lee was a Southerner."

What does Laura herself conclude from this? "I think my father was sort of inventing his own stories to fit himself into the family. As for my mother, I don't know. She may have thought he was just joking, but she never disputed what he said. For us, these stories took on an aspect of being very real."

Emily O'Herlihy Sargent, now in her early fifties, is more a Sargent than she ever was an O'Herlihy. She and Martin Sargent have six children. When their names draw from family tradition, it is always Sargent tradition, never the O'Herlihys.

Even as a teller of family stories, Emily is mostly Sargent. She does like to tell stories about her maternal grandfather, Karl Schroeder, who came from Germany to Bonterre, Missouri, in 1860 in hopes of making his fortune in lead mining, and did fairly well for himself, enough to become an established member of Bonterre "society." Emily is less enthusiastic about her other direct antecedents. Her father drank too much and earned too little from his gas station to make a suitable husband for Karl Schroeder's daughter. She acknowledges that when she married, she was looking not just for a husband but for a new family she could belong to.

Even after Emily's family moved out of Grandfather Schroeder's sprawling Victorian house into one that was small and shabby, she continued to feel at home among the elite. "I knew I was Bonterre class, such as Bonterre was, and that I was the equal of anyone." The family still had the hollow-stemmed champagne glasses Karl Schroeder had wrapped and carefully brought all the way from Germany, and the fine leather-bound editions of Byron, Tennyson, and Ouida that had graced his library. "I was Karl Schroeder's granddaughter, and my mother had been Freddie Schroeder.

"I knew I had to marry someone who had a future and some financial backing. I deliberately looked around—it sounds rather cold-blooded, and I do love my husband and I did then—and Martin was available and we had a lot of things in common. I knew if I didn't catch him in a hurry that would be the end of it. I would be stuck in Bonterre, Missouri, for the rest of my life. When I married Martin, he paid off all my debts, poor dear, and bought me a new winter coat. When we took off to the Ozarks on our honeymoon, I was never happier in my life. I said, 'Good-bye, Bonterre!' and never shed a tear. I had married an acceptable husband, and we were on our way."

There was more to it. Emily had entered the family she'd always wanted. The Sargent family had long carried a special charge for Emily because Martin's father was Dr. Edward Sargent, the Bonterre town doctor. He was an "elite" with a firmer toe-hold than Emily's own family, and, more to the point, he was the man who had delivered Emily herself. And therein lies a story that Emily had always known. "Dr. Sargent had taken care of me right along. When I was born, the nurses said I was cold as a snake. I was probably going to die, but Dr. Sargent fixed up some kind of broth with barley that saved my life. Then as a child, I had terrible asthma attacks, and he was right there to take care of me then, too. Dr. Sargent," she adds without prompting, "was a figure of some power and importance in Bonterre. He was director of the bank."

In short, when Emily O'Herlihy married Martin Sargent, she was quickly able to establish a spiritual genealogy for herself superior to the one she was heir to merely by biology. A story she would never have told had she married someone else became a story she would always tell when talking of her life. Edward Sargent was a better father to her than Dan O'Herlihy, and he had already proven it, beginning with the moment of her birth.

All that remained was for Emily to take on as her own the Sargent family lore and mores.

These days, Emily Sargent can still spin a good tale about Grandfather Schroeder, but she's just as happy telling about the time long before her own birth when Martin's mother, a gentle-woman from Hannibal, came to know Mark Twain, or the time even earlier than that when the Sargents came from Cornwall, bringing with them beautiful dishes and copperware. Figuratively or otherwise, they go rather well with the Schroeder hollow-stemmed champagne glasses.

All stories, including family stories, are told after the fact. In some cases, as in courtship stories that are the prologue to on-going marriages, the passage of time enriches the meaning of the original experience. Even in tension-fraught marriages a courtship story can serve as a lodestar.

But what happens when a marriage terminates in divorce? One man in his early twenties whose parents had separated when he was a child told me he had no idea how his parents had met. Obviously it wasn't an event either parent wanted to recall, much less celebrate. In other cases—for example, that of Polly Gardner, whose parents divorced when she was six months old—the courtship story goes rancid or shrivels up. The present casts its shadow back on the past.

This matters. Courtship stories, whatever else they do, are instructive. To the generation still at home and listening, such stories offer at least one possible way to enter into this intricate human dance; they suggest what to feel about love, how to recognize it, what to do with it. When a courtship story goes sour or when it dies, a resource is lost.

CHAPTER 4

UNDERGROUND RULES

I heard a report on the radio that a quarter of all American homicides occur at home. Intrafamilial killing apparently goes on every which way, the permutations including matricide, patricide, husbands killing wives, wives killing husbands, and so on. This is hardly desirable. Hence, long before emotions reach such a point, it is worthwhile for every family to have an understanding of what is or isn't allowed to be said, done, or felt, and by whom. What comes first, though, is the covert rule about how (and how much) anger is allowed to be expressed, and who is allowed to say or do what to whom.

In most cases, family members never explicitly state this code, either to themselves or to one another. But the rules that make up this family code are conveyed from very early on, by example of course but also highlighted in family stories.

THE EXPRESSION OF ANGER AND VIOLENCE

Depending on the combination of the culture and the individuals in it, there is permission to be expressive verbally and sometimes physically about anger, or not. If not, alternative styles of anger are suggested—irony or sarcasm, withdrawal or iciness. These styles are also, incidentally, usually congruent with what social scientists have to say about the varying ethnic groups and their handling of emotion.

As Ted Court sees it, "abusiveness and violence" are his family legacy, and he has a series of stories that come down the generations about the men in his family, passed along by their wives. This legacy, which begins with Ted's paternal grandfather, is one he says he would rather not have, one which is no help at all in his efforts at controlling his own quick temper. As Ted explains it:

> By the time my father was an adolescent, his father had quit drinking, but I heard a lot of stories about what my grandfather was like before that. I see in my mind scenes of my grandfather: he would come home highly mad, frustrated, pissed off and upset, and he would slap the kids around, push them around. He would abuse my grandmother verbally. I don't think he ever beat her up. But there are lots of ways of beating people up, rather than just hitting them. I have the image of him as someone who was really violent. He ran a group of men on the railroad, forty or fifty, and I see him as someone who was abusive and violent. I see that in my grandfather, I see it in my father— when I was a kid he used to come home drunk and bully my mother verbally—and I see it in myself. I'm abusive, too, when I get angry, though I'm aware of other options.
>
> About my father: The story I have here is that when my father was in his teenage years, he'd just about had it up to here with the bullshit my grandfather was laying down on the family. He felt morally indignant. So one day when my grandfather came in and began insulting my grandmother, my father went off on him. He said, "Look, you no-good son of a bitch, you're not taking care of the family, you're running around, you don't know what responsibility is, so why don't you shut up." He laid a whole trip on his father. He's the only family member who ever took my grandfather on, and so he's the only member that my grandfather confided in. After that he trusted my father. Also

the other family members gave my father some respect for that.

About me: When I graduated from college, I came home. I'd been hitchhiking and doing all this radical political work, and I didn't have a job. I was wearing long hair, blue denims, and a beard, and my father just kept getting on me. I was getting really pissed off at him and finally I exploded. I said, "Look, goddamn it, get off my back and shut up." So with that, he jumped on me, started choking me and beating my head against the wall.

This was in my house when I was twenty-one years old. So with that, I just pushed him. I knocked him flat on the ground, and I told him, "Don't bother to get up, and don't mess with me again." I packed my suitcase, and I've never lived there since. I lived in the Greyhound bus station, I lived in the park. Ever since that happened, my father will communicate with me—he tells me stuff he won't tell my brother or my sister or my mother.

Ted Court's initial lament about his anger is at odds with the power that comes of anger in the family stories he tells. Whatever reservations he seems to have about the tradition of violence in his family at the outset are vanquished after his first few words.

At least among the men in his family, violence has a strong positive connotation, and Ted Court learned this by example as well as by family anecdote: it is a way of being "morally indignant," and it is also characterized as a way of protecting other family members and getting their respect. Most significantly, among the Court men, an attack on one's father seems to be an approved and established rite of passage, a way of demonstrating one's manhood as well as a way of earning one's father's respect, as Ted Court's father did before him, and as he did as well.

In other families, the tone is decidedly more restrained when it comes to expressing anger. Nora Grenwald tells a family story which shows how her mother's family—adults and children alike—handled their anger at a runaway son when he returned, although when she told me the story she didn't think of it as exemplary.

It had stayed alive in the family because of a tragic coincidence. The uncle who had run away, hoping to get to sea, was later lost at sea. These stories may keep their private agendas to themselves but they are prescriptive nonetheless.

> When my mother was a little girl in Norway her older brother, Daniel, once took umbrage at some trifle and ran away to sea—this was at a rather tender age, perhaps thirteen. His family worried a good deal about him in spite of reassurance from the father that no captain would hire him on as he was clearly too young. Sure enough, some days later, the mother, looking out the window of their house, saw her errant son returning home, far down the road.
> She immediately marshaled her family and directed them to present a scene of complete calm: sewing, reading, or chess-playing with total absorption. They were not even to look up or comment when Daniel came in the door. Indeed, no one was to indicate in any way that the boy had ever been missed.

And that's the end of the story, one in which Nora Grenwald saw "a Norwegian kind of cool discipline." Daniel's way of displaying his "umbrage" is exemplary too. However momentarily divided Daniel and his family are, what they share is a style of anger which pointedly and deliberately avoids confrontation. Departing, as he did, or ignoring him, as the family did, are distinct but compatible. Both are "cool" expressions.

If some families favor expressing anger through icy silence, others prefer a more fiery style, whether through word or deed. Kevin Collins, his mother, Kay, and his sister, Cathleen, each (without being prompted) tell several stories about their "Irish temper" and its intersection with Irish irony. One story, which Kay Collins tells with real pleasure, has to do with a quarrel between a husband and wife. It is a story about her in-laws (including a father-in-law who died long before she met her husband), but one she has clearly embraced as her own.

> My father-in-law, whom I never met, was a bit of a dandy. He was the runt of the family, and the last born. He was

slight, with a little mustache, and he did love to dress. So
he went one year at Easter time and got himself all outfitted
in a new suit and hat and topcoat. Then he came home in
this outfit that he'd just bought.

Well, my mother-in-law took one look at him—she had
just two of the boys at this time—and then she got herself
into her coat and bundled the kids up and took them downtown. She went to the bank and drew out the money that
they had saved. Then she went to the store and used it to
outfit the three of them.

I always loved that story. When you heard about women
being downtrodden and stepped on and bossed around
—well, I never saw it in my family, and my husband
never saw it either. To me it means that my mother-in-law
didn't sit and weep or groan and reproach. She simply took
action.

At this, Kay Collins laughs heartily. Cathleen Collins, who
had listened to her mother tell the story with her own amused
smile, then offered a story of even later vintage about her own
parents that embodied exactly the same principles of battle.

I remember a story about my own parents that's roughly
similar to the one about my grandparents. I think they
hadn't been married that long and didn't have a lot of
money. Now my father was an optimist—he had expensive
tastes and felt competent about his ability to make enough
money to indulge them. My mother was always more worried. This is when they were first married, and my father
went out and joined a golf club. He didn't consult my
mother about whether they could afford it. It was beyond
reach, but my father wanted it.

Meanwhile, my mother had been scrimping and saving
and doing without certain things which she would have
liked to have. So when my father joined the golf club, my
mother went out and bought a set of dishes.

Here Kay Collins interjects, "It was a set of dishes I'd been
looking at and saying, 'Oh, I wish I had the money to buy it.'
I went out and bought them. If we could afford to join a golf

club, then we could afford the dishes." There is a certain "So there!" tone to her explanation.

Cathleen then picks up the thread and finishes the story. "We always called those dishes the golf dishes. To this day we call them the golf dishes. That story meant to me that there was an evenness, an evenhandedness to their power. They were on a par with each other."

The stories are intricate in that they not only suggest a style of fighting but, from a female point of view, encourage a particular stance between husband and wife and, by extension, between men and women. The message is that in the Collins household, feeling angry was not forbidden but actively enjoyed, at least by the women.

ILLNESS AND INJURY

THE ONLY GOOD CHILD IS A SICK CHILD

When Carrie Semple was a child growing up in Pittsburgh, there was a story she heard her mother tell over and over.

My mother's name is Marjorie, and apparently my grand-mother's brother had a child the same age who was also named Marjorie. The story is that when my mother was just a baby, the other Marjorie was left with my grand-mother for her to raise, too. So there were two Marjories in the household, and one Marjorie, the other one, was quite sickly. In fact when the sickly Marjorie was eighteen months old, she died. My mother always tells the story that her father always said to her, "Well, Marjorie, you raised yourself," because there were two Marjories and the sick Marjorie needed so much attention. I think my mother felt not well taken care of by her mother and this was one of her pieces of evidence that my grandmother was neglectful.

On the subject of illness itself, the story is inconclusive, containing nothing but the rule, common to all families, that mothers ought to take care of their children. But the tenacity with which Carrie Semple's mother embraced the story and the frequency with which she told it suggest that illness itself carries a charge. There is the suggestion that being sick is one way of guaranteeing that a child will be taken care of.

The cluster of other stories that pertain to illness begin to clarify what the story of the two Marjories meant to Carrie Semple's mother, however. The next story took place when Carrie's mother was eighteen or so. As Carrie tells it:

> My father didn't marry until he was thirty-five. It was always intimated that he led kind of a wild life. My parents met in a strange way. My grandfather, my mother's father, was a city fireman, though he always had another job to make money. My mother had graduated from high school and went to work for the local telephone company, but then she had a "nervous breakdown." In any case she couldn't work. My grandfather was working part-time for my father, who had started his own plumbing business, and my father took a paycheck over to my grandfather's house to give it to him. That's when he met my mother. Three months later they got married.

Never mind love, never mind passion. The conclusion that Carrie Semple's mother had apparently reached by the age of eighteen was that sickness was a reliable and appropriate way of getting the attention she needed, especially from a parent, and in the context of the story, Carrie's father, nearly twice Marjorie's age and her father's boss to boot, appears very much as a parental providing figure. Thus Carrie's mother began her married life with the clear conviction that a good parent is someone who takes care of a sick child, and conversely, that a child is someone who ought to be sick in order to demonstrate that the parent is a good parent. What remained to be seen is which of the two roles Carrie's mother would take on for herself. Would she be the sick child of her own parental husband? Would she be the good parent of a sick child? Or both?

The next story sheds light on the choice Carrie's mother made. As Carrie tells it, "Three months into her marriage, my mother got pregnant. My older brother was born two months prematurely, and my family was full of stories of how 'he was almost blind' because in those days they put premature babies in pure oxygen. Well, in fact he never came close to being blind, but the story was that he was *almost* blinded, and my mother was hysterical and upset, totally preoccupied with worry about this boy." In short, by having a sick child on her hands—her own version of Sick Marjorie—she could demonstrate to herself that she was a good parent. At the same time, given her worry and hysterical upset, she could continue to be her husband's sick child herself.

The plot hereafter thickened. Says Carrie Semple, "When my brother was eleven months old, my mother accidentally became pregnant with me. Two months into that pregnancy, so the story goes, she began to bleed. So my brother was sent to live with my grandparents, and my mother stayed in bed for the next seven months. Every morning, my father would carry her down the stairs. Then I was born and I was fine, and so she was still totally preoccupied with my brother."

So the family rule about illness, as Carrie Semple experienced it, was that the best child was a sick child. "I was always treated as if I were the older child. I dressed my brother and took him to school and picked him up after, as if I were the older child. My mother always said I was born eighteen years old, and she always said it in sort of an angry way—that I never needed anything, that I could always take care of myself." A child "born eighteen years old" is not much different from a child who "raised herself," and perhaps Carrie Semple's mother resented in her daughter the easy confidence she had never been able to muster herself.

At the same time, Carrie's mother's preoccupation and involvement with the illness and death of others continued to be a prominent feature in the family's life. Along with the more explicitly instructive cluster of family stories, it was part of the daily cue about Semple family rules. There was a little cousin of Carrie's who died when he was five. "My mother told the story a hundred times of the little boy laid out in the coffin in his sunsuit." Daily, with her morning coffee, Carrie's mother would read the obituary notices in the paper. "If she had known the person remotely, even twenty-five years ago, she would go to the wake at the funeral home and take us with her."

Yet despite all these cues as to how Carrie should behave—maybe stopping short of sunsuit and coffin—she refused, insisting on being steadfastly well. "My health was my defiance, and I was seen as 'the bad girl.' "

SICKNESS AS A FORM OF BLAME

In Ted Court's family, as in Carrie Semple's, using illness as a vehicle for all sorts of other feelings had gathered momentum twenty or thirty years before Ted was born, but through family stories as well as daily life, he received clear instructions about exactly what he had missed. In the Court family canon, illness first noticeably became a charged subject when Ted's father was born.

> My grandfather, my father's father, was an alcoholic, and a real heavy-duty Don Juan type with the ladies. There were stories I heard where sometimes my grandmother would plead with my grandfather, "Please, let's not have sex again," because she didn't want to have another kid. My mother told me that story—she got to be close with my father's mother.
>
> The bad story—which my mother also heard from her mother-in-law and which she would tell in bits and pieces and later deny—was that my grandfather had some kind of venereal disease. As a result, when my father was born, because they didn't use silver nitrate on him, that created some kind of eye problem. He was born with a white layer of skin over his right eye. In other words, it was the sins of the father getting visited on the son. Because of the way

my grandfather lived, getting drunk and playing around, his son suffered.

Putting aside questions about the medical accuracy of this story, it's clear that Ted's father's handicap was used by Ted's grandmother, Mary, to blame his grandfather. It was particularly valuable as a handicap because over the years she could build on it in a continuing reproach. Mary was a devout Catholic, and her dearest desire was that one of her sons should become a priest, and herein lies another family story. Says Ted:

> My father was the obvious choice. He was the only family member to go to college. Everybody else became a fireman or a cop or a garbage collector or a truck driver. So he was to be her offering to Jesus, her phoenix that rises from the ashes, and she groomed him for that, and he wanted that, too. So he went off to seminary. Academically I think he did fine, but one day—he'd been there over a year—the head guy at the seminary called my father in and they called my grandmother in and said, "Look, lady, we're going to have to ask your son to leave. We feel that his physical impairment would stand in the way of him becoming a good priest."

In other words, the sins of the father had continued to be visited on the son, so much so that he was disqualified from the calling his mother found most desirable. Ted Court confides that because of the turbulence in his own life, he went into therapy, and at one point his parents joined him for a family therapy session. During that session, says Ted, these series of stories relating to his father's "handicap" came up for retelling and examination. "The meaning I got from the exploration—and my parents even agreed—was that my grandmother really focused on my father's handicap, sometimes to take it and stick it back in her husband's face." Then he expands the insight to his own family and himself. "A lot of time sickness in our family means 'I'm sick. It's your fault. You're to blame.'

I can see it with my father and my mother, and myself some-times."

The Prohibition Against Sickness

In some families, sickness is permitted to some members but denied to others. In Sharon Medlow's family, she was not al-lowed to be sick or hurt or injured. In fact she felt she wasn't allowed to be dependent at all. And yet it wasn't that no one was allowed. In fact, throughout the generations there were stories of disastrous illnesses afflicting various members. The earliest, and most frequently invoked, says Sharon, took place when her father was a child of twelve.

> When my father was growing up, they lived in the west end of Chicago and they were poor. It was winter time, and my father's little brother, Louie, got sick. He had a cough, and they sent for the doctor, who came and ex-amined him. The doctor said Louie was sick, and that they had to watch over him. But then Louie got sicker and sicker. Finally, they got ahold of the doctor again in the middle of the night, and he said he thought Louie had pneumonia and that there was this medicine they should get. My grand-father went to get the medicine and Louie died while he was out.
>
> After Louie died, my father's mother withdrew into a corner near the window and sat there, just sat there. She was catatonic for over a year and did nothing to take care of the family.
>
> Another brother grew up to be real crazy—violent, hos-tile, definitely the black sheep of the family. He's now a man in his fifties who still lives with his father. He never married.
>
> So Louie's death brought psychological and emotional ruin to the family. Definitely. My grandmother always said that if my grandfather had gotten home with the medicine sooner, Louie would have lived. That belief was critical to their relationship. If it hadn't been for my great-grand-mother, who lived with them, the family couldn't have

survived at all. My father tells stories about his grandmother holding the family together after Louie died. She was the Rock of Gibraltar, and she peddled on the streets of Chicago to keep them alive. When everybody else was falling apart, she was always solid. My father, too. From the time Louie died, my father took over the family in very substantial ways.

Whether or not Louie's death was the event that shaped the family's sense of itself or whether it was just a pretext, no one will ever really know. But what's obvious is that the family became dichotomized into the Afflicted and the Survivors, Sharon's father and great-grandmother being cast in the latter roles. What's also clear is that as a result of Sharon's father's experience, he believed illness would always carry a terrible, powerful charge. A sick child was the first step toward utter family ruin.

But how did Sharon Medlow, born twenty or thirty years after Louie's death, become someone to whom sickness was not permitted? Those who theorize about how families work have an explanation that would apply to the Medlows. Says Norman Ackerman, "An individual relates to members of his or her nuclear family in the same manner as he or she learned to relate to the original family . . . relationships in the nuclear family tend to be mirror images of both extended families."

Applied to the Medlows, this means that when Sharon Medlow's father married and had children, he hauled out all the old costumes—Survivor and Afflicted—and dressed up his wife and children accordingly, obviously not without some collaboration from his wife. Sharon Medlow was an early choice for "Survivor" because to her father she seemed a reincarnation of his indomitable grandmother. "My father had tremendous admiration for his grandmother, which was real significant because he always told me I reminded him of her." Furthermore, his daughter reminded him of himself. "I was my father's kid. I was the kid that he decided to raise." And third and most compelling, "I was told that I was born different, that from the moment I was born I was different from my siblings: I was a kid who could take care of myself."

If anything, the circumstances of Medlow family life, as Sharon was growing up, confirmed that choice and laced her ever more tightly into her invincible Survivor's costume. In particular, Sharon's mother had a difficult time with her pregnancies. "I was the third child. My mother was twenty-five when she had me. They told her she would never have another child, and then after me she had a miscarriage. Then she got pregnant, but they didn't believe she was pregnant, so they told her she had a tumor. She had my brother, and then very shortly after— within the next year and a half—she did develop a tumor and had to have a hysterectomy."

In short, Sharon's mother, by obstetrical circumstance, became a candidate for the role of the Afflicted, as did Sharon's younger brother, the only boy and the erstwhile tumor. "My brother grew up as if he was a sickly child. But otherwise, my parents overreacted to anything being wrong with us healthwise. There was a whole drama around illness."

All children in all families stumble into their designated roles, but through family stories they are coached and encouraged, and they often grow into the costume so that it becomes a second skin. But the power of the Survivor costume to disguise not only Sharon Medlow but her actual state of health was made clear during an event that happened when she was eight. "What happened was I got pneumonia, and in fact I almost died. I knew I was dying, but my mother said, 'There's nothing wrong with you. You're not even coughing in the middle of the night.' As Louie had. Then when she found out I had pneumonia, she was real guilty, and I felt really gleeful." For once she didn't have to be the reincarnation of her great-grandmother. For once, she got to be sick.

Sharon Medlow is twenty-nine now. She hasn't lived with her parents and siblings for many years. But she still has trouble being anything other than the tough-minded Survivor, and she still has trouble being sick. In this family, stories were the tangible stage directions in her otherwise silent and subliminal Medlow script.

SUICIDE

Gerald O'Connor, like many men, wears his watch with the face over the veins on his wrist, so that he has to swivel his arm to see the time. Most men might have no idea why they wear their watches this way, but Gerald O'Connor knows exactly why.

"I said to my father—and this is perhaps as important a story as I might tell you, silly as it seems—'Why do you wear your watch that way, with the face up?' And he said to me, 'Because my father told me to.' I just craved the opportunity to say to a child of mine, hoping for the question, 'Because my father told me to,' so that I may pass it on. There is no reason to wear your watch this way, except that your father told you to do so. I only wear my watch this way because my father did. It's far more convenient to wear it the conventional way, where you don't scratch the crystal. But I would feel traitorous to my father."

But the rest of Edward O'Connor's instructive legacy to his son was not so benign, and Gerald—not a "traitorous" son at heart—is still wrestling with it. Edward O'Connor died at the age of forty-six, "of a heart attack," says Gerald, "complicated by alcohol." Gerald believes he knows the moment in his father's life when it began to be doomed.

> I want to tell you a story my father told me about his father and himself. He had returned from the Second World War and married my mother. His father was ill, very ill, with cirrhosis of the liver. Here's the scene as I imagine it from the story. My grandfather is perhaps on his deathbed, and my father, who was then twenty-two or twenty-three, with a young wife and perhaps a kid on the way, comes in. He is bright, a fine artist, with great prospects as a writer.
>
> He comes in and my grandfather says, "I want you to take over the family business." My father, through thought-lessness or lack of self-confidence, says O.K. He ends up spending his life in Holyoke, Massachusetts, working in a deadly boring profession—in a printing and lithography

business established by my great-grandfather. It is a profession for which he has no affection and in which he has no interest.

This story holds a good deal of meaning for Gerald O'Connor. "It had a great impact," he says, "in my thoughts about my father, about me, and about self-destructiveness," a self-destructiveness so marked that suicidologists would have called Edward O'Connor a "crypto-suicide," a man who steadily and deliberately inched his way toward death rather than leaping toward it as those who choose bridges do. "Self-destructiveness," continues Gerald O'Connor, "seems to characterize so much of my male heritage, and I see that in my father. I think his life was terribly sad. He was a wonderfully bright and inventive man trapped in a dull, dull life," perhaps like his father before him. Gerald's grandfather, at twenty-three, had been a Phi Beta Kappa graduate of Amherst, ready for more than his life subsequently offered him.

The male heritage that Gerald O'Connor refers to casts much of its shadow over the deathbed story he tells, limiting its possible meanings and making it seem clear that it amounts almost to a suicidal instruction from his father to him: to step into adult malehood, with its work requirements and its attendant conventionalities, is to beckon self-inflicted death in one's prime. The subtext of the story suggests that Edward O'Connor was no "traitorous" son either. He did his father's bidding, and his repetition of the story to Gerald implied that Gerald, too, should do the same.

Gerald O'Connor knows about the family self-destructiveness because of a whole vein of stories about the O'Connor men going back for at least three generations. His alcoholic grandfather O'Connor was dead by forty-eight, and his grandfather's two brothers—Gerald's great-uncles, Patrick and Francis—didn't even live that long. Says Gerald O'Connor:

Patrick and Francis were apparently mad. Alcohol figures into it. So does suicide. Both Francis and Patrick were apparently suicides. The stories were fragments, bits, and the details were unclear. There is a fragment about Francis. He had been set up in the family business, too, and he would get up in the morning and on his way to work, drink a pint of whiskey. One morning an employee walked into the storeroom, and there was old Francis. He had hung himself, just strung himself up. He was in his thirties. Patrick also died in his thirties, also a suicide.

The dark legacy of the O'Connors haunts Gerald, especially now that he is of the age to be susceptible to what he sees as the O'Connor destiny. He is a man in his thirties, with a family, with responsibilities. Perhaps his story legacy haunts him more than it might some others, since he is deeply tied to being an O'Connor. "I don't know to what degree people need to be connected to family pasts, but I clearly did and do. So little family history was discussed, whether from shame, a real wish to forget, or real bitterness. But these fragments of stories about these characters really are references for me. On the matter of roles and models, my identification with my father is at once deep, confusing, and unclear."

Nor can Gerald O'Connor find any relief when he thinks about his other recent male O'Connor relatives. "I always think about these guys—as definitions of masculinity, of how men should be. And these sad characters serve as a reference point. I don't want to be like them and yet one is attracted to that kind of romantic self-destructiveness. It's what's attractive and also repellent."

The pull of the O'Connor destiny is intensified because Gerald O'Connor sees his family destiny as ultimately anchored in the Irish identity. The two identities—being an O'Connor and being Irish—were more compatible and much more mutually reinforcing than Gerald O'Connor had initially anticipated, not only because of the shared fascination with alcohol, but with self-destructiveness as a masculine trait as well. "Irish kings," Gerald O'Connor says, "died violently in situations in which it's impossible to live. They quite literally fought naked because clothing might protect you from the wound. And to adopt any shield or weapon which would block an injury is less than manly."

So wherever Gerald O'Connor looked and whatever stories he heard, both within his paternal family and about the country they came from, he was greeted with instructions in favor of suicide, however romantically they may have been gilded.

With a legacy like this, Gerald O'Connor knows clearly what he's up against. "I've struggled a lot with this strange legacy of self-destructiveness—the romance of it, what's implied about life, and what's implied about ambitions and expectations. It's made me wonder about what men find when they mature, what my own expectations ought to be, what I can anticipate about the way I'll feel in ten or fifteen years."

Gerald O'Connor knows that beneath the "romance" lie some merely dreary human emotions. "It's no longer as seductive as it was. The wish to be a sort of romantic doomed young man is really gone." And yet to Gerald O'Connor, who wears his watch the way his father did, dispensing with the legacy is not only courting treason, it is confronting the unknown in an uncomfortable way. "I can't really believe I'll live to fifty years old because there's no track record. You learn such stuff from your father—how to cope, how to react." Instead, Gerald O'Connor will have to teach himself. "To dispense with my history will force me to make a person, to make a life, to throw away a lot of what seems preordained.

"And yet I think I would like to be around to see grandchildren and to live to be a funny old man. I would like to have maple trees and to live outdoors the way old men do."

Irene Goldstein, from an altogether different background from Gerald O'Connor's, knows a good deal about death, too, especially because she is the daughter of parents who spent World War II imprisoned in Nazi concentration camps, an experience which colored every subsequent moment of their lives and much of their talk. Every other relative on both sides of her family died at the hands of the Nazis: four grandparents, two uncles, one uncle's wife, and a cousin. That is quite enough to contend with. But Irene Goldstein says she has another legacy that is equally daunting. "Even well before the war, my family was full of suicides. I'm the fourth generation of suicidal women, and my response to this is one of tremendous fear. I don't like the legacy."

As Irene recounts it, the "legacy" of suicide began with her great-grandmother, her mother's mother's mother, whose favorite child, Heinzy, died of pneumonia. For a while she wept at his grave daily, then she threw herself out the window. "It was not a surprise to anybody," Irene continues. "Her daughter, my grandmother, subsequently went off and became an assistant to a dress designer in Vienna." She married soon after, in her twenties, but the marriage was annulled because her husband was syphilitic, and it was never consummated. Eventually, Irene's grandmother married a second man, who also, says Irene, came from a heavily suicidal family. But all these years, Irene is convinced, her grandmother continued to be what she was at twenty: "very very nervous, neurasthenic, constantly on the verge of fainting."

> Both my mother's parents kept threatening to commit suicide. My grandmother continued to have fainting fits and hysterical fits. She went off to sanitaria. I think of her as a Klimt woman—extremely sensitive, extremely sensual in a nonsexual way, and tremulous all the time. My grandmother's suicidal impulses appear to have been very inner-directed. They didn't seem to have much to do with what was going on outside. She had a very tenuous connection to life, which makes sense since she lost both her parents when she was nine years old.
>
> As for my grandfather, he kept a loaded pistol in his desk. His suicidal stuff [here Irene laughs wryly] was apparently geared to what was going on in the financial world. When the stock market went down, the pistol came out. My mother says she would walk into her father's study, and he'd be sitting there with his pistol out. In fact later, my grandfather, in addition to having a pistol, had a vial of pills in his desk which my mother discovered when she was fourteen. She was very worried about her father committing suicide, as I'm sure she must have been because her mother must have told her that *her* mother committed suicide.
>
> So at the age of fourteen, my mother went through her

father's desk, found the pills, decided they must be suicide pills, took them to a pharmacist, and had them analyzed. In fact they were arsenic and cyanide. So she had the druggist replace them with saccharine, and then she put them back in his desk. In 1941 or 1942, when the three of them were sitting on the floor in a deportation center waiting to get carted off to a concentration camp, my grandfather told my mother, "I have my life in my own hands. Here are my pills." And then my mother had to tell him what she had done.

He was in a total rage because my mother had robbed him of his own domination over his life. That was the last time she ever saw him, and she's been guilty about that all her life. She's never been able to forgive herself.

My mother survived the concentration camp, but as soon as she went back home after the war, she became suicidal. She wanted to kill herself the first year after the war, and then when I was a kid suicide came up again and again and again.

But is Irene herself suicidal? "No," she says, somewhat uncertainly. "But every time I get depressed to the degree where I feel hopeless, I think, 'Well, if the worst comes to the worst, I can always commit suicide.' It's always there. It's a family option. A reasonable option. I've never tried to do it, but I think I'm probably more interested than your average person in the subject. I read Alvarez's book, The Savage God, but I didn't have to read it. I was very interested in Sylvia Plath, not because she was a woman writer, but because of her suicide. I was always interested in Antigone for the same reasons. And Joan of Arc. Death doesn't really scare me."

As A. Alvarez pointed out in The Savage God, the children of those who eventually commit suicide are more inclined to suicide themselves—for example, Ernest Hemingway and John Berryman were suicidal sons of suicidal fathers. In part this is because, as Irene Goldstein pointed out, suicide becomes a "family option." It lurks about as a familiar presence. But it's not just that suicide seems familiar. There are two other explanations as well. The first, as Gerald O'Connor so clearly understood, is that suicide itself becomes a covert form of family loyalty. How dare one turn one's back on an option that is seen as running in the family? To repudiate the option seems a repudiation of a child's suicidal parent, and thus may engender guilt. This is how theoreticians interested in the subject of intergenerational family loyalty might explain it.

Second, there is the fact that in some cases suicide receives a rather flattering characterization, as in the Goldstein family stories about it. In Irene Goldstein's experience, suicide is chosen when one is faced with overwhelming grief at the death of a child, or when one wants to preserve some measure of autonomy in the face of malevolent oppressors. The cluster of Goldstein family stories carve out and delimit the possible meanings of the act, and do so in ways that enhance it as an option. It is likely that in families where there has been no suicide, the subject either doesn't come up at all, or else is dealt with in ways that reinforce prohibitions against it.

In her reflections, Irene Goldstein compared her family's experience with suicide over the generations to the curse on the House of Atreus in Greek tragedy. However the Greeks understood the idea of a curse that spans generations, Irene Goldstein understood it as the cumulative weight of the generations on her head. It was a psychological destiny she feared and wanted to resist. And not surprisingly, she thought the only way she could successfully resist it was by calling on the heritage from her father's side of the family, where there was no suicide. "It's a legacy of courtesy. I'm telling you," she concluded, "my mother's side of the family is crazy, and if I didn't have my father's side, I'd be a total lunatic."

Anger, illness, injury, suicide—these are some of the arenas where the family has its own series of rules, many of them covert, which it wants to have followed. Some of them are undeniably destructive, but ironically, they strive toward a certain kind of harmony. Any family has to do its intricate dance together for at least twenty years and sometimes longer. It helps, therefore, if everybody knows the steps.

As for secret rules extending beyond the life of one nuclear family through generations, these rules can be, and have been, teased out by family therapists through the use of what's called a "genogram." A genogram is an annotated family tree, with all the salient facts about nuclear and extended family members included, among them marriage dates, divorces, physical and mental illnesses, miscarriages, death dates, manner of death, and so on.

In the hands of a talented clinician, the genogram can reveal the patterns that have governed the family for three or four generations, even for a century. The genogram gives a picture of the family as it's known to the individual, a picture which has been constructed, pointillist fashion, from what the individual knows of his or her family stories. And what if the "true" facts, could they be miraculously known, are at odds with the facts brought in by the individual? It doesn't matter. The facts that we know, true or false, are the facts that we live by.

CHAPTER·5

FAMILY MYTHS

EXPLANATION MYTHS

My father was one of seven children—three boys and four girls—born to his parents over nearly twenty years. The eldest two had been born in Austria before my grandparents came here, in the first days of this century, to Ludlow Street on the Lower East Side. My father, William, was the first child born here.

My father's parents were very devout Orthodox Jews. My father always told me his father was a rabbi (though a sister of his whom I once asked said it wasn't so) and among their beliefs was a belief in arranged marriages. My father's first marriage had been arranged by his parents in his absence. He had run away to some cousins in Wyoming, and his mother, so the story goes, came and got him so she could bring him back and marry him off. My most benign assessment of this story is that she hoped marriage would settle him down, stop him from running away, as he had, on and off, since he was a youngster.

She did bring him back and the marriage did eventually take place, but it was not a happy one, or even a tolerable one. They divorced two years later. When my father later married my mother, he said his parents, considering him lost to the family,

96

sat *shiva*, a mourning ritual for the dead. His brothers and sisters say this isn't so.

Whatever the case, it is not in dispute that my father's next-to-youngest sister was Naomi, nor is it disputed that when she was in her late teens and of marriageable age, her parents arranged for her to be married to a man a good deal older than herself. Shortly after her marriage, she had a nervous breakdown and had to be institutionalized.

Later the family learned that Naomi's husband was impotent and that their marriage was never consummated. They explained her breakdown this way. Whether protracted virginity is enough to induce a nervous breakdown seems questionable, especially in light of what happened to Naomi later on. The second story takes place a few years later. By then, Naomi was married again and had become pregnant. Whether this was an arranged marriage or not, I don't know. At any rate, after Naomi's child was born, she went into a severe postpartum depression. This became yet another explanation for the next trauma that ensued. Naomi was again institutionalized, and this time was given a prefrontal lobotomy. She remains institutionalized to this day.

While it's true that lobotomies were in medical vogue during the 1950s, I find it hard to believe that these two separate events—an impotent husband and a postpartum depression—truly explain so much distress. But the fact remains that although I don't think of myself as psychologically naive, until now I have never challenged—even to myself—the explanations offered by the stories.

And I think I know why. My Aunt Naomi was not the only troubled member of that family. My father was an unstable and unhappy man. During his life, he was tormented by demons I didn't—and really still don't—understand, which made him drink too much liquor and swallow too many pills. Another member of his family, in my generation, also had to be hospitalized for mental illness. What was going on there? Was it the genes? Was it some psychic time bomb long ago planted on Ludlow Street? If it was, then I had to worry, too. I believed in my Aunt Naomi's first impotent husband with the same frightened fervor I believed in the story my mother told me about why my father drank too much. She said his drinking had become a problem while he was in the army during World War II.

Mental illness is a crucial event not only to the afflicted person but to the surrounding family members. It is a preoccupying event, an event to brood over, an event which can bring the emotional life of a family to a tense standstill while its members stare at it, transfixed by the event and worried about their own vulnerabilities.

Family stories, such as the ones about my Aunt Naomi, belong to a special category. They are family myths because, like classical myths, they are meant to explain why—why the flood covered the earth, why the desert is parched, why my Aunt Naomi wound up spending half her life locked up with only half a brain in her head, why my father annually tried to drink and drug himself into oblivion. If I challenge the myths now, it is only because—grown, with a family of my own, and still no demons in sight, at least not unmanageable ones—I can afford to. If I couldn't I suppose I wouldn't have noticed them at all.

The term "myth" also suggests that the explanation offered might well be untrue, or at least too limited, which all such explanations very likely are. But at least they offer possible, if not always plausible, explanations for emotional cataclysms within the family and can be an adroit solution to our worries. They offer a simple, one-dimensional cause, and in so doing, they seem to put a fence around the event, releasing us from our preoccupation so we can move on. And even if such myths of explanation don't succeed altogether in reassuring us, they perhaps make our uneasiness more manageable. They obscure our deeper conviction that what is in the blood will out, that shared blood means shared susceptibilities.

Furthermore, family stories, including myths, are well equipped to lull us. We accede to the nature of the genre, and enter into it on its own terms. As part of the oral tradition, family stories do not easily encompass intricate analyses or explanations of the many causes for an event. In fact, they obey the conventions of the oral tradition, reducing complex phenomena to single comprehensible causes. Because they are casually told and even more casually heard, we hear without alerting our more critical faculties. And so we may believe emotionally without truly assenting intellectually.

As Bruno Bettelheim explained in *The Uses of Enchantment*, simple fables speak metaphorically to the unconscious. "Fairy tales," writes Bettelheim, "convey at the same time overt and covert meanings, [they] speak simultaneously to all levels of the human personality, communicating in a manner which reaches the uneducated mind of the child as well as that of the sophisticated adult. Applying the psychoanalytic model of the human personality, fairy tales carry important messages to the conscious, the preconscious, and the unconscious mind, on whatever level each is functioning at the time."

And so it may be with family explanation myths, which, like fairy tales, deal in code with the important human issues of birth, death, sexuality, injury, and what used to be called madness. My Aunt Naomi, like some latter-day Sleeping Beauty permanently imprisoned, never awakened to or acceded to adult sexuality. At least her unconsummated marriage and her postpartum depression, functioning almost as symbols, suggest her deep uneasiness with sexuality.

And certainly there was enough in her childhood to occasion such uneasiness. She grew up in exceedingly cramped quarters on the Lower East Side. Certainly there wasn't a bedroom for every child, and undoubtedly there weren't even enough bedrooms to separate the girls from the boys, or for that matter, the children from their parents. In addition, a stint with an impotent husband did her no good, but it's unlikely that that alone was the direct cause of her turmoil. It's not unlikely, however, that the sexual climate of her childhood, filled with half a dozen adolescent siblings as well as her parents, was distressing, and perhaps distressing enough to account for her later difficulties.

The most metaphoric explanation fable I ever heard came from David Moses, a law student who grew up in a very well-to-do Black family. As in other cases, the myth he repeated was meant to explain the emotional illness that has made an ap-

pearance in some family member or other in almost every generation as far back as he can trace.

The risk of such instability's surfacing yet again seems truly
to haunt the Moses family. In fact, his father's fear of it dominates
even the story of David's own birth. "The story I've gotten is
that the first question my father asked my mother when I was
born was 'Is he O.K.?' meaning 'Is he disturbed?' They were
always wondering, 'When is that madness going to surface again?' "

David turned out to be quite sturdy in both mind and body,
though he says that one of his four sisters is "extremely fragile."
In his father's generation there is a troubled uncle, though David's own father, a Justice Department attorney, has never had
any such problems.

But the facts are quite different in David's father's mother's
generation. "My grandmother and her two sisters—all three of
them were crazy, though my grandmother probably had more
moments of lucidity during her life than her sisters. Her sister
Martine, who was a concert pianist, had a coming-out party at
the Plaza. It was her debut to colored society in New York, back
before World War I. The way my father tells it, Martine went
insane at her coming-out party and was put away as a result."

Those are the facts as David Moses knows them. It is in
explaining why the family is so susceptible to mental illness that
the Moses family explanation myth, and its coded metaphor,
come into play. According to what David has heard, such de-
rangement first entered the family through an illustrious white
ancestor, a slave owner, and this ancestor had something to do
with a curse. "Either a curse was put on him," says David, "or
he put it on his own illegitimate Black offspring."

This is all the explanation David has. As for decoding the
metaphor—it has certainly been the case historically that Blacks
in this country have been cursed and indeed driven crazy by the
conditions imposed by powerful white oppressors. This may be
even more true for those Blacks, like David's family, who are
extremely ambitious and therefore likely to come into the most
extended contact with white society. The Moses family explanation myth is unusual in that it offers the family no protection

at all against further psychic derailment, and indeed suggests such distress will be the family's perpetual legacy. But the myth does, in code, explain that racism is what has caused so many generations of the family so much distress, and indeed this is exactly how David Moses understands the story.

But families believe in their myths for reasons more compelling than respect for the versatility of metaphor. What the family tells us has a force and power that we never quite leave behind. What they tell us is our first syntax, our first grammar, the foundation onto which we later add our own perceptions and modifications. We are not entirely free to challenge the family's beliefs as we might challenge any other system of belief. And even when we do challenge, we half disbelieve ourselves.

MYTHS OF BLAME:
THE FAMILY SCAPEGOAT

Peter Mott is a successful nuclear physicist at a large West Coast university. He is an attractive man, with a full head of curly blond hair, bright, amused blue eyes, and the lean build of a born athlete. In fact, up until he was a teenager, his dream was to become a professional tennis player. He had the talent and the speed, too. But the dream came to an abrupt end when Peter Mott came down with polio. In time, he recovered well enough to get around, but not well enough ever to play tennis again. Especially when he's tired, he walks with a discernible limp.

Now in his early fifties, he's had time to make peace with his condition, but he still remembers—and still tells—the story that circulated in his family about how he contracted polio in the first place. "When I got polio, it was in the mid-1940s, ten years before the first polio vaccine began to be used. My mother always said that the reason I got polio was because we had gone to visit my sister at college, and while we were there, we drank water that was no good."

Peter Mott is an entertaining raconteur, and I had been sitting in his kitchen, having brunch, looking through old photographs and listening to his stories rather passively, willing enough for the moment to do nothing more than enjoy them. But when he got to the part about the water being "no good," I became more alert. It seemed an extremely odd locution for a scientist to be using about contaminated water. Maybe the child who had first heard that story would use that phrase, but not the scientist talking to me now. Besides, the whole story didn't add up. How could the Motts have known that Peter contracted polio from drinking water, much less pointed a finger at a particular faucet?

A rash of questions occurred to me, and I asked them. Had anyone else in the Mott family come down with polio as a result? Had any of the dozens of young women in his sister's dormitory become ill? Had his sister's university ever tested the water to find out whether it was contaminated or not? To all these questions, Peter Mott's answer was no.

The story turned out to be not just implausible but one with a covert agenda, comprehended implicitly by the Motts but, without a gloss, incomprehensible to anyone else. And the agenda focused on Peter's sister, Blanche. In every family, say family theorists, individual members have their assigned roles, which they may be well cast for or not. What determines the assigning of roles is not so much who the players really are, but who the family as a whole needs them to be. In the Mott family, Peter was understood to be "the golden boy" while Blanche, as Peter put it, was "dirt."

These are the sorts of destructive convictions for which family therapists reserve the term "family myths." The first to elaborate on the notion was psychiatrist Antonio Ferreira, who defined "family myths" as "beliefs shared by all family members, concerning each other and their mutual position in the family life." He asserted that these beliefs "go unchallenged by everyone involved in spite of the reality distortions which they may conspicuously imply. It should be noted that although the family myth is part of the family image, it often differs from the 'front' or social facade that the family as a group attempts to present to outsiders. Instead the family myth is very much a part of the way the family appears to its members, that is, a part of *the inner image* of the group, an image to which all family members contribute and, apparently, strive to preserve. In terms of the family inner image, the family myth refers to the identified roles of its members."

Ferreira further characterized the family myth by suggesting that family members may not subscribe to it absolutely. "The individual family member may know, and often does, that much of that image is false and represents no more than a sort of official party line. But such knowledge, when [and if] it exists, is kept so private and concealed that the individual will actually fight against its public revelation, and, by refusing to acknowledge its existence, will do his utmost to keep the family myth intact. For the family myth 'explains' the behavior of the individuals in the family while it hides its motives. . . ."

But why should a family hold on to a belief regardless of its truth? The answer lies in the usefulness of the belief to the individual members. Such beliefs, in whatever way, make other family members feel better about themselves; they allow the family to work, and in doing so, they preserve what Ferreira calls family "homeostasis" or equilibrium.

This is the case even if one member has to bear a socially stigmatized role as a result—as the "bad" one, the "sickly" one, or the mentally ill one. Given this approach, those who do therapy with families make the assumption that the "sick" one is the symptom bearer, the scapegoat, for the entire family. Cure the family and the "sick" one will get better. But this is not so easy to accomplish because all the family members—with the possible exception of the scapegoat—get something as a result of their unconscious conspiracy.

Now, in the Mott family, the central myth was that Blanche was the bad one, the sick one, and the story about how Peter came down with polio was one of many stories used to justify the myth and to keep Blanche tethered to her place in the psychic desert. As the Motts understood that story during the years when Blanche and Peter were growing up, it meant that Peter's polio was Blanche's fault.

Blanche's place in the family was not of course enviable and never had been, and Blanche did not escape the unhappy consequences of her role. If enough people think someone is incompetent or insane or stupid or sickly or bad, that someone may eventually oblige, even if he or she wasn't to begin with.

This is a truth about how families work that Hollywood and movie audiences have long since recognized. In that old film classic *Gaslight* (1944), Ingrid Bergman, as the young wife, is told so often by her husband and maid that she is losing her sanity that eventually she begins to. Similarly, in *Now, Voyager* (1942) and *Separate Tables* (1958), each "spinster" daughter is, at least initially, frail, homely, and invalided because each has dutifuly subscribed to her mother's "myth" about her. In each case, it is a myth the mother generates because of her own need to have a companion who won't leave home.

As for the real-life Blanche Mott, she was even more vulnerable than the afflicted young women onscreen. "When my sister was fourteen or fifteen," says Peter, "she had a nervous breakdown. She had shock therapy and saw a psychiatrist and tried to take her own life."

But how had Blanche come to occupy her unenviable role as both "the sick one" and "the bad one"? And how did Peter emerge as the family's "golden boy"? The answer, or at least part of it, lies with Peter Mott's mother, Helen; with events in Helen's life at about the time Blanche was born, as well as earlier; and with the way those events determined, apparently unconsciously, her vision and expectations of each of her two children. This perspective, which comes from Peter Mott, was one he arrived at after several years of analysis.

In the years just before Blanche was born, says Peter, their mother had endured too much tragedy. "My mother's father, whom she always saw as a comforter, had died," says Peter.

"Then her two sisters died—one of scarlet fever and the other of spilling boiling water on herself. Then my grandmother, my mother's mother, died of a heart attack. My mother was pregnant with my sister at this time, and so they named my sister Blanche, which had been my grandmother's name. In fact my grandmother's maiden name was Kane, and they named my sister Blanche Kane Mott."

The conclusion Peter draws from all this now is that at the time of the younger Blanche's birth, Helen Mott was emotionally devastated and totally depleted; she was not in any psychological condition to welcome or rejoice over her first child's birth. "My mother was in terrible shape," says Peter. "She was hospitalized—she had a nervous breakdown—and there was a nursemaid to take care of my sister."

The additional twist was that Peter Mott's mother had apparently miscalculated what she would feel about naming her daughter after her mother, however much she had liked, or wanted to like, the idea of so honoring her mother. Helen Mott had had a difficult, even stormy relationship with her own mother and now, having a little girl with the same name as her mother's, she seemed unable to keep the two separate in her mind. It was as if once Helen Mott lost her own mother, she took all the feelings she had had about her and transferred them, part and parcel, to her little daughter.

"My mother could never bring herself to use the name Blanche with my sister, so she called her Missy. It was just too much, the death was too much and the daughter was too much. Perhaps my sister was just too much of a reminder. But anyhow, my sister was the one in the family who could do nothing right. As a consequence, she was raised as if she were dirt, or incompetent, or terrible. Growing up, I didn't consciously recognize how my sister was being devalued, but one of the most extraordinary aspects of all this family stuff is that for most of my adult life, I dealt with my sister as my mother had dealt with her. As for me," says Peter Mott somewhat ruefully, "I was 'The Golden Boy.' The doctor told my mother to have another child to make her well. I was that child, and I could do no wrong." Perhaps,

too, Peter was the replacement for his mother's dead "comforter," her father.

There's nothing in Peter Mott's explanation to explain his
father's investment in having Blanche as "the sick one." According to Peter, his father was fairly involved with his own
parents, both of whom lived with the Motts. Maybe he was
therefore too distant to intercede in the *folie à trois* developing
right under his nose. But as for Peter's mother, despite her own
fragility, she could redefine herself as healthy once she had a
fragile daughter. For Peter, having a disabled sister certainly
made it less likely that there would be any encroachment on his
role as the "golden" child.

I have gone rather far afield here and made so many incursions
into the Motts' prior history—told to Peter as family stories,
along the way—to show how any one family story derives its
meaning not only from daily family life but from the family's
entire jigsaw puzzle of stories. The meaning of any single family
story will therefore appear as inevitable, from narrative context
alone, to the family members who know the story and tell it.

Relatively few such stories came my way, perhaps because I
didn't always recognize them for what they were, but also because
family members implicitly recognized their subversive nature
and, out of continuing family loyalty, kept them to themselves.
Perhaps Peter Mott could afford to tell the story because the
event it referred to had happened forty years earlier, both his
parents were dead, he was deeply ensconced in his own family
of a wife and four nearly grown children, and maybe he was
looking for a way to expiate his guilt for whatever part he had
played in his sister's long-ago torment.

Could Peter Mott have recognized the implausibility of this
family story decades ago? Many family therapists would say probably not. Such stories, as Ferreira points out, serve the family
as defense mechanisms serve the individual. "The myth, like
the defense, protects the [family] against the threat of disintegration and chaos. . . . Thus, to maintain oneself within a given
myth, a certain amount of insightlessness is necessary." But to
outsiders, the family myths that serve to keep a family's specious

convictions in place are recognizable by the same two elements that appeared in Peter Mott's myth—implausible logic and blame.

Another family-blame myth is a relic from a family now dismembered by the passage of time. The family myth concerns a mother who has long since died, a father, also long dead, and their baby, now a woman in her late seventies. The story was told to me by the latter woman's daughter, Maureen Kelly.

My mother, Cecilia, was an only child, and therein lies a story. The marriage between my grandmother and grandfather was not going well. I never knew my grandmother because she died three years before I was born, but she was a very domineering woman and as she grew older people called her a shrew. And so she went to her parish priest and asked him what to do to save her marriage. The priest said, "Have a baby." She did and that baby was my mother. My grandmother was thirty-five by then.

My grandmother really did not want children. She saw them as an impediment to doing what she wanted to do in life, which was work and get ahead. After my mother was born, she went ahead and did that anyhow, and my mother and grandfather were sort of buddies against my grandmother. My mother always felt she wasn't really wanted by her mother. Besides, the state of the obstetrical art was not what it is today. The story is that having my mother made my grandmother get a heart condition as a result of too much chloroform. She always blamed my mother's birth for her heart condition. She died at fifty-five of it. Now lately my mother has come not to believe that her birth caused her mother's heart condition. She thinks my grandmother might have either had a familial history of heart disease or that as a kid she might have had rheumatic fever.

As far as Maureen Kelly knows, aside from a few more scattered stories, there's not much else known of Cecilia's early life in the beginning of this century. But the story is a rich clue to the flavor of family life as Cecilia must have known it, rich enough to allow anyone who cares to, to reconstruct, almost as an archaeologist might, how that family must have worked.

At its center was the tight alliance between Cecilia and her unhappily married father, an alliance Cecilia's mother surely noticed and resented, especially since this was the child she had had in an effort to "save" her marriage and somehow reclaim her husband. Instead all she had was a heart condition, which progressively weakened her until she died at fifty-five. She must have felt bitter about a disabling condition that she believed was caused by giving birth to this child she hadn't wanted in the first place. And so she blamed Cecilia openly for her disabled body, and more covertly for her disabled marriage.

All these family myths, whether benign or destructive, are tightly embraced by the families telling them. At their best, they help foster a useful sense of family cohesiveness, uniting all the members under a given banner of explanation. At worst, they can be dramatically debilitating in their effects, especially to the individual who is singled out for blame. Good or bad, family myths are the family's most secret and intimate genre, highly influential in supremely invisible ways. If they are exposed to the light of day, one might expect them to lose at least some of their power because they do not stand up well to scrutiny.

But scrutiny and logic aren't what matter here. These stories are about matters of deep family conviction, conviction that exists prior to the story meant to exemplify it, conviction the family is most reluctant to surrender. The story is never quite enough to justify the conviction, but given the family's need for the conviction in the first place, a challenge to the evidence is unlikely to dislodge it.

PART·II

FAMILY STORIES AND THE WORLD

If my homework was done, I could sit with them and listen until ten o'clock struck. . . . I loved the sense of family warmth that radiated through those long kitchen nights of talk. . . . Usually I listened uncritically, for around that table, under the unshaded light bulb, I was receiving an education in the world and how to think about it. What I absorbed most deeply was not information but attitudes, ways of looking at the world that were to stay with me for many years.

—Russell Baker,
Growing Up

I have stories, and that's very important to a people who are colonized, who have no history and might otherwise think of themselves in the stereotype they see on tv all the time. You know—Frito Bandito, the Latin lover, Carmen Miranda with the banana on her head, the sleepy peon with the sombrero underneath the cactus with the flies buzzing in the heat.

—Carlos Morton,
PLAYWRIGHT, 35

CHAPTER 6

THE PECKING ORDER
AND
HOW TO SURVIVE IT

The happiest Bongiorno family stories were the ones where they were all at home—making fun of their piano teacher, Miss Asquith, whom they called Miss Broadbottom, teaching Brother Joe how to say "butter" correctly (to this day, he says it as if there were a mountain peak in the middle), or playing charades based on lines from Edna St. Vincent Millay.

The world certainly came into their family, but it did so manageably as far as they were concerned. It was when they had to go out into the world that they felt it as unfriendly. For my mother's family, one of the central and abiding preoccupations was the pain of being Italian in America, in a culture that made possible Sacco and Vanzetti's execution, equated Italians with mafiosi (or worse, organ-grinders), and had a closetful of derogatory terms to call them.

My mother's family always seemed to feel more self-conscious about being Italian than others of their generation and background did, and I think the major reason for their vulnerability was that they didn't stay long—I'm tempted to say long enough—on Union Street in Brooklyn's Little Italy, where my mother, her two brothers, and her three sisters were born. Union Street might have kept them insular, but it kept them protected. The only non-Italians they had known there were a pair of social workers. One was a Miss Hollarde, a name my grandmother rendered as "Miss Sola," like the notes in the scale. These two women ran the settlement house on their block, gave them books, and liked them because they were clean. With Miss Hollarde and her cohort began my family's excessive pleasure at any and all praise that came from WASPs.

The family moved to a neighborhood in Flatbush when my mother was four or five. Once they got to Vanderbilt Street in Flatbush they named their cats George Washington and Abraham Lincoln. And once their rather conservative father died, the process of assimilation speeded up immeasurably. No more DiNobilis and no more *Il Progressos* and everyone in the house spoke English. The younger children couldn't even speak Italian and barely understood it. And prided themselves on that.

They rushed to anglicize their names—Giovanna, Giuseppe, Annunziata, Bartolomeo, and Maria Elena became Jean, Joe, Nancy, Bart (Bartel for work), and Ellen. These were the only names I ever knew them by. Only my mother, Aurora, kept her name, and that was because the single alternative that occurred to her—Rory—struck her as even worse than what she'd started out with. By adulthood they had sloughed off Bongiorno in favor of their new name, Bonney. My grandmother and her sons adopted it legally.

The oldest boy, Joe, wrote poetry and sent it off regularly to *The Brooklyn Eagle*. Eventually they began to publish him. My mother, still a Bongiorno at the time, went to Hunter College for a few years and winced as her professors mangled "those unpronounceable Latin names." She eventually left (over chemistry, not her surname) and decided to become an actress. She played ingenue roles in summer stock at first, and then, during the later 1930s, found a haven among old-blood left-wing theater people with manageable names like Duckworth and Janning and Gilette.

Toward the end of the thirties, because my mother was talented, there was talk of screen tests, and then there *were* screen tests, an experience that years later still pained her. She was decidedly Mediterranean-looking—beautiful in a sulky, inno-cent way, small, with very dark hair, very dark eyes, a full sensual mouth, and a nose she thought altogether too broad. What they wanted was a pert nose, blue eyes, strawberry hair, and height. My mother stayed with her repertory company until World War II dispersed the members. After the war, she didn't go back to acting and hardly ever went to the theater again. She has never said why.

Many of my family's stories say how hard they felt it was to be second-generation Italian-Americans, but they don't say how it made them feel about themselves. But there is one story which, in a cryptic and covert way, does. It is a story, always told in two parts, of what happened when my grandmother tried to become a citizen.

The story, as it's always told, begins with a lapse in my grand-mother's memory. She had come here soon after her marriage to my grandfather in Sicily, though I don't know whether she came back with him or followed him soon after. But maybe because she was so excited at being a new bride in a new world, or maybe because she was just a teenager with other things on her mind, she could never afterward recall the exact date she arrived or the name of the boat which brought her to Ellis Island. She came here to stay, but without these details in hand, so the story goes, she couldn't do what she most wanted to do, which was to become an American citizen.

Not one to accept defeat so easily, she sent her son Joe to the place where such records are kept. She knew roughly when she had come—sometime in November 1905—so my uncle combed all the passenger lists of all the ships. He went back to August, September, October, and forward to December, Janu-ary, February. He went back a year. He went forward a year. But somehow her name had slipped through some bureaucratic crack. The result, according to the story, was that she could never become a citizen.

The second part of the story leaps forward to the days of World War II, when Italy was one of America's enemies. What this meant for my grandmother was that for each year of the war she had to register as an "enemy alien," a designation that shamed her. And even after the war, every year for the rest of her life she had to continue to register as an alien. Even unqualified, "alien" was an ugly word, and my grandmother was always humiliated by it, and always sad when that time of year came around.

This is the family story, but it isn't the whole story. In fact, there was legislation passed in the 1920s which permitted all foreign-born residents to become citizens. No documentation necessary. No questions asked. But apparently my family didn't know this. Leaving historical fact aside, there are several points to be made about this story and my family in particular, and about family stories and the ways of the world in general. The first point is that according to the internal logic of the story, my grandmother alone bears the shame and responsibility for her outsider status. If only she'd remembered the name of her boat and the date of her arrival, the outcome would have been different, and she could have become the citizen she so much wanted to be.

But the logic of the story is faulty, though I never realized it until I looked at it as an adult. Even if my grandmother had had a photographic memory, there simply was no record of her arrival. Her poor memory was altogether irrelevant to her status as an alien.

But the logic of the story is also revealing. It demonstrates that when people are accused of inferiority (or some symbolic equivalent), they not only believe it but obligingly specify the ways in which they are. Perhaps this is because collaborating in the judgment is more comfortable than opposing it, or perhaps it's because coming up with a reason makes people feel they have a measure of control that in fact they don't.

If my grandmother did feel any anger at her "alien" status, it never came anywhere near the story, though she should have felt it. By the late 1940s, she had lived here for more than half her life and had had two sons in the service during World War II, even strong-arming one of them into it who, by both temperament and conviction, was a Conscientious Objector. He was the proof of her patriotism.

People need to see accurate cultural reflections of themselves in order to feel welcomed and rooted. They don't need either invisibility or distortions. It makes them have to work too hard just to remember who they are or could become. Ironically, those in the throes of assimilating are likely to feel worse about themselves than those on Union Street. Not only are they exposed to more, but they are likely to have bought, or at least put a deposit on, a cultural package which denigrates them.

Ethnicity fades. Race doesn't. Blacks especially can't totally assimilate, no matter how educated or prosperous they become, no matter where they live. So far, they have remained outsiders in white America. But because they are so bombarded with white racism, they often can't resist it entirely. Sometimes self-hatred even infiltrates a family's own stories.

This was clear in a family story told by Marian Glover, a Black investment banker in her early thirties, educated in America's most elite institutions. Auburn-haired and gray-eyed, Marian is unusual among Blacks because of her background as well as her looks. She belongs to a family descended from free Blacks— those released from slavery before the Emancipation Proclamation of 1863.

By the end of the American Revolution, there were 59,000 free Blacks. Most had escaped but some were freed by owners newly inspired by the idea of liberty. By 1860, there were nearly half a million free Blacks. In the North, slavery was abolished. In the South, some slaves managed to purchase their freedom or to escape to the North or the Midwest. But sometimes they were the offspring of a slave mother and the plantation owner. These racially mixed children were often raised in the home, educated, acknowledged and loved by their fathers, and given their freedom. In rare instances, they were even given plantations and slaves of their own.

In our own century, the descendants of many freedmen have defined themselves as "colored" and have seen themselves as distinct from both whites and Blacks. They created their own subculture, which, in its select clubs and debutante balls, is very like white society. Up until the civil rights movement of the

1960s, they tended to marry only those from their own class and milieu. Many of the most well-known and successful Blacks have come from their midst, including singer Lena Horne, Supreme Court Justice Thurgood Marshall, Atlanta Mayor Andrew Young, former Georgia legislator Julian Bond, and writer and former Assistant Attorney General Roger Wilkins. Marian Glover's own father was a well-to-do Midwestern lawyer.

But part of the legacy of these Blacks may be a susceptibility to contempt for their own race. Certainly this emerges in one story told to me by Marian Glover. "There was one time," she begins, "when this man, Reginald Whitlock, came to visit us. I was very young, still in my crib, and he was the first truly *Black* man I'd ever seen. According to the story, I screamed when I saw him. I had been having recurrent dreams about seeing a gorilla at the front door, and though I don't remember the incident per se, I must have thought this extremely Black man was a gorilla. This was a story that was told and retold." Marian Glover sees the survival of this story as evidence of her parents' own racism, not against themselves but against those other Blacks. "My parents discriminated. They were very prejudiced people."

Family stories about aliens or gorillas are unusual. Most families don't have such ethnically or racially self-disparaging stories. They reserve their disparagement for others and often convey it through family stories. Folklorists have said that groups which are both large and distinguishable are most likely to prompt stories.

Those who are most often the subject of existing disparaging stories are the major immigrant groups of this century and the previous one—the Irish, the Italians, and the Jews of Eastern Europe—as well as Blacks and Indians, the last two groups racially visible. Furthermore, who told the stories about whom seemed to bear some relation to the conventional pecking order. Thus from WASPs I heard stories about the Irish, from the Irish I heard stories about the Italians and the Jews, and so on. There were a few twists: from almost everyone, I heard disparaging stories about Blacks, and from almost everyone, including Blacks, I heard disparaging stories about the Jews.

The stories I heard varied in details but seemed to have several motifs in common. The following story, included because it is representative, takes place around 1910, the decade of peak immigration, during which two million Italians arrived here, and was told to me by Kevin Collins, a man of Irish descent, whose grandfather had once worked in railroad construction.

> We all used to get together for big holiday dinners, and afterwards, the reminiscing would start. I remember one story that my grandfather Frank O'Brien often told about his experiences working on the railroad. The story was about this Italian guy, Antonio, who kept putting his hand in the railroad switch and just didn't get it out very fast. "Be careful, be careful, you're gonna cut a finger off," my grandfather would say.
>
> And Antonio would answer: "Eh, Fraanga. Donna worry. I gotta lots."

Those on the rung just below are often rendered as ridiculous rather than evil, as inept or boorish rather than malign. They are often located in a cartoon universe, with the kind of broken speech that suggests a cartoon nose, and endowed with only a diminished capacity to feel pain. The covert point is that "they" are not like "us," but lesser in their human capacities. They seem to be characters in ethnic jokes that over time have come to be permanently encased in a family story and presented as true. As a group, these stories also play on stereotypes: the thick, insensitive Italian, the brawling, drunken Irishman, the money-hungry Jew, the dumb or criminally inclined Black.

Thus through family stories is the social order announced, and preserved through them as well. These stories—the disparaging and condescending ones especially—are part of the family's defensive apparatus. They help an insecure and threatened family assert its own substantiality, its right to a rung it feels is, or may soon be, contested.

Kevin Collins is a college administrator rather than a railroad worker and firmly anchored in the America of the 1980s. He thought the story of "Fraanga" was mildly humorous and in poor taste, but it carried no charge for him. It is not a story likely to survive the next generation, now that the Irish are fully assimilated and the Italians more so than they were. But undoubtedly, this very minute, there is some family storyteller busy working up a story about the newest immigrants—the Vietnamese, the Koreans, the Colombians, and so on.

Native Americans are also the subjects of derogatory family stories, though with two qualifications. First is that most such stories seem to come from the West or the Midwest—Illinois, Iowa, North Dakota—while almost none come from the East. Second is that all the stories I heard were dated. None was less than a century old. Typical in its flavor was a story told to me by a woman named Mary Fellows—now fifty and a New Jersey resident—about her great-grandmother, who was a pioneer settler in Iowa.

> Great-grandma came to southwest Iowa sometime just after statehood. The family built a soddy and did as much of the housework outdoors as was possible, boiling laundry in iron pots over the open fire, making elderberry jelly, rendering pork, cooking cornmeal mush, and so on. As a result, the local Indians came to expect a treat from the big black cauldrons. The Indians were always hungry and—according to every story told in my family—very demanding.
>
> One warm prairie day, my great-grandmother was boiling not cornmeal but brown soap in her pot. As usual the Indians appeared and began gesturing insistently that they must be fed. Great-grandma shook her head, grimaced, and shouted "No good! No good!" Nonetheless, the Indians seized the long spoons and sticks at hand, and dipped in, slurping up great bites of scalding lye soap! Howling and spitting, they threw down their ladles and ran off across the prairie. And Great-grandma was never bothered by those Indians again.

Mary Fellows's family story was from a past century and several hundred miles away from her current life. As a result, the story's function was absolutely clear to her. "In every Indian story that went the rounds of my family, the 'natives' were portrayed as childish, untutored, unclean, and without manners. In every story, the white pioneers proved their superior right to the land—their 'manifest destiny,' as they believed. But as a child, I know I accepted all this without question."

Native Americans occupy a position in the American psyche totally unlike that of any other racial or ethnic group. Whatever Native Americans are really like, in the American consciousness they are split, as folklorists have observed, into two distinct images. The first is the bad Indian, who is, like the Indians in Mary Fellows's story, stupid, greedy, and so on. Historically, the negative images of the Indian peaked at the end of the last century and have since subsided. So it makes sense that most of the negative family stories about Indians were coined before the end of the last century. At the same time, as we shall see in more detail later on, Native Americans are also romanticized and symbolized in other, more flattering ways—in family stories and other forms of popular culture, such as advertisements, books, and films.

GOING AGAINST THE GRAIN

While a good many Americans devote at least some of their narrative energies to keeping ethnic and racial bigotry thriving, there are exceptions. In families that explicitly define themselves as liberal (or even as socialist) and in families that are deeply religious, there are often family stories which work quite deliberately against bigotry. These stories are more explicit and more didactic, probably because they are more self-consciously intended as correctives.

Lester Goldberg's father was born in Russia, his mother in Poland. In this country, they were members of a Yiddish theater company. "It was a left-wing theater that got started in the thirties by people who worked by day in sweatshops as cutters and seamstresses and who by night would get together to rehearse for shows they did on weekends," says Lester. "They did traditional secular Jewish stuff, plays by Sholem Aleichem, but also they did political plays—one about a revolutionary Jew, another about a corrupt U.S. senator. I guess you would have called my parents 'fellow travelers.' I was once visited by the FBI during the McCarthy days."

Lester Goldberg, now in his fifties, knows what he got from his family stories. "I think a social conscience was the biggest gift I got from my parents—a concern for other people, anger when there was injustice. A lot of this was conditioned by stories they told me."

One story goes back to Warsaw, where his mother went after she left her village. She was a young woman and the year was 1905. "She didn't see her first Black person till she came to Warsaw. A Black person must have been a rarity for everyone in Warsaw. My mother thought the woman was ill, that something had happened to her to change her color. My mother ran back to her mother and said, 'Help that woman! Help that woman! Something has happened!' "

It is a slight story, but one worth comment. First of all, if the story makes fun of anyone, it makes fun of Goldberg's mother for her naïveté. On a deeper level, the assumption behind the story is that the moral response to Blackness—or simply to difference—ought to be support, not attack.

"As I've gotten older, I've gotten more conservative," says Lester Goldberg, "but what has sort of kept me from going whole hog—and still makes me feel guilty for that change—is the powerful influence of these stories when I was still at a formative age."

Rowena Court's background is altogether different from Lester Goldberg's. She is a Texan from a fundamentalist Baptist tradition. Her father was an oil refinery worker until she was nine. Then, as a born-again Christian, he left the refinery and became a minister. Her mother's family has always been sternly Protestant. Her family's strong liberalism has nothing to do with political dogma, and very little to do with the tenets of Christianity, but seems to come from crucial personal experiences of various family members, now preserved in family stories. Together they comprise the family's liberal legacy, a legacy which has led her own parents to adopt four Black children, despite the fact that they are not especially well off themselves.

The key stories come from both sides of Rowena Court's family.

> My grandfather on my mother's side had no family. His parents both died when he was very young. He was somewhat taken care of by his sister, who was much older, but only somewhat. She had a lot of kids of her own and didn't have much time for him. I remember a story of how she'd buy him a suit three sizes too big, and he'd just have to wear it until he grew into it. By then, of course, it was totally shabby.
>
> The real nurturant people in his life were Black people, especially this one man named Oscar whom he had a lot of warmth for. He had played with Oscar as a kid, and Oscar's parents had taken a lot of care of him, especially emotionally. My grandfather died when I was nine, but I remember I would go with him to a building he owned that Oscar rented. There was something special between them. My grandfather transmitted a very liberal sense of racial equality to my mother, which was very unusual in Texas at the time. As a result my mother turned out to be very liberal and passed it on to me.

A similar story, this time with an Indian man as the nurturant protagonist, came to Rowena from her father.

> Dad as a little boy doesn't remember much love. His father worked in a flour mill and when Dad was five, he used to go up to the mill to ask his father for some money. Dad felt that his father generally had it but didn't share it.
>
> When Dad was about six, he went up to the mill to ask Granddaddy for some money. Granddaddy said, "No, I can't give it to you," but this young Indian man named Isaiah

who worked with Granddaddy said, "Let me give it to him."
After my father left, Isaiah said, "He's cute, my wife and
I don't have any kids. Why don't you let him come over
and stay with my wife and me."

My father was eventually raised by them. They didn't
have much money either, but they would do a lot of things
together. They'd save up their money and go to Fort Worth
and buy boards to make hardwood floors, or they'd save and
buy a sofa together. He slept in the same bed with them
till he was twelve years old. Dad is very fond of telling
those stories.

A third story, cut from the same fabric as the first two, Rowena
heard from her father, and it was about an experience he had
at the end of World War II. "During the war, Dad was in China
as a serviceman. He tells a story about meeting up with this
young Chinese girl who was trying to sell her baby brother
because she didn't have the money to keep him. My father
bought the baby—he gave her the money, but he let her keep
the baby."

Construed psychologically, this story may mark the beginning
of Rowena's father's efforts to pay back what he was once given
by an Indian man—a sense of reparations which culminated in
the adoption of four Black foster children. At heart, all these
stories reiterate the rescue of the unloved son. But Rowena was
neither unloved nor a son. The legacy of these stories left her
with a sense of compassion for oppressed people and a loathing
for racism or ethnic prejudice.

But Lester Goldberg and Rowena Court were not typical in
the family stories they told. Much racial and ethnic antipathy
still festers and broods beneath the surface of American life.

ILLUSTRIOUS ANCESTORS

There is another powerful vein in American family stories that
compensates for the disparagement suffered by some ethnic groups

and is indeed both exhilarating and valiant. Those who feel themselves to be insufficiently welcome in this culture have any number of ingenious ways—all of them evident in family stories—of making themselves more comfortable, of defending against slight and disparagement. One of the ways is by telling themselves stories of their illustrious ancestors. These stories boost family morale by pointing to a past family member's stature and reputation.

I knew about these sorts of family stories before I began talking to other people about theirs, because I heard them in my own family and took them to heart even as a very young child. Through family stories, my relatives countered the cultural image of Italian-Americans with a more appealing characterization. In fact, they tried to ignore their ethnicity altogether. There was a cluster of family stories that were toted out again and again, year after year with the Christmas tree ornaments and the holiday gumdrop tree. These stories were meant to reassure us not only that we were all right but that we were special because our ancestors had been.

One of the oldest stories, and to me one of the best, was about my great-grandfather, the musical postman. His musicality was a trait of such significance that in a version of this story told by one of my younger cousins he is not a postman at all but a musician. He could play, they said, any instrument he laid eyes on. He went on to sire a dozen children, and they all grew up to be musically talented as well. In fact, he taught each of his sons to play a different musical instrument, and in the evenings after dinner, he and his sons would go into the courtyard, each with his instrument, and they would play music together for several hours. People would come from miles around, so the story goes, just to listen.

My grandmother, the youngest of his children, didn't play any instruments, but she had a lovely singing voice, sweet and sure. When I was a very young child, she would bounce me on her knee as she sang a tarantella. I was the fifth grandchild, and as there were seven more after me, I stayed familiar with the tarantella.

There were several family stories about my grandmother's voice, the earliest of them set during her childhood in Sicily. One day she was at home with her mother, singing as she did some chore around the house. Suddenly, her mother looked out the window and saw the parish priest ambling up the road. "Be quiet! Be quiet!" she hissed to my grandmother. "The padre will hear you singing, and he will again tell us that we must send you to Rome for singing lessons, and you know we don't have the money for that."

By the time of another story, my grandmother had come to this country and had had six children. The family had been long gone from Union Street and was living on Vanderbilt Street in Brooklyn. They lived in a second-floor apartment over a grocery store run by a man named Mr. Petersen, and every Friday morning my grandmother would get down on her hands and knees and wash the tile floor in the first-floor entry hall. My grandmother loved opera, and as she scrubbed the floor she would sing one aria or another. As the story goes, Mr. Petersen would invariably stop whatever he was doing and hush his customers in order to listen to her without interruption.

As I cast a quizzical though friendly eye at those stories now, I can't help but see certain implausibilities. Where did a man with a postman's income get the money to buy his sons all those instruments? And is it really possible that a nineteenth-century parish priest in a small Sicilian village would encourage a family to send their preadolescent daughter hundreds of miles away to Rome? And would he do it for as secular an undertaking as singing lessons? As for the story about my grandmother's appreciative grocer, did he really grind his modest business to a halt in order to listen to my grandmother sing?

No one ever noticed the oddities in these stories, in part because these stories live in a strangely protected realm, half real, half fanciful. I think the more assaulted and the more ambitious my family felt in this country, the grander their forebears' talent became. There was another element, though. My mother and her brothers and sisters had an almost reverential regard for the arts. They not only wanted to appreciate them, they wanted to participate in them, and in the stories they valued, "music" was almost a generic term for the arts. I have often wondered about their zeal for the arts, and I think they were drawn to them not only because they had abilities—one as a writer, one as a painter, and my mother as an actress—but because the arts allowed you in without exacting the social dues required elsewhere. I think my mother's family also understood that in the arts there was a bohemian egalitarianism which made access to them more possible than, say, entry to the more stratified corporate world.

So the stories about their ancestral musicality gave them a feeling of entitlement. The stories both announced and vicariously satisfied their need for recognition, and gave them a feeling of continuity in a culture where they felt dislocated. For further support, other important ancestral figures materialized in the family pantheon, and regularly took their seats around the holiday table. They were good company, too. There were court musicians whose exact relation to the family or to any royal court was predictably fuzzy. There were a cardinal and an aide to Garibaldi. There was even a prince of a pre-unification Italian city-state, though when I ask about him now, no one recalls him. They say I made him up, and maybe I did.

In other families, in other stories, the ancestors wear different clothes, speak different languages, and have different talents than my ancestors did, but the impulse to fashion a grand ancestor remains constant. Such ancestors appear most regularly in family stories told by those from twentieth-century immigrant backgrounds, but they also appear in family stories told by people from every imaginable background. Perhaps this is because for all but the very few, status and stature in American life seem so uncertain and conditional.

This tendency toward ancestor inflation, if not worship, may after all be the thread that links all American families, regardless of race or class. It's certainly not new. When Alexis de Tocqueville visited America in 1835, he noted with some irony that most Americans claimed illustrious ancestors. "There is a hardly an American to be met with," he wrote, "who does not claim some remote kindred with the first founders of the colonies; and as for the scions of the noble families of England, America seemed to me to be covered with them." It may be that a culture with such an urgent pull toward the future has to balance it with an anchor way back in the past, even if it's moored to nothing more substantial than fantasy.

And it may also be that those who are no more than two generations away from steerage still need their ancestral paragons, as both guides and sources. Elizabeth Cantor, now in her early forties, grew up in Washington, D.C., the daughter of a physician. Her father's father, a Russian-Jewish immigrant, had been a pharmacist, but that profession, as Elizabeth Cantor's father often told her, marked a temporary generational deviation from what Cantors had always been.

> On my father's side, they seem to be doctors all the way back to the medieval times, practically. I have a story about my great-great-grandfather on my father's side. A Cantor. Whatever the words were, I long ago translated it into an image: my great-great-grandfather is standing in a little courtyard behind his house in Patava in Russia, where he was a doctor, renowned far and wide for his skill in removing cataracts.
>
> The people are coming in droves, lining up, to sit on the chair he stands beside. My grandfather has a knife and he is removing cataracts from people's eyes with it. I don't know if the part about the courtyard is right, but I know the part about the knife is true. This is a story about skill and professionalism at a time when Jews weren't allowed to be professionals. But everyone, Jews and gentiles alike, came to him to be taken care of. His ingenuity was such that he became famous for being able to remove cataracts without ever injuring anybody.

One can imagine the power this story must have had for Elizabeth's father as a young boy, the child of Jewish immigrants early in this century; this story must have been a beacon from the past lighting his future. In going toward a career in medicine, he was simply doing what his ancestors had always done. He was in Washington, D.C., not Patava, but the approbation his antecedent got from those Russian "gentiles" must have assured him that he had a chance at being accepted by these other "gentiles" in whose midst he found himself.

The need for an illustrious ancestor is apparently so pressing that people will go to any length to make sure they have one. Cathleen Collins didn't find the ancestor she needed until she began to research Irish history on her own as an adult. Then she read about the Irish Republican Army and the Easter Rebellion of 1916, and along the way she came across a photograph of a man named Michael Collins.

Cathleen Collins is now convinced that Michael Collins is an ancestor of hers. He comes from the same county as her Collins relatives did, for one thing. "Also he looks like we do," she says. "There's an existing photograph of Michael Collins, and his arms are crossed exactly the way the Collins men, including my brother, Kevin, cross their arms. Plus Collinses are executives, they know how to delegate responsibility. And Michael Collins knew how to do that, too. He's the guy who really got the Irish Republican Army going. It had existed before, but he really fired them up." Cathleen Collins has so far persuaded two of her Collins cousins that Michael Collins is their relative, and she has at least half persuaded her brother, Kevin. One can see that it will not take very long before the force of the shared conviction turns a hope into a certainty.

So far, all the family stories reach for self-esteem through the existence of an esteemed ancestor of the same ethnic background as the family. In a related strain of family stories, the point is that the ancestor is someone of "better" ethnic or racial ancestry, and sometimes, but not always, illustrious to boot.

Marian Glover—the woman who as a child had mistaken a Black visitor for a gorilla—tells a story about a white antecedent which has been handed down in her father's family over many generations.

> The point of this story was to instill in me a fair amount of pride so that when I would run into prejudice from people, I could feel my own underlying current of "I really

am better than you are"—not in a bad way, but in a factual way—"so you really have no right to look down on me."

I heard this story from my father a lot. I heard it as a little girl, and it never changed. It's about the first relative I'm conscious of: a white man who was the governor of North Carolina and before that a U.S. senator. I have no idea who the woman was who was the mother of his Negro child, only that she was a house slave and that the child was raised in the house along with that man's other children and was educated along with his other children as his child.

I know that this boy's relationship with his father was very good. He took this child, this Black child, to Washington, D.C., with him to see the Senate, as he'd taken all his other children. They went to the hotel, and they checked him in, and the bellboy treated the child like he was a servant, but his father said, "No, this is my son. He's going to be staying with me."

That was something that instilled pride, because in those days there were other people in the same situation where the father would not acknowledge the child or take responsibility. The point to me was that this man was very responsible and he had a lot of courage. He acknowledged his paternity when he could have easily turned his back on him and told him he was a servant. Later this little boy had an arranged marriage with the [racially mixed] daughter of another slave owner. I see this as a loyalty which is pretty much a trait in my family, and I always kind of fantasized that that was where it came from.

The point here is that Marian's ancestor was not only white but illustrious and willing to use his power and status on behalf of his child, Black though he was. Marian Glover's family made a connection between themselves and whites, without regard to the particular ethnicity of the whites in question. When whites tell the same kinds of stories, the ethnic group they want to be part of—as in Marian Glover's case—is always one which carries more social prestige, and often the one which has most oppressed them.

From a family of Irish ancestry, I heard one such story, and the illustrious ancestor was, not surprisingly, English. The Hopes from Kansas believed their earliest known ancestor, James Hope

(1840–1900), was a Protestant duke's disinherited son. "Because James had championed the Catholic cause in Ireland," said a family member, "he was disowned and escaped to America with his life. He was either the oldest son or the only son, and the claim was that he was the rightful heir to the dukedom." It was a family skeptic who told me the story, but she said the family believed it wholeheartedly. Their evidence was that the Hopes had a family tradition whereby the oldest son of the family is always named James. "Whenever one of us has traveled to Europe," she added with some resignation, "we have always been asked to go to London and research this dukedom."

A similar story has worked its way into the written genealogy of the Mayock family, who came from western Ireland to northeastern Pennsylvania in the 1870s. Says Peter Mayock:

> The surname Mayock is a unique and uncommon family name. The area of its greatest popularity seems to be in Addergoole Parish, Ireland. In 1840 there were sixteen families by that name in the whole county. At the present time, there are about six Mayock families in Addergoole Parish.
>
> The founder of the Mayock name, as the story goes, was an English earl or lord who fell in love with a lady-in-waiting. They were unable to marry because of their different stations in life, and so eloped and fled to western Ireland. So that they would not be discovered they took the name Mayock, possibly from Mayo, and the abbreviation for county, CK. This tale has been told throughout the generations of Mayock descendants.

Maybe this story is true, maybe not. To the family members, veracity is never the main point—what's important is what could be rather than what actually was. While for the Irish, English are especially appealing, and while for Jews, someone Christian may be of special value, those not in need of so pointed an acquired ethnicity often choose the French. Often just a whiff of plausibility will do.

In my own family, for instance, my grandfather's looks alone set off fanciful speculations. He had been dead since 1929, but everybody liked to talk about how he was six feet tall with red hair and blue eyes. These physical details were happily toted out in order to suggest that we weren't "really"—or "only"—Sicilian because everybody knows that Sicilians are short and dark (as in fact my grandmother and all her six children were). Some of us knew enough about the history of Sicily to know that among its invaders over the centuries were the fair-haired Normans. And that's how it happened that, for a while, our Sicilian heritage was seasoned with a pinch of French. For a while maybe we half believed it.

There are others like us, eager to pick up French ancestry in the absence of something more pointedly relevant. Dan Vernale, a social worker and administrator, is by heritage both Northern and Southern Italian. The story about his maternal grandparents, the Northerners, was that they were French orphans who were somehow brought to Italy.

Two other ethnic groups, though their members have come in for some rough treatment by this culture, seem to have emerged as particularly desirable, and even exotic, ethnicities. The first is Chinese. One woman, Russian Jewish in background, told me that she believed her great-grandmother was Chinese. She said she had included this putative strand of ethnicity in several employment applications in the hopes that she could be considered as an Affirmative Action job candidate.

The second ethnic group, which at least half a dozen of my interviewees, both white and Black, claimed a connection to was American Indian. Regardless of the fact that Native Americans, as a discernible group, have surely not thrived in the culture educationally or economically, the *idea* of the Indian, as I said earlier, seems in our time to have been apotheosized into a powerful symbol, especially since World War II.

The earliest sign was when the whooping and hollering "bad" Indian of cowboy-and-Indian movies of the 1920s was replaced by the "good" Indian, the noble Indian of *Broken Arrow* or *The Lone Ranger*. By the 1960s, the Indians had been appropriated by the counterculture, summoned as a symbol for values ranging from ecology to a belief in the superiority of intuition over mere reason.

Chief Broom, of Ken Kesey's *One Flew Over the Cuckoo's Nest*, is one such figure. By the 1970s, even Madison Avenue had claimed the Indian as an ecological symbol. Overall, the ascendance of the Indian as a symbol may suggest our nostalgia for a more bucolic life, especially in the face of increasing urbanization and technology. In literature, the Indian (connotatively distinct from the Native American) is suggestive of our mourning for our lost preindustrial Eden.

Among Blacks, to have Indian blood is considered an ethnic enhancement. And there is good historical plausibility for the claim. Many escaped slaves took refuge among Native Americans and were accepted by them, and there was considerable intermarriage between Blacks and Native Americans in the postbellum South. Some Blacks who claimed Indian ancestry did so because they knew and had seen grandparents who said they were wholly or partially Indian.

In one case, the claim was no more persuasive than my claim about my Norman ancestors. This was from a Black woman who had heard a story about how her mother, as a child, used to stand for hours at her great-grandmother's side, combing and combing the older woman's waist-length hair as she sat at her vanity facing the mirror. As mine was a redemptive story about fair hair, hers was one about straight hair.

The white claims seemed, as a group, more farfetched. One woman, of white Southern background, said her family believed they were related to Pocahontas. Stephen Griffith, of old New England stock, said his family believed there were Indian ancestors in the family's eighteenth-century past. He had long sympathized with liberal causes and felt uncomfortable at the privileges his WASP background gave him. For him, Indian ancestry offered the opportunity to ally himself to a less exploitative ethnic background.

In family stories about possibly apocryphal relatives, there is almost never information about how the story got started or who handed it down. And of course there is never any familial memory about how the story may have changed over time. But a clue as to how an Indian—or any member of an unlikely ethnic group—may climb into the family tree comes from a zealous amateur genealogist named Stanley E. Perin, who had long wondered why his family believed themselves to have Indian blood, especially since none of the blond, blue-eyed Perins that he knew looked even remotely Indian.

But in all his investigations, Perin found that the only Indian blood his family had encountered was in the context of bloodshed. Perin eventually discovered that one of his forebears, Captain Moses Rice, had been killed in Massachusetts during an Indian raid in 1755. Moses Rice's son, Asa, had been taken captive during the same raid. Perin also discovered that at some later date Asa Rice had apparently been released. "Imagination," he wrote, "fondled the idea that Asa might have married some Indian girl while a captive and perhaps had a [child] who brought the Indian heritage into the Perin family."

But further historical research proved pretty conclusively that Asa hadn't married an Indian woman at all, especially since he was only ten at the time of his release. He later married a young local woman, and she had no Indian ancestry either. So there it was: in the course of two centuries, a family story about an ancestor captured by the Indians had become totally transformed into a family story about having Indian blood.

Perin himself speculates that the transformation may have come about because of two factors. The first was that "Asa may have been, as other captives were, adopted into some Indian family. His reported reluctance to return to civilization would indicate that his lot among the [Indians] was not unhappy. In later life a tendency to dwell upon the pleasant side of his captivity, combined with a natural aversion against recalling the tragedy with which it started, could have left his children with an inverted notion of the truth."

Second, after 1811, the family scattered westward. With one generation now separated from the other, there was no one around to keep the story in place, as it were. What's interesting here is where the collective Perin imagination apparently wanted to go with the story, what they wanted it to be. Bitten by the same bug as Hemingway, Kesey, and, no doubt, thousands of other Americans, they wanted the blood of the only really true Americans coursing through their veins.

GETTING EVEN

Given the ethnic and racial hierarchies of American life, there are those who dish it out and those who have to take it. Some get to dish it out without ever having to take it, some take it from those above and dish it out to those below, and some find themselves in the position of always having to take it. Such a position is, psychologically and emotionally speaking, almost unbearable. Rage and despair accumulate with no place to go.

But it is one of the functions of stories—and the oral tradition of family stories surely belongs to the genre—to allow for vicarious pleasures. Through family stories about revenge, those who are especially vulnerable to insensitive treatment can have the imagined pleasure of righting wrongs and settling scores with those who make them most miserable. As one Black folklorist put it in an introduction to an account of her own family's stories, "Our folklore was the antidote used by our parents and our grandparents and our great-grandparents to help us counteract the poison of self-hate engendered by racism."

Glenda Dixon, a Black woman in her twenties, grew up on Manhattan's Lower East Side, but most of her mother's family, one generation back, was from the South of the 1940s. One story they brought with them is about Glenda Dixon's great-grandfather, who, so the story goes, was a servant for a Jewish family in North Carolina around the turn of the century. According to the story the family ordered their servant into the kitchen to make tea for them one morning. "They used to treat him so badly—hollering at him, calling him all sorts of names—

that this time while he was making the tea, he peed in it. They drank it right up, licking their lips and all. They asked for another potful when they were done. He came home hysterical, laughing."

Glenda Dixon's story, as well as being a story delineating a particular set of ethnic tensions, is also a revenge story. In fact it is a double revenge, first because Glenda's ancestor got his employers to drink contaminated tea, but even more because he made utter fools of them: they liked the tea. They thought the tea was so good that they asked for more. It is a story which not only allows the pleasure of witnessing a revenge, but itself teaches a style of stealthy revenge against those who have power. To the powerless in our culture such passive aggression is often the only safe option available.

A story with the same style of revenge was also told to me by Marilyn Johnson, a Black New Yorker now in her fifties. It is a story about a particular incident which took place in the 1940s but, more explicitly than Glenda Dixon's, it teaches a style of revenge as well.

> This is a story about being on a subway. The lady sitting next to my mother began trying to inch her off the seat. My mother said she would move over a little bit, and then the woman would give her another shove. Finally the woman gave my mother a pinch. My mother took out a hatpin, and she quietly gave the woman a jab, and of course the woman said, "You stuck me!" making a fool out of herself. My mother said she looked at the woman blankly as if to say, "Did something happen?" My mother didn't look like the kind of woman who would stick anybody with a hatpin. [Here Marilyn Johnson laughs.]
> What that story means is that for me and I suppose for most of us the right way is to take the road of least confusion. Somebody else might have started a fight or caused a commotion. You don't let the person get away with it. The point is to avoid outright confrontation.

Not frequently, but every once in a while, an explicit and overt revenge story finds a place among the stories that families tell. From David Wills, whose ancestors were Black and Native

American, I heard such a story. In fact it was a piece of folklore about his grandmother's hometown, but over time it had become included among the stories the family told about itself, and it was a story that gave him great pleasure.

David Wills's great-grandfather was a Creek Indian, a member of a tribe that had clustered around Alabama and Georgia until they were defeated in 1814 at the Battle of Horseshoe Bend by Andrew Jackson. This defeat cost them most of their land, and eventually they were forced to relocate to Indian Territory, now Oklahoma, Nebraska, and Kansas.

But David Wills's great-grandfather did not live exclusively among the Creek.

> He was sort of integrated with the Black population which a lot of Indians did, and the story I have took place about the time the Indians were going to be dragged off to Oklahoma. My grandmother came from this town in Alabama which, when she was growing up, was called Burnt Corn. She says her father told it was called Burnt Corn because when the whites came there to take the land, the Indians apparently burnt their corn rather than let the whites take over the land. I remember that story with pride. I like being part Indian, but even more I like the fact that they at least made a stand before they got wiped out.

This is not really a revenge story—the Indians were burning down their own corn—but it has the quality of bravery and self-assertion which, from David Wills's point of view, makes it gratifying and one he is proud to have.

SURVIVAL STORIES

Deeply embedded in the soul of every family is a vision of what the world is like, and every family has a set of ideas about how best to survive in it. It may have to do with literal survival—

staying alive till the next morning—or it may have to do with achieving and maintaining dignity, psychological comfort, or inconspicuousness.

Whatever a family's particular experience, all families concerned with some sort of essential survival have family stories— sometimes intricately coded, sometimes boldly explicit—about an encounter with the enemy. In all cases, the power or authority is always deaf to reason and incapable of sympathy. Whatever or whoever the enemy, the family stories offer an approach to survival, a strategy that seems almost designed to have an application beyond the particular dramatic moment.

The archetypal survivor is the trickster, and his strategy is wily cunning. A staple of both oral and written tradition is the rogue trickster, the *pícaro*, who lives by his wits from one day to the next. Odysseus had such ingenuity and survived. So did Gil Blas, Tom Jones, Huckleberry Finn, and Brer Rabbit. And so did Solomon Ballow, a short but strong Jew from Odessa. This is the opinion of his grandson, Danny Ballow.

"There are many 'clever' stories in my family," says Ballow, "and many of them are about my grandfather. He was really kind of a character, a *pícaro*, almost like those Indian stories about Crow, the sneaky Crow. The earliest story is about the time he was about to be drafted into the Czar's army." Solomon made immediate plans to escape to America, but he still had to get through the night and the next morning's search by the cossacks. What did he do? He hid in a rain barrel outside his house, armed with only a drinking straw. When he needed a breath of air he raised the straw, periscope fashion, up through a hole in the rain barrel lid. The cossacks came. They searched everywhere for Solomon, ransacking the house in the process. But Solomon sat tight in his rain barrel, and after the cossacks had left empty-handed, he made his escape. In other Ballow family stories, Solomon gets what he wants by hiding, lying, and feigning. His adversaries include still more cossacks, a border guard or two, a rabbi, and a pugilist.

Can these stories be of use in the present to Danny, who lives on the Upper West Side of Manhattan? Danny believes they

have shaped his sensibility, and had already done so by the time
he was an adolescent living in the Bronx. Like his grandfather
Solomon, Danny is both small and quick-thinking. Once, on
his way home from junior high school, he was cornered on a
subway platform by three bigger boys who believed the money
in Danny's pockets belonged in theirs. But Danny had no such
notion himself. "Money?" he said, furrowing his brow. "What's
money?" His adversaries explained. But the more they explained,
the less he seemed to understand. Soon all he could do was
shrug and shake his head in bafflement.

Finally, in disgust, they left him standing where they'd found
him, departing in search of some other prey. Danny's approach
to the situation was the only one that even occurred to him.
Through his stories about his grandfather, he had long ago learned
to survive by his wits. Nor is the Ballow approach to survival
likely to die out. Danny himself has two young children, always
eager for exciting stories. And when he tells them the stories
about Grandfather Solomon, he always finishes off with the
newest wily installment—the story about himself.

Sarah Levine Richardson is a New England Jew, born, raised,
and educated in Providence. But unlike Danny Ballow, Sarah
Richardson has a story which makes it clear that the best survival
strategy is assimilation. The story, set in the early 1940s, was
told to Sarah Richardson by her mother.

My mother was a medical librarian in a hospital where,
at the time she worked there, there were very few Jews on
the staff. She wasn't exactly a "token" Jew, but she was
the-Jew-on-the-staff. The hospital was having to schedule
something and realized there was a big Jewish holiday coming up and that they were going to have to schedule around
it. No one knew anything about the Jewish calendar so
word got around that they should ask my mother. My mother
didn't know, but she said, "Wait. I'll call my mother. She'll
know." So my mother called her mother and said, "Do you
know when Rosh Hashanah comes around this year?"

There was a pause. And then my grandmother said, "Wait.
I ask the butcher."

Richardson's own analysis of the story acknowledges that it places limits on just how Jewish it is acceptable for the family to be. "The story acknowledges that my mother was happy to be the-Jew-on-staff, but it also said, 'I'm not that moved by it that I have all that information on the tip of my fingers. I think we maintain a food connection with Judaism. But it's not a pompous set of directives. We don't wear things around our neck and proclaim, but we keep up in a very domestic immediate way.' "

But beyond the domestic, the Levine family and Sarah herself did not keep up in a very immediate way at all. "I didn't know I was Jewish till I was thirteen," says Sarah Richardson. "No one much talked about it. Everyone assumed I was Protestant. We had Rosh Hashanah, but we had Christmas, too. It just never occurred to me that religion was an issue on which people divided themselves." And when Sarah Levine grew up, she married Matthew Richardson, the son of an Episcopalian minister.

Most of the families whose stories abet their survival believe in what they're doing. While they know that the practices, attitudes, or stances they've adopted are useful, they shower them with conviction. Classically, this is what assimilation means. But sociologists also talk about acculturation—a more self-conscious effort to do as the Romans do but without the attendant conviction.

From Carlos Morton, a Mexican-American playwright who grew up in Chicago, comes a story about how his grandfather first got an economic toehold in this country and what he had to do to get it.

> My last name is Morton, and that's really an English name. Everybody always asks me, "How the hell did you get a name like Morton?" Sometimes I tell different stories, but the official version which came from my grandfather via my father was that when my grandfather came to this country in 1917, he went to Chicago. That's where he went because there were the foundries and the factories, but he couldn't get a job. They wouldn't hire him because his last

name was Perez. They just wouldn't hire any spics, I guess.
[Here, he laughs uneasily.]

So my grandfather, so the story goes, got out of the
employment office, and he looked up, and there was this
billboard there, and it said, "When it rains it pours." And
there was a little blond girl under an umbrella. It was Morton salt. My grandfather just took the name, and at the
next employment office, he got a job in the factories.

My father told the story as an irony, he told it caustically.
Sort of "Too bad he had to do it, but he did it, and now
we're stuck with it. So what are you going to do, change
it back to Perez?" I was born Charles Morton—that's what
it says on my birth certificate. I was named after my uncle
Carlos, but you had to pass, you couldn't be obviously
Mexican. Later, I thought, "I'll just take back Carlos and
let it go at that." [He laughs again.]

Carlos Morton's story, though pithy, is both rich and covert.
When Morton's grandfather made allusion to the "little blond
girl under an umbrella," he was telling his family something
about the ethnic sources of safety and protection in this culture.
The Perezes couldn't of course become blond, but they too could
find space under the umbrella, nominally at least, by attempting
to "pass." It wasn't until fifty years later, in Carlos's time, that
his generation could afford to reclaim some of what had been
lost in stepping under the umbrella. But only some.

Carlos's story is ironic and self-conscious, but the most knowing and perhaps most disturbing family story about survival comes
from a northeastern Black family with roots in the South. The
story is told by Adele Withers and its cast of characters includes
her father, her grandfather, and her grandfather's boss, who
owned peach orchards in rural Alabama.

At the time of this story my father, Simon, was maybe
ten years old. He was mischievous but not bad. It was the
time of year when the peaches were ripe and so my father
climbed right up into a peach tree and had himself a little
feast. He just let the pits fall on the ground below.

Then he fell asleep right up there in the tree. A couple
of hours later, the boss was walking through. He saw the

pits, he saw my father, and he put two and two together. Well, he was mad! He pulled my father down from the tree, and dragged him over to his father, who was working on the other side of the orchard, and told him what had happened.

My grandfather listened to the boss. Then he said, "I'll take care of it." Without another word he took off the heavy black leather belt he always wore and beat my father till he was half dead. Then he went back to picking peaches.

Adele Withers tells this story about a beating that took place nearly a century ago with quiet emotion. "My grandfather beat my father till his skin nearly fell off, but my father always said his father saved his life. This was the rural South, don't forget, where white men could do anything they wanted to Blacks. The story was meant to let us know that if we had the chance, it was better we should punish among ourselves in the family— even if it was too severely—than let it get out of our hands."

For Irene Goldstein, growing up in New York City in the 1950s, stories were really all that was left of her familial past. Her parents, both Austrian-born, were the sole survivors of Nazi concentration camps in each of their families. No relatives had survived and no mementos had survived—no photos or rings or silk handkerchiefs or embroidered antimacassars or anything. Only family stories. Irene Goldstein's parents, her father especially, told these stories over and over as if enough repetition could provide them with clarity about their lives or the meaning of what they had endured.

The offspring of concentration camp survivors, as Helen Epstein has written in *Children of the Holocaust*, grew up expecting the *next* Holocaust. The world was presented to them with a certain *film noir* quality, and this was the world they were raised to live in as best they could. They were always on a kind of adrenaline alert.

The children had a difficult time living with the legacy of dread, heirs to an acute sense of danger which seemed to have no source in the world of the 1950s. Meanwhile their parents still wrestled with their own past. Part of what was so devastating to Irene's father was that he couldn't understand why he had survived. It was pure luck and therefore purely terrifying, since there was nothing, no immediate strategy for survival, that would have done him any good at all had not luck come his way. And so what he did was rehearse his bemusement and his numbness with stories that he told Irene repeatedly.

> There were lots of concentration camp stories, mostly about luck. The best one was when he went to Auschwitz, and they got into this big room where they were asked to form three lines to volunteer for three different work details. There was line A, line B, and line C. My father went into line A, and then at the very last minute, at the very last *second*, just before you could never change your mind again, he moved from line A to line B because a guy he knew on line B beckoned to him. In line A, everybody got killed, in line C, they got sent off to the mines and nobody returned, but in line B, his line, 96 out of 100 survived.
>
> And my father's moral . . . there *was* no moral. He'd just say, "What was this? Was this luck? Was this God? Was this just my friend saying, 'Come over here'?" And he could never make up his mind. He had a real puzzlement in the face of events, an inability to make sense of them. And I think this is part of my own detachment, part of my ability to distance myself.

In a world which is uncontrollable, it does make sense to retreat into oneself, to cope by emotionally departing from the event. But it is intolerable to imagine a world which is so totally beyond one's control, and so there was a second strain of stories Irene Goldstein's father told, and in this set he provided his daughter with an alternative to passive dissociation and bemusement.

What he conveyed to Irene Goldstein and her two brothers was a psychology, almost an ideology, about the body. Before the war, Irene's father had been a swimmer of national reputation and Olympic caliber. Had no war come along and had there been no anti-Semitism in his early years, he might simply have passed on to his children the advantages of being an athlete and staying in shape. But his athletic prowess dovetailed with his particular experiences, and his body, for him, acquired almost magical power.

If the body was just about all you could count on, and if you were disconnecting emotionally from the world, then the body became the haven to retreat *into*. If there was anything at all that Irene's father could say had actively contributed to his survival, it was his body.

This came out in two stories that Irene's father told often. In the first, there were elements that made it seem to Irene not just a story about her family, but a story about the Jews.

> The town my father lived in was on the Danube River, and they used to go swimming there. My father said that whenever the Jewish kids went down to the river, they'd get stoned by the Christian kids. And I would always say, "Well, why did you keep on doing this?"
> And my father would say, "Well, I really loved the water, and I really wanted to show them, to prove to them that Jews could swim."
> But in the way he told the story, it was very hard to imagine the stones really landing on him. There's this Jewish folktale about the rabbi who walked between the raindrops, and that's how I saw it—I saw my father walking between these stones that were coming at him. He never said, "One time I got hit in the eye" or "One time I got hit in the chest." It was always "Well, we walked through this hailstorm of stones, and then we swam, and then we walked back."

Irene sees herself as someone with a strong investment in the body. She doesn't feel healthy if she can't get her body going. She jogs regularly, she swims, she skis, she plays tennis. "My father had a very clear identity in his body. He liked his body, and I think the message my brothers and I got was that if you exercise your body"—here Irene laughs—"you can essentially withstand stones."

And even more than stones, because the second story Irene

Goldstein's father told about his body had to do with another experience at Auschwitz.

> What my father said was that he had to go past this doctor, Dr. Mengele, "The Angel of Death." Mengele said to him, "Are you healthy?" and my father said, "Yes."
> One of the reasons Mengele asked was because my father had very skinny rickety legs (just like me). Then Mengele said, "But are you *really* healthy?" And the way my father would embroider on this story was to say that he was a swimmer and an athlete and that this was what made him really healthy. And then the story went that Mengele said, "Go to the right," which meant to life.

Irene Goldstein does not see her father's bemusement about his survival as being incompatible with his certainty that he survived because of his physical well-being. "The idea we got was that the reason my father survived the war was because he took care of his body. The implication was you had to have your own world, you had to be self-sufficient in that way. That's what allowed you to look at everything that happened and not get knocked over. My father couldn't say why he had survived the concentration camps or what part luck had played—that was beyond his control, mysterious. But he *could* pinpoint the fact that because he was in good shape, he survived. That was within his control."

Literal physical survival is often a matter of *doing*—of hiding in rain barrels, or beating one's child, or keeping oneself in good physical condition. But there is also the related matter of emotional survival—of coming through with all one's faculties intact, of keeping a grip on hope or the future or some fundamental human vibrancy. These are matters of *being*—internal psychological maneuvers—rather than doing.

Those who survive best emotionally do so partly by the gift of their inborn temperament. But psychological or emotional strategies for surviving in the world—for keeping a stiff upper lip, for believing hope is a thing with feathers, for not crying over spilt milk—are also learned, just as Irene Goldstein learned from her father the psychological style of emotional dissociation. Probably these stances are communicated by adults to their children a thousand times a day in the most grossly clichéd as well as in the most subliminal ways, but we often catch them at work most powerfully in family stories.

Growing up in Kansas as a child, Paulette Berry had to have a strength, endurance, and dignity unusual in a child. As a result of *Brown* v. *Board of Education of Topeka*, the 1954 Supreme Court decision which said that segregated schools were inherently unequal, Paulette and her younger brother were among the first Black children to attend a formerly all-white elementary school in Topeka. It was one of the schools that had prompted the court case in the first place. Even as an eight-year-old, Paulette Berry was aware of the swirling passions surrounding the decision, and knew that at their new elementary school she and her brother might be in some danger.

Her grandmother took her and her brother to school that first morning, and on the way Paulette Berry remembers hearing a story she had heard from her grandmother many times before. "She would tell me and my brother about my great-great-grandfather Dodge, who was a slave in Tennessee. He was an organizer, and to make an example of him, they cut his stomach open, just cut it right open. The last they ever saw of him, he was running up the road holding his guts in. He still kept his dignity."

For the Berry family, this ancestral slave was exemplary, a model for them to emulate. The word "guts" is the key to the story. It suggests courage, and in the context of the story, the notion of a dignified power of containment. There is no promise of safety in the story at all, or even a suggestion of how to physically survive danger.

The point is to keep from being *emotionally* vanquished. However wounded Paulette Berry's great-great-grandfather was, physically or psychically, he did not "spill" his guts. He turned his back on "them" and held his guts in. It was a powerful image, powerful enough to have helped an eight-year-old schoolchild cope emotionally. "When something came up where they didn't want me and my brother to waver, or where they were afraid we would waver, they'd tell us that story," says Paulette Berry. "The idea was that if he could put up with *that*, then we could put up with whatever little thing was required of us."

Whatever the character of the world, it falls to the family to help its members make sense of the part of the world that is theirs, and then to negotiate it as well as they can. American society may be more difficult than most to get a handle on because there is so much rhetoric about democracy, so much public denial of social hierarchy.

But the social hierarchies exist—by consensus—which means those of little power and status and those of great power and status tend to confirm one another's position. It is the first job of the family, through its stories, to explain to its members where they are positioned socially. Or as Walter Benjamin once put it, "Every real story . . . contains, openly or covertly, something useful." Forewarned is forearmed.

CHAPTER · 7

OF MONEY, SELF-WORTH, AND LOST FORTUNES

I know of no country, indeed, where the love of money has taken stronger hold on the affections of men. . . .
—ALEXIS DE TOCQUEVILLE

What is the chief end of man? . . . to get rich. In what way? . . . dishonestly if we can; honestly if we must.
—MARK TWAIN

It is a hot summer day as James M. M. Terrell strolls with me through the modern art wing of a major northeastern museum. A small wiry man with sharp blue eyes and a puckish smile, he is at home amidst the Brancusis and Duchamps, the Braques and Picassos.

All of them had belonged to his great-uncle Oliver, who had begun amassing his large and famous modern collection in the early days of this century. Many had hung in Uncle Oliver's home until the 1950s, when he gave them to the best museum in his state.

James guides me down hallways and around corners as if he were the lord of this particular manor, at the end insisting on buying me a book about the collection, at the museum shop. He does not announce himself to anyone and seems to take pleasure in his anonymity. I try hard not to look awed and am relieved when I manage to appear nothing more than suitably impressed.

Great-uncle Oliver is just one of the members of the Terrell family oriented to a kind of philanthropic social service. Surrounding all of them is the aura of money. Lots of money. These have been people born to extreme privilege. James is a lawyer who works in state government instead of the firm begun by his grandfather and continued by his father. He wanted to make his own way, he says. Still, he isn't having quite the career he had envisioned for himself. "My man lost the election" is all he really says by way of explanation.

James M. M. Terrell does not think of himself as a rich man, although he is. "My family has sufficed on several million total capital quite nicely for over a hundred years—as opposed to the forty or fifty million some of my cousins have. The money we have—less than ten million—strikes me as a modest amount." Though James is a man of keen humor and even keener self-irony, he is exercising neither as he says this. He is simply comparing himself and his immediate family with the families he knows—the family of his first wife, who recently came into her own five-million-dollar patrimony, the families of those who attended his sister's debutante party on the grounds of his parents' home, or those who sent their sons to Harvard this year.

Money is such a powerful symbol in American culture that people must take some stance in relation to it. They can save it for a rainy day, let it burn a hole in their pocket, use it to keep up with the Joneses, throw it away, neither borrow nor lend it, or turn their back on it altogether. Whatever they do, they must reckon with the idea of money as well as with however much or little money they happen to have.

Since James and his family are the Joneses, with nobody to keep up with, one might expect their views about money to differ from most people's. "We don't *care* about money," says James. He makes it clear that pursuing money is distasteful but having money is morally neutral. He believes that old money is better than new money. Given a choice, he would prefer five million of old money to fifty million of new money "every time, every single time," he says.

Money is so much a given that James doesn't seem to really know where it comes from, only that the current supply has been enriched by a steel-related family endeavor. "There is no single Horatio Alger story that I know of in my family," he says with just a hint of pride, perhaps because it shows just how old the money is.

James and his family have so many ideas about money because they have so much of it. However, one question seems to interest him especially, and it is: What are you supposed to *do* with all this money once you have it? For the Terrells a good many of the obvious answers are irrelevant. Says James, "What do we need money for? To get into the golf club? We're already in the golf club. So we could buy a house in the best neighborhood in town? It was where the family had always lived. To get into Harvard? How could I not go to Harvard? As long as I got decent grades in prep school and behaved myself, I was going to go to Harvard," where his father, grandfather, and great-grandfather had gone.

For the Terrells, the question of how to act in relation to money is a pressing one. Or seems to be, since a huge swarm of their family stories buzz persistently around it. One of them is a cautionary tale about the widow of James's great-uncle Andrew. "Aunt Sally left her personal estate of several hundred thousand dollars to a home for wayward Dalmatians. A posh dog orphanage! I'm not making that up. The family tried every way we could to break that will. That was just too silly. You're supposed to *give* money away, not *throw* it away." In a related story about what not to do with money, another great-uncle leaves Stutz Bearcats he didn't actually have to each of his great-nephews. That was, says James, another disapproving story about "showy and grandiose" uses of money.

What makes the family happiest is when a member behaves with absolute morality-play uprightness, coupled with altruism if possible.

My mother's family lost all their money in the Depression. They were bankers, exceedingly wealthy, much more so than the Terrells. Mother was in her teens when the family bank failed, and a big bank it was, and private.

Her grandfather, who was then the president of the bank, paid out 100 cents on the dollar. He didn't *have* to do this; he was not compelled by law to pay back everyone's account. But he did it, thereby bankrupting himself and impoverishing the family. The point was that nobody criticized him for it. What he did was the right thing to do. It shows honor, no matter what the money involved is.

James M. M. Terrell had thought so much about money because he was so rich, while Marilyn Johnson thought about it because she wasn't. A Black Brooklynite in her middle fifties, widowed several years earlier, Marilyn Johnson was by no means poor. She lived in a home of her own on a well-kept street, and added to her regular income by taking in foster children.

Money was the thread which ran through Marilyn's stories about her brothers, sisters, parents, and their earlier life, many concerning events which had taken place long before she was born. She had a vaster store than most, too. "In my family," she says, "I'm the one who remembers."

Her mother's family had lived in New York for at least three generations, and her father was an immigrant from St. Kitts. The earliest story she knows about her father—about his first moments in New York—stresses his immediate recognition of the economic differences between whites and Blacks. "My father said he saw the whites going to school, and he thought, 'White men go to school.' He knew Black men had to work." She shrugs. "I guess he thought, 'This is the way things are.' They had the opportunity and he didn't."

This is more resigned than the rest of Marilyn Johnson's stories. In another one, her sister is suffering from tuberculosis of the bone, which she died from when she was four. "My mother and father were glad they had Liberty Bonds because it meant they could get my sister decent medical care. That way they would never have to say to themselves, 'If only we had had the money.' "

Many of the other stories are about thriftiness—buying day-old bread rather than more prestigious brand-name varieties, making sandwiches out of peanut butter and jelly, not roast lamb like their neighbors, walking extra blocks to buy an ice cream cone for a penny less. Yet Marilyn's world was one in which this thrift was rewarded. Their roast-lamb neighbors lost their house, while Marilyn's family did not. "I suppose what it showed was that counting the pennies really paid."

Marilyn Johnson's mother was thrifty and passed it on to her children, emphasizing its value. "It was a big message," says Marilyn. "I was talking to my niece not too long ago, and she said, 'Auntie, if after all of Grandma's talk you haven't saved any money, then I feel sorry for you.' So it's filtered down three generations now.

"My mother had two messages: one was always put something aside for a rainy day. The other was always have something that is yours alone and not your husband's. Even though marriages were solid and you trusted your husband, you should always be able to put your hands on some money. She would say, 'If a man should leave, he has his pay, but you'll have nothing.' My husband and I had a good marriage, but one of the things we settled long beforehand was that I would handle the money. I didn't think I could live with a man giving me only what he wanted to. A woman handling money—that's the only way a family gets ahead."

James Terrell and Marilyn Johnson come from entirely different worlds. His concern is with wealth, hers is with getting along; his is with what to do with money, hers with how to hold on to it. Yet for both of them, as for almost everyone, the presence of money, whether a lot or a little, jingles its way through stories about death, love, and illness. It is there in stories about men and women, family saints and family sinners, in stories from earlier centuries and those coined yesterday.

In fact, whatever family stories people tell, they often turn out to be stories about money, even when they aren't intended to be. The reason for it, say social scientists, is that at the heart of the American experience lies the conviction that money is a sign of worth, whether individual or familial.

As James Terrell put it, "No one can deny us." But Marilyn Johnson, too, felt that money was related to her family's worth. "If I were to describe my mother, I would call her 'thrifty.' My father, I would call 'solid.' The stories about them that impress me the most are those that show that they came from next to nothing and wound up owning their own house." James Terrell and Marilyn Johnson, despite the obvious differences between them, nonetheless play by a shared set of rules.

Anthropologist Margaret Mead had an explanation as to how money became so disproportionately important in American culture. She felt that ours is a dynamic rather than a static society, hence there is no enduring ideal of what is good. As a result, every new generation has to come up with a way to assess worth. Monetary success, because it's so easily measurable, became the only enduring standard.

Mead's analysis is compatible with an understanding based on the Puritan roots of American culture. Among the Puritans, though extravagance was unacceptable, the presence of hard-earned wealth—with the emphasis on hard-earned—was taken as a sign that the earner might be among the saved, preordained by God to receive grace. This belief took some mental maneuvering since the dogma, as articulated by John Calvin and promulgated by American theologian Jonathan Edwards, said that one couldn't really *know* if one was saved or not. As a way of contending with what had to be an intolerable uncertainty, hard work that resulted in wealth took on a salvific power. Among many seventeenth-century Puritans, a little more leeway about the value of good works in salvation was allowed. There seemed reason to hope that they might be a sign of one's selection by God after all.

Building on the New England tradition, but in a secular manner, Benjamin Franklin's *Autobiography* was nothing so much as an early how-to-make-money guide, a seed which in our own time has sprouted the likes of *Money* or *Sylvia Porter's Personal Finance Magazine*. By Franklin's day, money-making had severed its connection with religion and had become a good in itself.

This analysis of the symbolic importance of money rests on the assumption that the world we live in is as plentiful as Eden, and that all that is required is effort, regardless of class origin. It is an attitude that deeply permeates James's understanding of how the Terrells acquired their wealth in the first place. "When the Terrells arrived in this country, they went into manufacturing and were successful. After the Civil War until 1930, it was virtually impossible *not* to make money. If you did manufacturing, it was going to be successful." Historically, this was true for many. Alexis de Tocqueville, writing about America earlier in the nineteenth century, reported that the second generation usually achieved all the material comfort they possibly could have hoped for.

To some degree, all Americans, regardless of class, accept Tocqueville's view of unlimited plenty there for the taking by those who make an effort. When they fail to make money, they turn the blame on themselves rather than challenging the hypothesis. It is only in the last few years that this assumption has come to be explicitly challenged, but we have not yet revised our deepest myths accordingly. The culture at large promotes money-making through its invocation of Horatio Alger. So powerful and recognizable is Horatio Alger as a symbol that many who invoke him assume he is the protagonist of his rags-to-riches tales rather than the author.

Within the family, meanwhile, money-making is reinforced as admirable through stories featuring relatives as the heroes. One, for instance, comes from Catherine Browning, a New England lawyer now in her thirties.

> There are a lot of stories of the Horatio Alger type associated with my grandfather, Edwin Gordon. He was a small-town bad boy. He dropped out of the eighth grade, but before that he was a truant of long standing. He used to take the truant officer's long underwear and run it up the flagpole. But he had a lot of gumption—and the vision to break out of small-town New Hampshire. Plus he was self-reliant.
> After he dropped out of school, he started selling sandwiches and newspapers on the Boston and Maine Railroad. I don't know what his first business ventures were, but he

must have been one of the few people who did well during the Depression. The way he ultimately made money was through gasoline. He had an independent chain of gas stations in Massachusetts and a few small home-heating-fuel businesses on the side.

By the time the last of his kids were growing up, they had pony carts and maids and motorcycles and a huge house. The recollection I had of my grandparents' house was that everything was big. Big, big, big. The Christmas tree was twenty feet, the turkey was big.

He died when I was seven, but he remained a mythic power in our family, and he's still a presence. He represented the ability to do well in the world. By yourself. From scratch.

As a matter of historical fact, in Horatio Alger's fiction, the key trait his nineteenth-century ragamuffins exhibited was virtue, the residue of the Puritan tradition in America, as well as Alger's own personal legacy—his father was a Unitarian minister, and Alger attended Harvard Divinity School and eventually became a minister himself. But in Catherine Browning's "Horatio Alger" account, virtue is not part of the success recipe.

Catherine Browning's grandfather came by his wealth honestly, and in this he participates, at least loosely, in the virtuous Horatio Alger ideal. But there is a darker side to the American money-making ideal. The acquisition of wealth is so important that it is preferable to come by money dishonestly than to pass up money altogether. The culture's implicit admiration for the robber baron makes itself felt even in family stories, and demonstrates how totally the pursuit of money has become unhinged from the Puritan ideal.

Ballard Mason, a journalist in his late forties, comes from an old "upper-middle-class prosperous" New England family, one that was here before the Revolutionary War. "The family has always had the myth of the American dream about them—that you can start your own business, that you can be a success, and by that they mean a material success. And they have always done that."

Accordingly, Ballard Mason has a rash of family stories about money-making centering on his grandfather, known as Shep. Even as a child, Shep had learned to cut corners, and his efforts are preserved in a family story Ballard Mason heard from Shep himself. "My grandfather had his own chickens as a kid," recounts Ballard Mason, "and his father would pay him a penny an egg. So every morning, he would go out and collect the eggs and carry them in for a penny. Then his mother would go out and hide the eggs again in the nest without her husband knowing, so Shep would then collect twice on the same eggs."

There is no hint of judgment—one way or another—in the story, but the story tilts in favor of approval simply by the presence and collaboration of Shep's own mother. In the context of the story, the double collection is cast as admirable. And this is Ballard Mason's own conclusion as well. "The Yankee trader bit is strong in there," he muses by way of comment.

In any case, Shep learned well at his mother's knee and grew up to be even more skilled at commerce, a fact demonstrated by a later Shep story Ballard Mason tells.

> One of my grandfather's competitors in his lumber business was a man named Ezekiel Higgenbottom. Now Higgenbottom was no good. In fact he was probably a drunkard and certainly dishonest. So if my grandfather could trade woodlots with Higgenbottom and get the better end of the deal—give him a woodlot with all dead trees, but make Higgenbottom think he was getting a good lot, and get a woodlot from Higgenbottom that was terrific, but he didn't know it—well that wasn't dishonesty, that was shrewd Yankee trading!

The belief in cutting corners crosses both class and race lines. A similar story was also told to me by Keith Tompkins, a college-educated New Yorker who came from a rural Southern sharecropper background. "My family," he says, "they admire the rogue, the man who can go out there and get the money. It's O.K. to play an illegal number but it's not O.K. to become involved in any activity that would lead to jail because, let's face it"—here Tompkins laughs—"you can't make any money while you're in jail."

The hero in his family is his mother's brother, Uncle Measo, who still lives in South Carolina. "He's your typical rags-to-riches story," says Tompkins. "The American pioneer. Third-grade education. A millionaire."

Uncle Measo began with bootlegging, an activity in which he demonstrated a stunning aptitude for amassing slightly shady profits. After a while, he changed occupations.

> You know what he used to do? He used to swindle people out of their land. Poor Blacks down South are not aware of the tax laws, and not aware that they stand to lose their land by not paying the taxes. What Uncle Measo used to do was secretly pay the taxes for them—for five or ten years at a time—and then he would present them with a bill. Naturally, they didn't know from Adam. They'd never have the money anyway, so in this way he accumulated quite a bit of property. He sure knew how to get over.

Call it getting over or call it shrewd Yankee trading, the two phrases have in common a tie to the more shadowy side of the American Dream. While it is preferable to come by money honestly and preserve it by thrift, it is rakishly acceptable to extend one's fortunes by deviousness. This is a considerable message about how to make one's way in the world, and it is often attractively packaged in the stories that circulate in American families, regardless of the social class of those families.

But for the vast majority of Americans who are nowhere near wealthy, or even economically comfortable, the ideal, though they subscribe to it at least nominally, causes problems. If there's so much out there, and they haven't gotten a huge share of it, then something must be the matter with *them*. Their "failure" subjects them to shame.

Some families reckon with their own lack of wealth by attempting to devalue wealth itself, as my family did. This maneuver may or may not work. In other families without wealth, such as Marilyn Johnson's, thrift is celebrated as if it were wealth itself. In her family, the celebratory story is about walking six blocks to get day-old bread rather than buying a more expensive brand around the corner; in another, it's about a whole warm double-bed-sized quilt made entirely out of scraps; and in another, it's about rubberband balls, string balls and yards of used wrapping paper.

Why should such stories survive? Part of it is the family's pleasure that it has weathered adversity and weathered it ingeniously. The value placed on thrift may stem from a Puritan admiration for frugality, but it's reinforced by the value placed on wealth in the first place. John D. Rockefeller's thrift was notable only because it demonstrated how every little bit helped his fortune grow. Because of its association with wealth, it has acquired a value it would not otherwise have had. In a way, thrift has become the poor man's wealth.

STORIES OF LOST FORTUNES

A much more serviceable variety of family story is what folklorists call "the lost fortune story." It is useful first, because it establishes family worth—and hence individual worth—by reference to an apocryphal fortune that the family used to have, and second, because it testifies to the blamelessness of the current generation in the loss of that fortune—"they" lost it, they are responsible.

One of the most common sorts of lost fortune stories is the "almost" story, as in We Almost Made a Mint. Mimi Runkle, a Chicago radio producer, tells me a story about how her father came that close to pie in the sky.

> My father is a very open, trusting person who made his living as a baker. In the 1950s, my father had an idea for making a frosting that housewives could use at home on their home-baked cakes. Daddy made this recipe, and he

worked and worked and worked, and he experimented and experimented. He did this in combination with a man named Mr. Sullivan, who was a sugar dealer. After years of my father's hard work, Mr. Sullivan just ripped off the recipe. He sold my father's recipe to one of the major cake-mix companies, which then became the first company to market ready-made frosting.

A second and closely related genre, serving the same purpose, is the story of the family fortune, once in hand, that now is lost. Whether true or apocryphal, these stories are most effective when the agent of loss is a swindler or, even better, a catastrophe of major proportion. Floods, fires, wars, and droughts are among the most useful.

A story about a fortune lost to war was told to me by Maria Stacken de Filipi, a woman of Spanish ancestry who lived in two worlds as she was growing up. One was the fairly impoverished world of her childhood in upstate New York, which included a stint on welfare. But Maria's mother attempted to mute the family's daily difficulties by conjuring another world based on her own family's illustrious economic past, though these were not so much stories of events as they were an ongoing inventory of a material world the family had once been immersed in.

"In Spain we were *hidalgos*—allowed to sit in the presence of the king. The de Filipis were a very old, very aristocratic family. We owned *fincas*—very large estates on acres and acres of land. We owned half the property the Prado sits on today. We owned enameled watches inset with gold and diamonds. And [manuscripts of] old Gregorian chants with the goldleaf stamps of Isabella and Ferdinand.

"Then there was the Spanish Civil War and the houses and land and titles were all lost. And," she says gropingly, "things happened." Pressed, Maria de Filipi could not explain why her grandparents had left Spain and so much comfort during the 1920s, well before the Spanish Civil War. But the conjured golden world Maria's mother provided did allow her and her two brothers to fulfill their *hidalgo* destiny rather than what their more ordinary Buffalo existence held out for them.

Maria went on to become a dancer with one of the most highly regarded American ballet companies. Her two brothers are both cellists with well-known symphony orchestras. As an adult, Maria de Filipi went to Spain and found, to her relief, that the stories her mother had told her of the family's lost fortune were in fact all true. But perhaps it wouldn't have mattered had they all been invented. They served their purpose— bolstering the family's self-esteem while sparing them all responsibility for their losses, reassuring them that the golden past would surely be succeeded by a golden future.

One of the best lost fortune stories came from Ballard Mason, grandson of Shep, the shrewd Yankee trader. In this story about Shep, he is a grown man and the prosperous owner of a silk mill. The agent of destruction is a flood, and Shep emerges as such a hero that it's only Ballard's coda that reminds us that this is a story about the end of the family's prosperous times.

> The big crisis for my grandfather came in 1927. I guess he was fifty-five by then. It was October and it was raining. It rained day and night, for four or five weeks, and it just didn't stop.
>
> My grandfather had a silk mill, and he had a reservoir that supplied water to the silk mill. It rested on a plateau directly over the village as a sort of menacing water bomb. If the dam broke, the village would be in big big trouble. My grandfather had had the reservoir inspected and it passed inspection. But he was worried about it anyway in all this rain and began checking it himself.
>
> One night at about three o'clock in the morning, he had a premonition. "Jeez," he said to his wife, "I gotta go up there." So he went and got his foreman and three other guys, and they drove along Main Street up into the hills. Just as they got to the reservoir and pulled up in front of the dam, they heard a tremendous crack! A thunderous crack! And at that very moment the dam was going!
>
> So they turned the car around. The hubcaps were already covered with water. They drove about a quarter of a mile

down the road, beeping the horn madly the whole time, and stopped at the first house. A guy came out and let my grandfather use the telephone. My grandfather called the town switchboard operator and woke him up. "Listen," he says, "I want you to do two things. Call my wife, get her up, tell her the dam broke, tell her to get out of the house, and then call everybody else in town."

So he did. He started calling everyone in town. Meanwhile my grandfather got back in the car with the other guys. The water was coming down right behind them! So they just leaned on the horn all the way down the hill into town. They got every single person out of their houses safely—the townspeople didn't have to go too far—just a little up in the hills into their backyards and they were safe. Just in the nick of time, too, because just then the water came roaring down and knifed through a lot of houses on Main Street, just sliced through them, sometimes taking off the living room or the sitting room. The flood took furniture and coins and valuables in one room, and left everything that was in another intact.

So the next morning the people were sort of stunned and looking down at this wreckage of their little town. And one of my grandfather's employees came up to him and said, "Well, sir, what are we going to do?"

"What are we going to do? I'll tell you what we're going to do," said my grandfather. "We're going to start rebuilding."

They called my grandfather "Paul Revere of the Warrentown Flood," and Monday morning they did start rebuilding.

But this was the beginning of the end, really. As he put it, he'd watched $50,000 of his land get washed away in fifty seconds. All the other stories he told me were stories about work and success and hard work, and in the end, triumph, but here he didn't triumph. From the 1927 flood on, things were downhill. After that, it was always a struggle. He died by no means broke, but the good times, the really prosperous times, from then on were over. It was never the same after that.

I heard fewer stories about the great fortunes lost in the Depression than I would have expected. This was because most people who lost money in the Depression blamed themselves for their

losses. In *Hard Times*, Studs Terkel comments on how pervasive
this sense of personal failure was. "The suddenly-idle hands
blamed themselves, rather than society," he writes. "True, there
were hunger marches and protestations to City Hall and Washington, but the millions experienced a private kind of shame
when the pink slip came. No matter that others suffered the
same fate, the inner voice whispered, 'I'm a failure.' . . . It was
personal guilt."

The only exceptions Terkel found were among Blacks. One
elderly Black man told him that there wasn't much difference
for Blacks between now and 1932. Folklorists have observed that
Black Americans are less likely than anybody else to have lost
fortune stories because, while the culture might hold up achieving wealth as a universal possibility, they themselves didn't share
in that belief. The implication is that race and class values helped
determine a family's response to the Depression. The more comfortable classes who had previously had a sense of their own
power in the world suffered a more personal sense of self-
diminishment than did those who'd never had much money and
thought it was all a matter of luck anyhow. Thus, paradoxically,
the most useful and exculpatory Depression lost fortune stories
tend to come from those who were least likely to have had a
fortune to lose anyhow.

There is one more strain of lost fortune stories. In them there
are no floods or fires and nary a swindler in sight. Just one lone
ancestor standing in the spotlight without anyone or anything
else the current generation can blame.

Ricardo Nuñez grew up in New Mexico. His mother's family
was a mixture of German, Italian, and Mexican, and he tells a
story about a family fortune they don't have because of his great-
grandfather.

> The story begins with my great-great-grandfather's will.
> It was written in Gothic script and apparently there was a
> lot of money. His son, my great-grandfather, had three
> sisters, and he had fought in the Franco-Prussian War and
> was left for dead in the Alsace-Lorraine, in the snow. But

he found his way back to Hamburg. His father died, and he had a big falling-out with his mother and three sisters, which is why he left. Apparently they had servants because there was money left for the servants. Money was left to my great-grandfather, but he never collected it because he broke away from his family.

The Nuñezes don't make any attempt to blame Great-grandfather's sisters or mother, though there is certainly room there to embroider if they cared to. They seem content to let Great-grandfather be responsible. But if he is responsible, he does not seem to be blamed. The ultimate mildness of the Nuñez judgment is palpable, unexplained, and has everything to do with the story's structure.

The story is oddly shaped. What bearing does Great-grandfather's military service have on his falling-out with his family? Why is that military anecdote there at all? The answer has to do with the story's unstated purpose. The first and second parts of the story have no inherent relationship to each other. You don't have to be a brave soldier to lose your share of the family fortune. But the presence of the military details are useful because they establish that Ricardo's great-grandfather is a hero—with a few fairy-tale trappings including death and rebirth in the snow. Thus while the story seems to hold him responsible for the "falling-out," it also establishes him as so exemplary that we forgive him before it even occurs to us to blame him. Since he and his descendants are thereby exempted from any blame for the family's current financial position, it is just as useful a format as the ones involving crooks and catastrophes.

At the heart of the American experience, there has always been the assumption of plenty—a chicken in every pot, a car in every garage, and the sky's the limit. Given these assumptions, the belief that money is there to be acquired has always been an integral part of the American Dream. Therefore, like the Eskimos with all their words for snow, Americans have always made fine distinctions about the money they do have—old money, nouveau riche, land-poor, cash-poor, and the like. Money means status, money means power. Every family maneuvers so that it can perceive itself in the most complimentary terms possible. And in this regard, family stories are extremely functional. At the very least, they provide the family with some clear stance of itself in relation to money, even if that stance involves a dismissal of money's importance.

PART·III

FAMILY STORIES
AND
THE INDIVIDUAL

Inside a family, people have mythologically simple characters—there's the angry one, the bookish one, and so on, as if everyone were getting ready to be elevated and turned into a constellation at any moment. Notions of character were much less mythical once you got outside a family usually.

HAROLD BRODKEY,
"LILA" IN Women and Angels

It's absolutely funny to me—the predicament of having to be ourselves, and yet the facts are that large hunks of you are someone else, and you can't do a thing about it. The family is the ultimate debunker. Everyone wants to be infinite and the family limits that.

—B. C. HEINZ,
INDIANAN, 26

Now everybody says, "My goodness, you are such a sociable person," but in the core of myself, I think I am not. I really am not. In the core of my mind, I'm always avoiding people. The first word I ever uttered was good-bye. Sayonara. I didn't even say it right. I said Chayonala. My mother and older brother told me this story. I always wanted to be alone.

—JANICE HOSHIDE,
WEST VIRGINIAN, 53

CHAPTER·8

LEGACIES

Once upon a time, almost fifty years ago, there was a magazine advertisement for Sanka coffee. To this day, Ted Stephens, a fifty-three-year-old English professor, recalls the ad in detail because it became an integral part of a family story told about him on the Iowa farm where he grew up. "The ad," he says, "featured Mr. Coffee Nerves, who was a vaudevillian-style evil character who twirled his mustache and wore tuxedos. I was told, ever since I can remember, that I said I would never drink coffee because it made you 'nerfus.' It was supposed to be a joke because I mispronounced the world 'nervous.' "

Why should the Stephens family have seized on this as an event worthy of becoming a story? And why should it have survived as a story for as long it has? Children say clever things every day. Usually the latest charming remark becomes enough of a story to last until it's passed along to other family members who would want to know.

But when a family story about a child's clever remark becomes a part of a family's active story repertoire, and survives for years hence, something more is afoot than the mere charm of the child's remark. It survives because it hits a particular family nerve or confirms some deeply held family value, or because it serves as an omen that the child is exactly what the family most wishes—or most fears—he or she will be.

There was a reason Ted's clean-living, devoutly religious family mirrored the story back to him, and Ted understood the reason and obeyed the story's unspoken admonition. "For a long time I didn't drink coffee because of that story." he says. "In fact I didn't drink coffee until I was twenty. One of the things women, especially, do in the family is try to nurture character, and they try to guide children into being this or not being that."

Thus, Ted Stephens's family was not only giving him a family instruction about what he could do; they were also advising him who he should be by reminding him of, and holding him accountable to, a remark that, given his age at the time, could only have been idle. The particulars involved coffee, but in a broader context the family's preservation of the story was part of their effort to "nurture his character" so he would habitually turn his back on casual pleasures the rest of the world might take for granted. "My people," he adds, speaking of their religious abstemiousness, "believed dancing was right from the devil, as was card-playing."

The particulars vary from family to family, but what went on in Ted Stephens's family goes on in families everywhere, especially when the children are still young enough to be shaped. In time, most children obligingly become much of who they otherwise might not be at all. As family therapists Lily Pincus and Christopher Dare put it, "As the child grows out of infancy, he tends to take over as his own the needs and expectations that other people have of him, particularly the people who are important to him. Subsequently, in time, the person can be as loyal in pursuing the needs of these others as of his own wishes, longings and self-expectations." Indeed these expectations of others can become the individual's own self-expectations.

Later on, we may file our own edges here and there, or design coherent, if changing, narratives about our lives. But we can never be entirely self-invented. Our very deepest sense of our own identity—the deeply familiar flavor in our mouths when we use the word "I"—is more a matter of conviction than a matter of fact. If we believe we are kind or smart or good or bad, competent or incompetent, mean or dumb, valuable or worthless, on the strength of our convictions, we are likely to become so.

In Jean-Paul Sartre's biography of French playwright Jean Genet, he describes an experience Genet had in his kitchen when he was a child. As Genet rummaged through a kitchen drawer, he heard the epithet "thief" hurled at his back. It became the central story Genet told about himself, the story he lived by. It was, says Sartre, the first moment Genet knew himself to have being, and it was coeval with having the nature of that being announced to him. For the rest of his life that pivotal "moment of awakening" remained with him.

One would think that since matters of being, of identity, can't be easily measured, they might eventually be more easily discarded. But this isn't at all the case. In fact, when conviction and what would pass as fact are patently at odds with one another, it seems easier for someone to alter the fact to accord with conviction than to change the conviction so it fits the fact.

The most extreme example of this has to do with gender identity—the sense of sexual affiliation one subscribes to, the cultural significance of what it means to be the sex one is. In practice, the gender we believe ourselves to be matters more to us than the overt clues given by the body we have. Transsexuals such as Jan Morris and Renee Richards have found it simpler to change their bodies than to change their minds.

For better or worse, and whether we collaborate with our families or not, we are shaped by our families' notions of our identities, particularly that part of our identities which exists as an idea beyond the reach of measurement. The image they mirror back to us exists earlier and more substantially than we ourselves do. And among the primary vehicles families use to mirror us to ourselves are the family stories we hear about ourselves. These stories, especially the earliest stories about our life in the womb, our birth, and our early days of life, are a record of our family's fantasies, often unconscious, about who they hope we are or fear we are.

The power of these fantasies, and not their accuracy, is what ensures their survival. These stories influence the specific traits we later demonstrate, they become portents and omens of the careers we may later choose, and, most profoundly, they tint or taint our deepest and most intractable sense of our own being—the sense that we are either good or bad, welcome or unwelcome in the world.

AND BABY MAKES THREE

Some of the family's impulse to create stories comes from its need to make a place for the newest member—to welcome, define, or identify the child so she or he can exemplify and embody the parents' deepest hopes and expectations and some-how fit into the family and its definition of itself. Given these needs, the inchoate personality of the child—especially before birth and in the first weeks after birth—runs counter to the family's need to perceive the child as more articulated than he or she initially is.

Consequently, the parents often seize on anything as a portent which confirms their wishes. Kate Turner's experience was an example of this. As a child, she heard story after story testifying to the "spunk" and "stubbornness" of the Turner family. That was how the family thought of itself, and it prided itself on those traits. During her childhood Kate often heard stories about her-self in which she was cast as both spunky and stubborn. There was one in which she determined, at the age of five, that she would run away from home. Not content with freeing herself alone from parental oppression, she decided to run away with her baby sister, carriage and all. In the denouement of the story, she packs her belongings and her sister in the carriage and, without a backward glance, marches down the street.

In another story, of an event which was reputed to have taken place at roughly the same age, she is involved with some imaginary friends. "I had these imaginary companions called the Snookies, and I used them in a very controlling manner, I suppose. My room would be a mess, and my mother would come in and say, 'Clean it up,' and I would say, '*I* didn't mess it up. It was these Snookies.' "

When Kate's father told her these stories about herself, he always told them in a very "approving manner," making Kate feel pleased about her stubbornness and pleased about her obvious connection to the Turners. So the family stories, as told by Kate's father, were part of a family syllogism: Turners are stubborn, Kate is stubborn, and therefore Kate is a true stubborn Turner.

Had that been all there was to the stories and their telling, today Kate might well think of herself, altogether benignly, as a stubborn Turner. But families are complicated, especially in their messages to their children about who their children seem to be and what they think about them. As Kate experienced it, her mother—not a Turner and not so pleased at having a stubborn daughter—told Kate these stories about herself more judgmentally.

"My mother," says Kate, "always made me feel improperly socialized, far too scrappy, stubborn, and impossible to deal with. Now it makes me wonder how my mother wanted me to turn out. I think she had mixed feelings about me. She told the same stories as my father did but not in the same approving manner." The result was that Kate did indeed grow up feeling that a key to her identity was the Turner brand of stubbornness, but even now, having incorporated both her father's approbation and her mother's judgment, she is ambivalent about who, in this regard, she is.

There is another family-story strategy by which families find a place for new members, which also tells them who, in essence, they are. In this method, a child is perceived as the reincarnation of a grandparent, usually one of the same sex, and is often reminded of the likeness.

Kevin Collins was often told he was "a good listener," just like his grandfather Frank O'Brien.

> My grandfather O'Brien was a justice of the peace. Everybody admired him. There were all sorts of stories about how state troopers would bring drunken drivers to him or how the local police would bring men who had been thrown out of their house by their wives. People who were in trouble and didn't know where else to turn would say, "Frank, can I come down and talk to you."
>
> My mother told me over and over how his style of listening was to let the person in front of him get it all out. Then he would sort of repeat it. He would let the other person have a catharsis, and then he would try to guide that person to his own solution. He talked to them without scolding them. He had a kind of gentleness and equanimity.

In the Collins family, Kevin was not actually told stories about how he, too, was a good listener. The family worked more telegraphically: "Whenever they saw me listening, or doing something kind or gentle, they would always say, 'That's the O'Brien in him,' or 'That's Frank all over again.' In a way it was positive. He was put up as a model, and in some sense I've accepted him as a model. I feel a little bit bad when I don't keep my calm. I worry about my temper. I say, 'Wait a minute. This isn't the way Frank would do it.' So when I'm 'like Frank,' I feel it makes me likable, it's something in me to cherish."

In fact, Kevin Collins has grown up to be an exceptionally good listener, both in his personal relationships and in his work as an administrator. But he isn't altogether at ease as a reincarnation of Frank O'Brien. "The Irish always link you up to somebody, which is bad in a way because it means you're no longer yourself. You're a composite. You're one quarter Collins, one quarter O'Brien, one eighth Crowley, and so on. If you start thinking genetically, it's almost like predestination. It puts limits on you."

In Laura Holmes's family, the story system was similar to the Collinses', though in Laura's case the comparison with her long-dead grandmother was even more unwelcome. "I used to get a lot of headaches, and I was told, 'You're just like your grandmother. She got nervous headaches.' They labeled them 'nervous headaches.' They said, 'She didn't like crowds either, just like you.' They would say, 'You're the quiet one, you're the sickly one, you don't like crowds, you get nervous. Just like your grandmother!' My mother and my aunt would say this to me.

"My grandmother died when I was five. Boom! I'm the frail one! But it turned out I wasn't at all 'just like' my grandmother. I had appendicitis. I had ear infections. There were *real* things wrong with me. But even when I was going to the hospital to have my appendix removed, I was being told, 'You're just like your grandmother.' "

Even a negative sense of oneself has its uses, however, and early on, Laura discovered a use for, and thereby embraced, her "frailness," in a way corroborating what her family had always said about her. "My family's tag line for me was 'onset of incurable disease,' and they said it because when it came time to do the chores, I usually didn't feel well, especially right after eating. If it was my turn to do the dishes, I would usually lie down. My 'disease' would usually miraculously disappear when the chores were done."

Despite its usefulness within the family, Laura Holmes chafed under the yoke of reincarnation, but nonetheless the sense of herself as frail and nervous stayed with her for quite a long while. "I kind of fell for it for a long time. I would get nervous in a crowded place, and I would get headaches. It wasn't until I was well into my twenties that I said, 'I don't need to get headaches, and I don't need to get upset in crowded places. Maybe it's not true.' "

Laura Holmes says she has now shed the sense of herself as frail and nervous, but a sense acquired so early and reinforced so vigilantly—as it was by her mother and her aunt—doesn't shake off so easily. These days Laura will go and eat dinner in a crowded restaurant, but she doesn't just do so without thinking about it, she does so deliberately.

OF SACRED SONS
AND
SCORNED DAUGHTERS

David Copperfield begins to tell his own story by first referring to a family tale about his birth. According to what he's been told, the nurse who delivered him said he was destined to be unlucky in life, but that legacy is ameliorated by another: David was born with a caul over his head, which was supposed to bestow gifts, like a prosperous future and protection against drowning. His is a mixed legacy, unusual for a son.

In Peter Mott's family, the very first story about him was coined even before he was conceived. His mother had had a nervous breakdown following the birth of his older sister. He was planned as his mother's cure. "After the breakdown," says Peter Mott, repeating what he had often been told, "the doctor said to her, 'Have another child, and devote yourself to the raising of that child, and that will bring you out of your problems.'"

The next event in this family story is consistent with the beginning: Peter Mott was "amazingly easy to conceive," a fact that was often repeated to him as if it suggested something conclusive—and undeniably positive—about his existence and potential. After Peter Mott was born, he apparently did nothing to prevent the fulfillment of his parents' deepest wishes. Or more likely, their wishes, revealed in the story of his beginnings, determined how they would regard him and treat him. As a result, says Peter, he grew up feeling as if he were "the golden boy . . . the holy child."

But what if Peter Mott had been a girl? Could a daughter have been regarded as "holy" and "golden" in the Mott family or in any American family? Certainly there are parents who wish fervently for a daughter and are ecstatic when she arrives, and just as certainly there are sons who are not enthusiastically welcomed. But there are two reasons that make it likely that such sacred appellations and enthusiastic welcomes will be directed most often at sons.

First is the fact that most families would rather have sons than daughters. This preference is so marked that some fear the possibility that amniocentesis will be used solely to learn the sex of the unborn child so that a healthy child of the "wrong" sex can be aborted—"wrong," of course, meaning female. There is no evidence that this has occurred in this country, but the concern underscores how marked the preference for sons has become now that the American family size has shrunk, making it less likely that the desired son will be one of the family's 1.7 or so offspring.

The second reason has to do with the fact that, culturally speaking, our most powerful stories both fashion and reflect our feelings about sons. Baby Moses in the bulrushes, baby Jesus in the manger, honest young George Washington, education-bound Abe Lincoln are stories reinforcing the preference for sons and offering form for expressing those feelings, or even generating them.

Something of this sort happened to me during my first pregnancy, even though my preference was for a daughter. It was late December and my husband and I had just learned that the child I would give birth to in the spring was a healthy boy. That evening we went to hear "The Messiah," motivated more by a love of the music than religious sentiment. But at the words "and he shall be called Wonderful, Marvelous," a thrill, total and involuntary, coursed through my body. I remember feeling astounded at how involuntarily and powerfully my very nerve endings had absorbed the suggestion that sons are indeed sacred and special. Whether I ever tell my son this story, it certainly exists as a story to be told, and it wouldn't had the baby been a girl. Undoubtedly it colors my deepest feelings about him, feelings I was developing months before he was even born.

Peter Mott's family was Jewish, and the ritual that attends the birth of a son, the bris, singles out sons for special recognition, encourages the expectation that a son, even if he's not the Messiah, will be special. Although his family was not particularly religious, they were susceptible to the metaphor whereby "holy" became a synonym for "special." And Peter Mott, having been told early and repeatedly that he was special, went on to become so, at least in secular terms.

An aura of holiness and specialness also surrounds stories of the birth and early childhood of psychoanalyst and family therapist Craig Fouassis. A dapper man who exudes an understated but unmistakable self-confidence, he is a practicing Episcopalian, but his parents were more mystical. They were Rosicrucians, though not, says Craig Fouassis, the sort one sees ads for in pulp magazines. They'd met in a phrenology class. By the time Craig was born, they were heavily involved in the mystical practices of Rosicrucianism. "In our home," Craig recalls, "they had these highly polished wooden cubes, two or three inches square, on which were all sorts of numerals and symbols. There were maybe sixty or seventy cubes, all many colors, and my parents had a table on which they worked their cubes. Whenever my mother would sign her name—or any name, my name, too—the middle initial would have three dots, like a triangle, around it."

There is no single story about Craig Fouassis's actual birth, but there is a small cluster of family stories about his early childhood that told him he was special and was destined to be miraculously protected from physical harm or injury.

The first story, not about Craig Fouassis himself, seems to establish the premise that there is indeed danger in the world. "Somewhere around the age of ten or eleven," says Craig, "I heard that my mother had had a stillbirth, a male child, before me." He also knew that his mother's five brothers and sisters

were all dead by the time she was sixteen, although he didn't
know how they had died. He knew, however, that this had
caused her departure from Catholicism.

So Craig Fouassis was born into a family which, at least from
his mother's point of view, seemed especially subject to danger
and harm. Of his infancy, there is no surviving family story, at
least none that he knows of. But there are several stories about
his early childhood.

> There's one vague one about how my mother had a dream
> and somehow thought that I was going to be run over by
> a car that day. And they were very protective of me the
> entire day. That's the only story of vulnerability. But oth-
> erwise, it was pointed out that I never had any medicine,
> I never had any vaccinations, and yet the only contagious
> illness I ever had was the three-day measles.

In others, there are dangers he miraculously survived.

> There's another I vaguely remember about falling into a
> little goldfish pond at about the age of two. This was at the
> house of a friend of my mother's. Supposedly I would have
> drowned if the dog hadn't pulled me out. Then there was
> another one about a large stack of trays that would have
> killed me if it had started to fall, but my father or somebody
> grabbed me and pulled me out of the way at the last minute.

For Craig Fouassis, all these stories testify to the fact that he
was special. "I always felt I had a special destiny and a special
future. I was treated as if I were very special, though it wasn't
clear in what way." What seems clear to an outsider, however,
is that in the Fouassis family survival seemed a precarious business. Craig, an only child "and the only male child out of six
cousins," was indeed special—he survived. And that became
transmuted into its converse: he survived because he was special.

Also noticeable is phrasing one would expect in the Bible. In
both the story about his mother's previous miscarriage and in
the account of his place among his cousins, he uses the phrase

"male child" rather than, say, the more colloquial "boy." But "boy" does not carry the same connotative weight as "male child," or the same sacred allusiveness.

Craig Fouassis's deep and abiding feeling of being specially graced has persisted. The conviction has perhaps facilitated some of his achievements, but even more to the point it has certainly colored the way he perceives himself and how he therefore fashions the thumbnail version he offers of his life story. He graduated from college when he was only sixteen, specializing in science and math. Then, having decided on medicine, he went back to school. Now as a psychiatrist he feels he is special. "I do both psychoanalysis and family therapy and act as a go-between between the two camps. No one else" among his colleagues "is accepted as both." Even more dramatically, he survived a heart attack at thirty-seven and went on, phoenix-like, to create a new life for himself. After his heart attack, he and his first wife were divorced. Subsequently, he remarried and is now, with his second wife, in the throes of raising his second set of children.

By all appearances, Craig Fouassis lives a good, useful, and comfortable life, but not what most would call a remarkable life. What is remarkable, however, is how his very early experiences seemed remarkable to his mother and were reflected back at him through family stories. That feeling about himself has remained with him and has provided him with the vision by which he lives and assesses his own life.

Donald Tomlinson IV was also his family's first living son, although not an only son. His parents went on to have five more after him. In his case, as with Craig Fouassis, he has the feeling, through stories told to him, that his is a special life.

> I did a number of extraordinary things before I was two. I nearly killed myself. I fell down a series of steps from the attic. I was unconscious and had to be taken to the hospital. That story is supposed to account for my alleged intelligence—that's how it's always cited. It's an important story for me. It shows that my life was in jeopardy at a very early age, but somehow or other it was determined that I should go on living.

He does not say by whom it was "determined," but his phrasing suggests the grand hand of destiny. For Donald, as for Craig Fouassis, the fact that there was a stillborn son who preceded him is a fact of great significance.

> The child who was stillborn would have been Donald Tomlinson IV. That child died, so I picked up the name, though I would otherwise have been Robert, the name of my parents' second son. I'm the first child, but not really the first born. I'm not automatically Donald Tomlinson IV, but I was told: "This is the fourth generation. Your name is Donald Tomlinson. There was a Donald Tomlinson, your father; there was a Donald Tomlinson, your grandfather"— and I was very much impressed with him—"and there was a Donald Tomlinson before that."
>
> That has an effect on me: destiny. And I don't mean that in a cavalier way. It means you fit into a kind of sacramental and solemn progress of the generations in some historical context, and that maybe there is a role for you because of that.

Donald's name alone, especially given the numeral following it, constitutes a coded family narrative. It says that sons are important, that first sons of first sons are especially important, and that there is a place for him in the world. "There's the feeling that the ground on which you stand has been prepared for you," he says, "cleared away for you in some way because of these three other Donald Tomlinsons." As legacies go, it is a useful one.

Unlike Donald Tomlinson IV, Dan Vernale is neither a first child nor a first son, but, like Donald, he is a special son.

> Oh yes, there were lots of stories about my birth. I came after two brothers who died at birth—a gap of ten years. So my birth, as I was told, was awaited with great anticipation. You know—"another baby may die." So there was a kind of joy when I was born—joy that these were better times, joy that I wasn't dead. There was a certain investment in my birth. I had a much older sister and two much older brothers, and I think my father already felt that noth-

ing much was going to come of my brothers. I kind of felt my father had given up on them.

I was the only one born in a hospital and much was made of that. It was like I was the one who was going to take on the modern role, I was the inheritor of the experience in America. The message was: "You're special, you're unique, you're going to make it in America." I knew I was going to make it big. The family almost invested its own success in what I would do.

Like Craig Fouassis, Dan Vernale took the "feel" of his family's expectations of him as the beginning of his own story, and experienced later events in his life in a way consonant with that beginning. He went to college, the first member of his family to do so, and became a social worker. Later, as an administrator of a social agency, he was often called upon to make after-dinner speeches to assorted colleagues and associates.

In a story he tells about himself, he recalls one occasion when, with his mother in attendance, he made a speech at the Waldorf-Astoria. "I was speaking before a Jewish audience, and in her eyes, Jews were the ones who made it big, the ones who were my father's bosses, the ones who represent success. And here was her son talking in a building that her father had worked on to an audience of applauding Jews. To her"—and to Dan Vernale himself—"it was the moment in time that she understood we had made it in three generations."

And there it was: the legacy of a family story about his birth had been instrumental in establishing for Dan his sense of himself as someone who would make it big. It encouraged him both to venture further than he might have, and more important, to experience his own ventures as special and successful. And thus it was that an evening's after-dinner speech seemed a confirmation of the special destiny that awaited him as his parents' son coming into his own in America.

In Dan Vernale's case, as in the cases of Peter Mott, Craig Fouassis, and Donald Tomlinson IV, the facts alone—whether real or wildly embellished—do not account for the special and sacred auras which they believe surrounded their birth and early childhood. Daughters, too, are born after their parents have endured stillbirths. They, too, have survived their mothers' difficult pregnancies and have sometimes had a perilous time of it early on. But these facts, even when they appear in family stories about daughters, don't seem to mean the same thing or add up to the sense that their lives or their futures are of special significance. In fact the same elements in family stories about the births and early lives of daughters seem to become part of an altogether different genre, a genre quite apart from that reserved for sons and one often suffused with disappointment.

The disappointment is never frankly stated, though it often saturates the anecdotes. Cheryl Katernik, a woman in her late forties, tells a pair of stories she often heard about her birth and early childhood.

She characterizes the first story as "a perfect story about love"— the love between her parents—without remarking on the fact that it is a distressing story about herself.

> A month before I was born, my mother fell, and she jammed me into the birth canal chest first. When she did go into labor—she was in very hard labor for three days— they came out and told my father he had to make a choice about whether he wanted my mother or wanted me, and he said, "We can always have another child, so do whatever you can do for my wife."
>
> My grandmother Dinlager had been there with my father and my other grandmother for three days, and they were all very haggard. My grandmother Dinlager was German and talked very broken English. She grabbed my father, Jimmy, and said, "Yimmy, let's play, let's play." He thought she wanted to play, but she was trying to say, "Let's pray." She got down on her knees with my other grandmother and they just prayed silently for two hours with their arms around each other.
>
> The doctors couldn't make up their mind what they were going to do, and finally I came out of the birth canal, and my neck was ten inches long, and I looked like a giraffe. They didn't think I would live, but they were sure my mom would be all right.
>
> My father said, "Just so I can hold my baby, for just a

few minutes." They put me on pillows and brought me up
for him to hold me before I died. And my father just cried
and cried.

The story, hardly positive, is at best equivocal. The tears,
prayers, and pillow attempting to ameliorate and distract from
the central fact that Cheryl Katernik's father made the choice
to save his wife at the expense of his daughter, freakish and
giraffelike with her implausible ten-inch neck.

But the attendant stories Cheryl Katernik tells further diminish the sense that she, their daughter, was a child of value.
When Cheryl was a year old, her father, beloved to her through
stories she's heard about him, died in a motorcycle accident. By
then, her mother was again pregnant and five months along.
Her grief so overwhelmed her, says Cheryl, that she lost the
child she was carrying, a son who she had hoped would be the
reincarnation of her dead husband.

> My mother got so confused after that. She'd drive down-
> town with me, and go into the store, and then she'd forget
> that she'd driven down and that I was still sitting in the
> car seat. Then she'd walk home, and her family would say,
> "Well, where's Cheryl?" And she'd say, "Oh my god, she's
> still downtown in the car." Out of my father's death, she
> got angry, and then she got even angrier about what hap-
> pened to my brother. They all wanted her to give me up
> and leave me and just come East. But she wouldn't.

In Cheryl Katernik's cluster of stories, two motifs, in addition
to her father's choice, seem metaphorically to devalue her. One
is the motif which renders her as more animal than human, and
the other is the motif of forgetting her existence entirely, leaving
her downtown in a parked car. There is no doubt her abandonment testifies to the magnitude of her mother's grief at her double
loss. It is odd not that her mother reacted that way, but that it
was preserved as a story to be told to Cheryl. Surely hearing the
story cannot have enhanced her self-esteem.

In the dozens of stories I heard about birth and early childhood, I never found these motifs threaded through stories about sons—though surely some sons, sometime, must have actually been momentarily forgotten—but I heard variations on them frequently woven into stories about daughters.

Hannah English has a birth story similar to Cheryl Katernik's, a story which she says was told in her family in a rather "jovial" fashion.

> A couple of days before I was born, my mother was out hanging clothes on the line. She jumped to touch the line, and the cord became wrapped around my throat. Apparently that can happen. As a result of this, she had a very hard time giving birth, and I was blue. My mother almost died. I was very ugly, very very ugly. When they put me in my mother's arms, she said, "Oh my god! She looks like a moldy sausage." My father apparently said, "How can you say that? Look at her eyes. Big dark eyes. They're asking, 'Why did you put me here?' " My father told me that part of the story, and my mother told me the other part.

Hannah English's story, like Cheryl Katernik's, is marked by a good deal of ambiguity, represented by an ending in which the father's actions attempt to undo the central fact of the story— the daughter's faultiness and undesirability. Nonetheless, Hannah seems to accept at face value her mother's assessment of her ("I was very ugly") rather than her father's.

Another story that Hannah English tells also conveys the feeling that she was not essential, at least to her mother, though it is couched in the context of how well behaved she was. "I was a very good child," Hannah English says, "and when I was growing up, it was believed that children have to have lots of fresh air. They would put me outside in the carriage for two hours, then bring me in for lunch and then take me out again for another two hours. And I was such a good child that they forgot me once. They left me outside until ten o'clock at night."

What is striking about these sets of stories is how complacently the narrators tell them, how convinced they seem to be that the stories are "perfect love stories" or "jovial" stories, when to the disinterested listener they seem nothing of the sort. My suspicion is that the tellers deny the impact of the stories even as they relate them. They protect themselves by keeping a great emotional distance from the stories. But still they tell them, suggesting how deeply the stories have burrowed into their psyches.

Hannah English, for instance, is a registered nurse. Surely with her background she must have known that her mother's jump to reach a clothesline could not cause the umbilical cord to become wrapped around her neck, particularly so late in the third trimester. But the critical faculty that would have alerted her to the unlikeliness of the story, if the child were anyone other than herself, is totally absent, a sign of her own intention to keep the story at arm's length, even while she tells it. And the same must be true of Cheryl Katernik, a mother of five who surely must have known that it's impossible for a child to be born with a neck ten inches long.

Had there not been such a proliferation of stories about daughters who seemed so poorly welcomed in the world, so inconsequential to those who were supposed to care for them, especially their mothers, I would have been more likely to accept these stories at face value. But the motif of the abandoned daughter appeared so often. I heard it from Sharon Medlow, for instance, and in her case, it was unequivocal that her parents desperately wanted a son. "When all three of us girls were born," she confides, "they didn't have names picked out for us because they wanted boys, and they had a name, Richard, prepared for each of us. But by the time they had him, they were so sick of the name that they named him Joshua."

As for the story about Sharon Medlow herself, it seems she was an independent child, and that became the apparent point of a story told about her.

> I was a kid who could take care of myself. That's the way my mother tells it. She says that one afternoon she went to visit one of her friends. As she tells it, "I went there with four kids and I came home with three. You were so good about amusing yourself and taking care of yourself—

you were off playing someplace by yourself in a corner, and I just forgot about you. I got home, and after I was home for a while, I realized that I didn't have you, so I went back to get you, and you were just fine."

So while Hannah English was "good" and Sharon Medlow was "independent," neither could avoid playing a central role in a story about abandonment, the point being that the ascribed temperament of the child has less to do with the story than the sex of the child. Sharon Medlow's independence was perhaps so unexpected—at least in a girl—that it apparently made her mother uncomfortable, and the consequences of her mother's discomfort made life harder for Sharon. "The image I used to get from my mother," says Sharon, "was that I was some kind of monster who was going to eat her up if she went near me. So the whole image is of me having to take care of myself."

Are girls left behind—forgotten in their carriages or car seats—more often than boys? The question is impossible to answer. But the fact is that girls, more often than boys, are *told* that they were forgotten and left behind. And so the telling itself is a transaction between mother and daughter. It may be that when the mother is the teller, she is prompted in part by guilt and the relief that confession brings, but regardless of the teller's motivation, such stories cannot make the daughters feel that they were enthusiastically welcomed or deeply valued.

Furthermore, such stories of birth and very early childhood take place at a time in the daughters' lives they cannot remember themselves. Hence they cannot counter the painful impact of the stories with memories of their own which otherwise might help them resist the impact, or even mitigate it with a recollection of their own that might carry some more positive feeling.

What about the metaphors in the stories in which the newborn daughter is rendered as an animal or piece of bad meat? Metaphors reveal feelings rather than fact; neutral as a form, they can either sweeten or sour the flavor of a story. When they are used in ordinary conversation, they're not used self-consciously, and hence they may indicate feelings that the teller might consciously choose to conceal or even be unaware of holding. Clearly, in the birth stories about daughters here recounted, these metaphors devalue, and the devaluation is a function of the teller's point of view rather than any event per se: it says how the newborn daughter was *seen*. They are not ways in which anybody would choose to be seen. And so the point seems to be that the feelings that suffuse stories about sons and stories about daughters exist prior to and separately from the anecdotes that are later developed to contain them. While not all sons report stories of sacred births and while not all daughters are told stories about births that have made their mothers sick, the fact is that sons alone participate in the aura of the sacred, and daughters alone do not.

OF SONS, DAUGHTERS, AND GENDER IDENTITY

Most children understand by the time they're two or so what sex they are. The physical facts of their anatomy make the acquisition of that knowledge fairly straightforward. But their understanding of gender—what a given culture means by the appellations "masculine" and "feminine"—is a more elusive matter.

It's fairly well documented by now that there are really very few traits that are universally designated as either "masculine" or "feminine." As Margaret Mead demonstrated throughout her books, certain traits and activities may be designated as "masculine" in one culture, while the same traits are designated as "feminine" in another.

In a culture as complex as our own, it can take a whole childhood to tease out and understand which traits, mannerisms, names, dress styles, body decorations, colors, occupations, and preoccupations are customarily designated as "masculine" and which are termed "feminine." Ours is a culture deeply uneasy with what can't be immediately gender-sorted—hence the mania for color-coding even infant pillows—and so what often may be intended as descriptive becomes prescriptive.

I saw this determination to piece together an understanding of the complex nature of gender in my son when he was about three. Almost daily he asked some questions about gender, questions which had nothing to do with sex per se, as do, say, biological questions about who does what procreatively. Instead, his questions all had to do with the social and cultural consequences of being the sex one is. He was equally quick to pick up on what he perceived as signs of "deviance." Why did Christopher wear shoes with black straps across the front? Were Aaron and Erin the same name? Why was one a boy and the other a girl? Why was the Indian man wearing an earring? Could boys wear nail polish? How could a girl be a fireman when it's "fireman"? My son, like all children that age, had already discovered that his gender is the most significant facet of his identity, and having learned that, wanted to make sure he got everything sorted correctly.

Young children begin by demonstrating many, if not all, traits in the gender smorgasbord. According to Eleanor Maccoby and Carol Jacklin's study, *The Psychology of Sex Differences*, few of the stereotypical traits we respectively ascribe to men and women are present in young children in the ways we might expect. The implication is that all children gradually learn to forsake traits that the culture designates as inappropriate to someone of their sex, and try to embrace those that seem to be more suitable. But how does this subtle telegraphing of what one should be occur? It takes place in a thousand ways, a thousand times a day, largely through the experience of daily family life, and it is pointedly reinforced and underscored through family stories.

Early on, all little girls learn that it's important to be beautiful, as beautiful as one can be anyhow, and that beauty coupled with a mixture of flirtatiousness are two of the staples of female power—at least in relation to men.

Linda Rudolph, according to the testimony of early family stories, was both beautiful and flirtatious, even as a very young child. She had long flaxen hair and big, round blue eyes. These, she knew, were important traits because they made her her father's favorite (in comparison to her sister, who was not quite so beautiful) and the favorite of all the men she met. Her beauty and its usefulness were made clear to her through two family stories which she heard throughout her childhood.

"My mother says she would take me for a walk in my carriage down the streets," says Linda Rudolph. "She says that from the time I was a baby, I flirted with men, and that men were always admiring of me. She didn't say that to my sister."

The second story, a suitable companion to the first, is set during the early days of World War II, when Linda's father was in the army and away from his family for several years. "When my father was in the war, she took a photo of my sister and me—she told me it was a 'pin-up'—and she sent it to my father. It was like we—and especially me—were the sex objects."

This is not a story that gives Linda Rudolph any pleasure; in fact it is a story that makes her cry as she tells it. "Being beautiful was a burden," she explains. "My mother created the 'beautiful daughter' a little bit for my father and a little bit for herself. Being beautiful wasn't something I learned from her: she almost deliberately made herself unattractive. She admired me and deplored me for my attractiveness—either one, but she didn't love me."

Hence the double bind attached to being appropriately feminine rears its ugly head again. From Linda's point of view, she became the beautiful little girl her mother wanted her to become, but then paid the price of her mother's disapproval and perhaps jealousy for having been so obliging. Her father may have been less ambivalent about having a beautiful daughter—and Linda says he was—but during a sizable block of Linda's childhood, her father was overseas.

The tension between Linda and her mother is reminiscent of the state of affairs between Snow White and her stepmother, in that each older woman is envious of the young daughter's beauty. And this is inevitable, perhaps, in a culture which accords women status on the basis of a beauty which, by definition, is yoked to youth and therefore is ultimately ephemeral. Hence, in a culture which ties femininity to beauty, there may be an inevitable tension between mothers and their daughters, an inevitable ambivalence in mothers toward their daughters. Linda Rudolph states the tension and the reasons for it more outspokenly than any of the other women whose stories about birth and early childhood appear in these clusters, but the emotional aura, more blatant or less blatant, remains a fixture. And the result seems to be that daughters, unlike many sons, rarely feel special and almost never feel entirely acceptable, even to themselves, because they never felt entirely acceptable to their mothers.

As Susan Brownmiller points out in her book *Femininity*, girls are perceived as behaving appropriately when they are sentimental, empathetic, and vulnerable. The message that underlies all of these traits is that girls should be "good," a goodness requiring a kind of docility, a willingness to subordinate their own needs, impulses, and wishes to others. Many of the family stories told about daughters implicitly underscore and reinforce the presence of such a self-defeating goodness.

A second look at all those family stories about daughters left in their carriages or car seats reveals that these are messages about docility as well as abandonment. Hannah English and Cheryl Katernik were so uncomplaining—or so the stories go —that nobody even noticed they were missing. The further suggestion is that even when they were right under their parents' eyes, they were generally uncomplaining. Otherwise the silence when they were absent would surely have been noticed.

As for Sharon Medlow, her goodness was couched in terms of her independence, but the doublespeak notwithstanding, the message to her was surely that to be good was to be an appropriate little girl, even though for her, as for the others, it resulted in her abandonment. This is consonant with Brownmiller's assertion that to be a "good" and appropriately "feminine" little girl is to be in a no-win situation.

Many of the storytellers I encountered recognized the element of social control and tacit coercion embodied in the family stories about their daughterly goodness, but their recognition had come long after childhood.

Amy Dace, a woman of forty, knows a story about herself as a very young child, and it isn't one she likes.

> This is a story that still dogs me—and really bothers me. As a very young child I was amazingly obedient. I almost said "witlessly." The story is that they didn't have to take the playpen when they took me somewhere. They could take only the playpen pad and I would stay on it because I was so "bright."
>
> The gloss on the story was that I was so bright that I understood them if they told me to stay somewhere. But I was being terribly manipulated. The story was repeated to me as I was growing up as if it revealed a wonderful feature about myself. It took me a long time to realize that it was really godawful. I was deeply into pleasing people, there's no doubt about it.

Hannah English had no objection to the story about herself whiling away the hours in the backyard in her baby carriage, but there are a few additional stories—testifying to her saintly selflessness—which now enrage her when she thinks about them. Nonetheless, they are stories that got their hold on her early and deeply. One concerns a childhood birthday party.

> I don't remember this story actually happening, but it was a story that was often told in my family. I went to school and each year I had a birthday party. The year I was going to turn seven, my mother asked me if I wanted a birthday party, and I said yes. My mother invited a couple of her friends to help. They put up streamers and got hats and baked a couple of cakes.
>
> I invited seven girls from school because seven was how old I was going to be. I brought these kids home, and they were all real losers. They didn't know how to eat right or sit right or anything. So we had the whole party and then

after my mother asked me why I had invited them. I told
her they were the ones no one else would invite.

These days, Hannah English likes to think of herself as rebellious. She moved thousands of miles away from her family
when she was twenty-one, and never went back home. Soon
after, she married. Ten years later, she left her husband and
their two children and moved in with a lover a few towns away.
Now a nurse and one of the chief administrators of a local
hospice, Hannah sees herself as a medical rebel. "The kind of
work I do is at the periphery of establishment medical care, and
I'm always taking risks with my job for the people under my
care. As a nurse, I'm not supposed to change, increase, or de-
crease medications, but if the people are in pain I certainly will
do that, even though it could cost me my license."

And yet, Hannah English hasn't at all exiled from her heart
the seven-year-old who invited all the class losers to her birthday
party. With a smile which is half resigned and half ironic she
says, "How good can you get? I work every day of my life with
people who are dying. People look at me almost like I'm a saint."

Adelaide Lewis, now in her late forties, was also a "saint."

All the stories about me are about how "good" I was. I
was potty-trained when I was one year old. That's one of
them. When I was two and a half, I was so good and so
responsible that my mother sent me to the store alone to
buy a loaf of bread. Then there's another story about how
my mother once had to go to New York, leaving me behind
in Roanoke. When she was in New York, she called to find
out how things were going. I got on the phone, and I said,
"I'm fine. I'm eating liver, but I don't like it."

But eat it she did.

As an adult, Adelaide Lewis suffered bouts of mental illness,
and she is convinced that swallowing her family's view of herself
as utterly good was a factor. "I don't want to blame it on my
parents, but I think I got a pretty strong load of having to be
that good." The result was, says Adelaide, that there was no

room, in her view of herself, for anything that wasn't good. Her sense of herself was so compartmentalized that she had to be sick in order not to be "good."

It was during these "psychotic" bouts, she says, that she enacted her "badness" in as extreme a way as she had enacted her goodness. She spent money wildly, she says, and went through periods of marked sexual promiscuity. Adelaide Lewis believes that she was constitutionally, even biochemically, susceptible to mental illness, but she also believes that the environment had to collaborate with her susceptibilities, and the first step toward her illness was her conviction, internalized very early in her childhood, that she was utterly good, compliant, and responsible.

One may wonder, after this depressing rash of stories, how it happens that any little girl grows up into a woman of strength and substance. Part of the answer is that even if we look at the influence of family stories alone, the child—a daughter as well as a son—draws from a rich and mixed source. However much Kate Turner's mother deplored her stubbornness, Kate knew that Turners were spunky and stubborn, and so she was equally entitled to those traits. And the same was true for Hannah English. Despite the fact that her mother left her in the carriage, she believed that she came from "a long line of strong women" and so she went on to take her place among them. It is a mixed narrative heritage and not unequivocally benign to be sure, but certainly it helps offset the influence of the negative legacy alone.

There's a contradiction here, however. Why should a mother who proudly conveys to her daughter that she comes from a long line of strong women undercut the strength she is also trying to foster? The answer may be that a mother is assigned the task of making her daughter into a culturally "appropriate" woman, and in doing so she faces the same double bind that has faced women in other cultures who have had to bind their daughters' feet or perform clitoridectomies—that is, she must turn her daughter into something that she herself may inwardly deplore, or else run the risk of being seen as an inadequate mother. Looked at in this light, the "strong women" tradition of family stories is every daughter's subversive legacy. It offers her an alternative to the constricting and often damaging stories her mother may be telling her about herself.

And the second factor that gives daughters a way out is that at least some of the time their fathers either participate in the stories daughters hear about themselves or actually tell them in a way that softens the blow. Cheryl Katernik's story of her birth is manifestly depressing—her father straightforwardly chose her mother's life over hers, but the denouement of the story shows him cradling her lovingly.

And the same is true of Hannah English's birth story. The bulk of the story typecasts her as a "moldy sausage" who imperiled her mother's life, but her father added a loving addition to the story when he challenged her mother's characterization—"How can you say that?"—and focused instead on her "big dark eyes."

It also seems that every once in a while a father has an independent story contribution, one that the mother doesn't tell. Not always, but sometimes it offers the daughter a view of herself which contains much more latitude. Beautiful Linda Rudolph, her father's army "pin-up," says her father often told her a story which proved she had "spirit" and that the way her father told her the story showed how pleased he was. "He adored me," she says. "There's a story about that, too. He would come home from work, and I would always go get his slippers and put them on him. One evening he came in, and he yelled at me to go get his slippers. And I wouldn't do it. He ended up hitting me, and I never went and got those damned slippers again. He loved to tell that story because he admired my spirit."

What happens to sons during these same years? How do they learn the fine points of masculinity in our culture? I heard relatively few stories about males' acquisition of masculinity, and I think there are at least two reasons for it. First is that fewer sons than daughters participate in the family storytelling tradition.

But the second reason is that, in our culture, "masculinity" is a far less constricted role. Boys may have to learn to repress their more vulnerable sides ("Boys don't cry," etc.), and this surely costs them a great deal, but they don't have to be taught to manage their looks, develop their charm, suppress their expansiveness, expand their empathy, or devote their lives to being good. Since there is more latitude to the masculine role, less instruction is required. And the family stories that do exist are often stories of affirmation, reinforcing what already is, or simply testifying to the son's generic "specialness."

Michael MacDougal, a twenty-three-year-old college student, says there were a great many stories about him as a little boy, almost all of them testifying to his independence, an independence that was well received.

> One story is about the time I was four years old and my family was living in the Palace Hotel in Japan because my father was there on business. My parents went out and left my sister and me with the Japanese babysitter. The Palace Hotel was a wonderful place because it had about twenty-five stores and six different restaurants. So we all went down to the tempura restaurant, where they served sake. The babysitter didn't want hers and my sister didn't want hers, so I drank all three of them. I got rather drunk and terrorized the whole hotel, and then slept until noon the next day. It was a totally affectionate story. A lot of my childhood stories were "cute" stories, and I was given a lot of leeway.
>
> Then there was another story about the time we were driving to Canada. I was just sitting on the floor in the back. Right next to me was a bottle of antihistamines, and I just ate up the whole bottle. But they couldn't get me to throw up. My father called the Poison Control Center in Canada, and they said, "Make him throw up." But they couldn't make me throw up. I just wouldn't. There was a real admiration for my talent as a child—getting into things, being a little critter.

What is interesting about this story is that Michael MacDougal's inability to throw up the antihistamines is transformed into his stubborn refusal to throw up, as if he had made some decision about the matter. And so the story invents a "stubbornness" as his motivation and then rewards the invention with approval. Nonetheless, Michael MacDougal grew up believing he was stubborn and that it was just the way he ought to be.

Aaron Kane, a Kansan in his mid-thirties, often heard a family story about himself as a child—about an incident he doesn't actually remember—and even now he laughs when he tells it. "My mother had taken me with her to the grocery store, and we ran into an elderly man whom she knew. 'My, my, what a nice little boy,' he said, and patted me on the head. My mother said, 'Aaron, say hello to the nice man.' But I didn't say hello. Instead, I made a fist and socked hard. The problem was that my fist was at about the level of his groin. I guess the point was that I was a little hell-raiser. The story was always told very affectionately." Whatever disapproval or chagrin Aaron Kane's mother may have expressed at the time is lost. What remains, however, is her amusement and implied approval of his boyishness."

This does not mean that boys never hear negative stories about themselves. They do, especially when the issue is their expression of fear or their display of a trait that seems, to their parents' worried eyes, to suggest effeminacy. Thomas Garcia, now a college professor, has one such story about fear, but he hastens to add that it was not a "typical" story about him. "There was one time when I was a kid, and I was taken to the Thanksgiving Day parade. They dealt with the hassle of the subway and then pushed to the front of the crowd, getting into a fight in order to do it. Then, finally, when success had been achieved, and we had made it to the front of the crowd, I refused to open my eyes because I was so scared."

But Thomas Garcia clearly understood the story as admonishing and went on to explain that, in practice, he was not often the way he had been in that story. "I was a shy kid, but not a frightened kid," he says. "In fact I've always been pretty aggressive. When I was a kid, I was always fighting, always on the streets. I was a street kid, and always a leader, too." His tone suggests that aside from this minor Thanksgiving Day lapse, which his family apparently brought back to haunt him, he was always an appropriately "boyish" boy.

But B. C. Heinz, an aspiring playwright, was never quite boyish enough, and in his family there are a rash of stories that are "told and retold." He says:

> A lot of them are about my sister, Teddi, and me. We're as antithetically different as two people can be. My sister was a tomboy and a hellion as a little girl. She was two and a half years younger than I was. I was the "good" one, the quiet one, and I didn't like playing outside too much. And it absolutely befuddled my parents because they had very clear wishes for my sister and me—and we frustrated every one of them. They wanted me to be the ballplayer and all-around boy in the family, and they wanted my sister to be the petite and good one. In my family there's a good deal of respect for hell-raisers, for people who have enough spunk and wherewithal to do what can be told in stories later. It was curious to them that their boy wouldn't do it and their girl would. And I've gone on to be the writer and my sister has gone on to be the gym teacher.

One of the earliest stories is based on the events of a Christmas morning when B. C. Heinz was three and his sister was still in the crawling stage.

> Teddi was just out of her crib, and my parents had let her crawl around to play with her toys. I had opened all of my toys already. Well, my sister's toys were not good enough for her, so over the course of Christmas Day, she ignored her toys but managed to break or impair every single one of the toys I had received for Christmas.
> My mother always shakes her head at this point and says, "You poor soul. Every time she'd reach for one of your toys, you'd give it to her, and then she'd break it, and then you'd give her another one." As the story was told I was very gentle and self-effacing, and she was out to damage everything that she could.

Several companion stories B. C. Heinz heard were subtle, but he got the point all the same. "The stories told about me, when they are told, are usually to illustrate how strange I was, or how I frustrated my parents' expectations of me." In two of them, the uneasiness is perhaps prompted by the American tendency to equate an interest in the arts with insufficient masculinity.

> There are two stories they always tell together. In the first, I was a baby—on my stomach—and they would have friends over to the house. They would turn on the TV, and the baby—me—would just lie there peaceably, not really paying any attention. But then the commercial would come on, and during that moment of silence between program and commercial, I would click on. I would turn and stare unblinkingly at the screen for the duration of the commercial. The second it ended, I would roll back over and spit up again. It was like clockwork. It was just a curiosity of the baby.
>
> Later it manifested itself in another way. Every Saturday night we would watch Mitch Miller, with the bouncing ball. Mitch Miller always had a very characteristic conducting style, with his hand in the O.K. gesture. My parents would sit and watch me because I would always leap up to conduct with Mitch, singing at the top of my lungs.
>
> The two television stories are often told together. The second one means "Oh no! We thought we would raise a musician."

Now and then our legacy of stories is exactly what we need. This is especially true when it comfortably serves as a prologue to the life we have freely chosen for ourselves. But more usually our family stories about ourselves are passed along to us without special regard for whether we want them or not. Often, it seems—especially when the legacy concerns sexual stereotyping—it is not at all what we wanted but a burden we either live with uncomfortably or struggle later on to get rid of.

CHAPTER 9

FAIRY GODMOTHERS
AND
PATRON SAINTS

I happened to meet Amy Dace at a pivotal moment in her life. Just recently, she told me, she had legally acquired the right to shed the last name of her former husband and to resume the use of her birth surname. As we sat and sipped lemonade on the backyard patio of the house she shared with an English professor she would soon marry, she was clearly proud and pleased with herself, savoring the sense of independence and autonomy symbolized for her by the reclamation of her name. She told me she would keep her name even after her new marriage.

However tethered Amy Dace still was to her earliest sense of herself—as a good girl who would please others, staying on the playpen mat, even without the playpen—she was very much in the throes of inventing herself, and that included determining what she would be called.

But how, at the age of forty, was she going about defining herself? What were her sources or resources? For Amy, her mother had never been any source at all. "I don't think I have a real mother for the woman I want to be," she confided. "My own mother was kind of a graceless wacky tomboy person," unattractive, insecure, and heavily—perhaps too heavily—dependent on Amy's father. "All this made me want to have distance from her—not be like her."

But Amy Dace was by no means a spiritual orphan. These days her grandmother—ninety-three and still vigorous—was very much on her mind. But as we talked, it became clear that the grandmother Amy had in mind was not her grandmother as she was now but her grandmother as she emerged through the family stories about her when she was younger. The woman in those stories represented the kind of woman Amy wanted to be, and, even more, thought she *could* be, because her grandmother had a "sweetness" which Amy recognized in herself.

"I know she has a temper," said Amy, "but I've never seen it. My mother has a story about her parents moving into a new apartment. My grandfather—he was selfish, always inside his own funny world—came into the kitchen and asked her to do something *else* for him, and my grandmother turned and threw an egg at him. It's an amazing story, first because my grandmother is physically tiny, and second because she's always sweet." Amy lapsed into a silence for a moment before she spoke. "I dream about her; she's my fairy godmother when I dream about her."

Amy Dace has a second resource as well, in her great-grandmother.

This is my mother's mother's mother. She lived in Colorado and died at eighty-eight on her descent from her fourteenth climb of Pikes Peak. I knew her well, very well, and she was amazing—this little old lady who was always dressed in black with this little porkpie hat, no makeup, and dark tan leathery skin. She had white hair, and seemed to me to be kind of a Georgia O'Keeffe figure.

By the time I knew her she was a naturalist. When she would visit us in Galveston, she'd go to the beach, and she'd come back with rocks and shells. She would go to the salt flats with my little sister's red wagon, which she would pull around behind her so she could collect specimens. She would come back with rather strange vegetation.

Amy Dace also knew a few family stories about her great-grandmother's earlier life.

> She had two children, and then she divorced that hus-
> band—that would have been before the turn of the century.
> She divorced him because he was kind of a charming ne'er-
> do-well, a gambler and a kind of feckless person. She couldn't
> manage financially with her children, so she left them with
> her husband's family. After a time, she remarried a Mr.
> Roberts, and had four more children. Mr. Roberts didn't
> continue to be part of her life. Maybe he died. But my
> great-grandmother was an independent woman. She just
> made her own way; she taught and she nursed, and by the
> time I knew her, she was into rocks and flowers. She was
> tough.

Of all the family stories Amy Dace carries around with her, she
says it is the ones about her great-grandmother which affect her
most. "I wouldn't have said this ten years ago, and my answer
may be different ten years from now, but I feel a real strong
affinity and attraction for my great-grandmother—divorced,
climbing mountains, living her own life. I feel real proud of her,
though I think I'm not really like her. I think I'm too much tied
into monogamous relationships, and she was really independent
of that."

Amy Dace didn't say so, and I didn't ask, but the implication
was that in her prior marriage she had been too much the good
girl, too markedly the compliant wife. Now on the verge of her
second marriage, she was combing through the bits and pieces
and oddments of everything she'd ever heard, and probably her
memories of everyone she'd ever met, looking for solutions, ways
of thinking about herself, so she could marry without marriage's
becoming a playpen mat. In her search for herself, she had settled
on these two family figures to pattern herself after. And they
seemed more promising choices to her than a more distant figure
such as Georgia O'Keeffe. The women on her mind were her
antecedents, and she shared their blood, so if they could live as

they had, perhaps she, too, could live as they had, with her own modifications.

The family stories Amy Dace told me about her grandmother and great-grandmother were not, in content, any different from any other family stories people told me. What distinguished them was the active use Amy Dace was making of them.

Up until this point, all the family stories I've recounted have been stories which the individuals who heard them absorbed as passively as if they had been radiation. Whether they were stories about the family, the ways of the world, or themselves, the people who heard them had simply absorbed them without actively or consciously reaching out for them.

Throughout our entire lives, we remain affiliated with the families we grew up in. We remain, however uneasily, loyal and connected to, and profoundly identified with, those families. But at the same time, all of us are profoundly eager to be just ourselves, valuing an individualism, or at least an independence, encouraged by our culture.

And that gives rise to a dilemma. How are we to break free, begin to realize whatever ideals we may have set for ourselves, be who we need to be and want to be, and yet at the same time remain connected? And how are we to fill in the voids we see ourselves as having or to outwit the prohibitions that have been bequeathed to us without, at the same time, seeing ourselves as too uncomfortably rejecting or rebellious?

The urge to invent oneself begins early and is perhaps coeval with the advent of any sort of self-consciousness. I see it daily in my young son, whose recognition of himself is inextricable from his recognition of a vulnerability he would rather not have. And so, in his Superman pajamas, he tears madly down the hallway, cape flying, in an effort to appropriate for himself at least some of the dauntlessness he believes his superhero to have. He tells me of the miraculous feats he has performed just out of my sight—lifting beds up in the air, or saving his younger brother from evil adversaries. He flexes for me muscles he alone can see.

Whether we call them role models, fairy godmothers, patron saints, ego ideals, inspirations, or guides, all of us at some point

in our lives—and probably at many points—look outside ourselves at others in the hope of becoming something of what these
figures are or at least seem to be. These models need not be
people we know personally. The more remote they are, in fact,
the more serviceable they may be as archetypes or embodiments
of what we wish we were and what we hope or strive to become.

Such figures exist in fiction, film, and fable. But most con-
veniently, they exist in family stories—particularly, but not exclusively, in our most ancestral stories. These figures offer us a
way of achieving independence and of realizing our most personal
ideals without jeopardizing our connectedness to our families.

To return to Amy Dace's experience, she had heard these
stories about her egg-throwing grandmother and mountain-
climbing great-grandmother from her own mother, a woman who
was as dependent and compliant as her daughter and who, even
more to the point, had trained her daughter from infancy on to
behave the same way. Call this an over-the-counter transaction
between mother and daughter. It was Amy's mother's responsibility to offer up to the culture an "appropriate" female and
she did so, as mothers everywhere do.

But at the same time, a second strain of stories about Amy's
grandmother and great-grandmother had more subversive meaning. They offered Amy an alternative vision of what women are
like and Amy was now seizing on those stories as if they were
stolen goods, using them to make hereslf something she believed
ran counter to what her mother actually wanted her to be.

Amy Dace's experience is typical of the experience of many
women I interviewed. Through admonition, instruction, and
family stories, women are trained by their mothers to be good
and compliant. But in many families, there exists a second strain
of family stories about vigorous rebellious women, also told by
women, which the daughters latch onto as an alternative vision
and ideal. In doing so, they invariably believe they are defying
or outwitting what their mothers want them to be. And perhaps
their mothers believe it, too.

It was Melanie Reinhold who first made me aware that women
invent themselves by drawing from their own mother's subversive

stories. Her mother, like Amy Dace's, had raised her according to the unambiguous standards of the 1950s—to be a sweet, gentle, passive, and compliant woman and to accept the constraints of being female because it was dangerous to do otherwise. "I was always being told that I couldn't do something or be something because I was a girl," she recalls. "My mother always said that things were harder for girls, and that there was a whole rash of consequences for not following the rules. It was different for a boy to do it than for a girl, whatever the 'it' was. Somehow it was all tied up with sexuality or sex roles. You had less leeway because you were female. That was one message—and the up-front message—that I got."

However, the family stories that Melanie Reinhold heard from her mother—often stories about her mother—did not seem to confirm her mother's instructions.

I would say, "Tell me about when you were a little girl," and then she'd tell me things. Like the day she tried to sneak out the back door to go ice-skating without her long stockings on, and how mad they were. Or the story she told me about whistling. She told me that when she was a little girl, her grandfather got very angry when he heard her whistling because it wasn't ladylike. The message was that boys could do those things, but the other message was that she hadn't liked not being able to do them.

A lot of her stories had to do with being Jewish. They had this terrible Hebrew teacher, Mr. Bromberg. Mr. Bromberg was this enormous man who looked a lot like a frog. He had these bulging eyes. Every single day after school, they had to go to Hebrew school, and this man was terribly mean, though mostly to the boys. He would box their ears. After the eighth grade, my mother refused to go at all. She was quite the little rebel in her own family at that time.

Then she told me about how she met my father. One summer my mother went to Denver to spend the summer with her sister working in the hospital. My father happened to be stationed at Lowry Air Force Base, and they met through the local rabbi, who was the chaplain for the Jewish soldiers at the base. They had a blind date and that was the beginning of their romance, though the story is that

my father was so insensitive to the fact that they were
supposed to be the ones having the romance that after the
first date he called up and wanted her to go on a double
date with him—but he wanted my mother to be the date
for his friend.

My mother agreed to go at first because she was so surprised, but then she thought it over and realized that that
wasn't what she wanted to do. So she called him back and
said no. He gave her a lecture about not breaking dates
and about keeping commitments, but she still said no.

I think she told me a lot of stories about how she wasn't
passive and how she always asserted herself.

As a child, Melanie Reinhold, however reluctantly, was inclined to do and be what her mother wanted her to do and be.
The stories registered, but since they seemed to be at odds with
her mother's less ambiguous instructions, Melanie didn't know
quite what to do with them. "I think I was surprised by the
stories. The fact that she could tell those stories benignly showed
me a side of her that I didn't see. Her authority when I was a
child was pretty unquestioned. The stories gave me only the
slightest hint that it might be possible for her to accept something
different from what she was telling me. But it was pretty confusing for me."

And so, as Melanie Reinhold tells it, the stories remained
with her, subordinate and dormant, so as not to cause her conflict. It was only as an adult—"maybe in the last ten years"—
that Melanie Reinhold took them out again and examined them,
and she did so because, like Amy Dace, she had reached a point
in her own life—her middle thirties—when she needed to take
herself into her own hands and do some refashioning.

For Irene Goldstein, also in her middle thirties, the fairy
godmother in question is her paternal grandmother, and her
story about her grandmother serves to demonstrate just how
much that is usable one can make out of almost nothing if one
needs to. In Irene Goldstein's case, she has seized on one or two
wispy allusions to her grandmother as urgently as one might seize
on an antidote to poison. The familial poison, from Irene's point

of view, is her frightening maternal legacy, which she describes as three generations of suicidal women.

Irene never met her father's mother. She, like all Irene's antecedents on both sides, died in a concentration camp during World War II. But Irene has resurrected her. "My grandmother, Irena Goldstein, is the woman I'm named after. There were lots of stories—well, not stories so much as attributes, really—my father told about her because she was my name grandmother, and so I was told these things as if they were somehow imbued with my name. I always had the idea that I had to do these things that my grandmother did because I was named after her." But what's clear as Irene Goldstein talks is that she did more than quietly step into her grandmother's shoes. Given no more than a shoelace, she created an entire world, complete with an emotional texture.

> The story was that whenever any of her children had diarrhea, she would distribute these semisweet chocolates from this cache she had. It's a legacy of rural benevolence, very even-keeled. It's a legacy of courtesy. The courtesy doesn't really come through the stories; it's from the world that the stories suggest.
>
> You see, the stories in my case are so sketchy. I had my grandmother's name, but I had nothing else of her. There were maybe one or two pictures of her, but there was no other trace of her anywhere, except in my father's memory, which is where she existed.
>
> The chocolate story is my father going to the top of the staircase and yelling down this long oak staircase, "Mommy, I have diarrhea. Give me some chocolate." And she'd turn up with this wonderful chocolate. So that's the sketch. What I've done is fill in all around it. If there's a staircase, there's got to be two floors, right? And then where did the chocolate come from? There's got to be a pantry. But there's a way of life that's suggested by the story. I think in my fantasy of my grandmother, she was a healer, a caregiver.

And a lady. "One of the attributes of Grandma Irena was that she never whistled because if you whistled you weren't a lady, and if you whistled before breakfast you'd marry a crazy husband. But," adds Irene, "I never got the sense of her being a coldly aristocratic lady. The image was very warm, involved with people, and very much governed by feeling in a noncrazy way. It's perhaps an idealization of the maternal."

Irene Goldstein's allusion to the maternal suggests what links her experience with the experiences of Amy Dace and Melanie Reinhold: each woman feels that her own deficits, shortcomings, and limitations stem from being shortchanged by her mother. What each mother gave either wasn't enough or wasn't good enough. But although the daughters get on with business and take their lives into their own hands, they don't entirely experience themselves this way. Instead, below the surface they preserve a fundamental sense of themselves as existing *in relation*, inventing new or better mothers for themselves so that they can become the nurtured daughters they'd like to be. It's as if the I-Thou sense of self persists in women throughout childhood and into adult life. To change the "I," women posit a new "thou" to exist in relation to, the "thou" then redefining the "I."

If there is anyone one might expect to be permanently enmeshed in the intricacies of family life, even at the price of individuality, it is Yolanda Mercutio. She grew up during the 1950s in a large Italian family, surrounded by parents, grandparents, aunts, uncles, and various grades of cousins. It was a family that valued the idea of family and at the frequent family gatherings, story upon story poured forth, almost all of them testifying to the importance of close ties and the need to subordinate one's own personal strivings for the good of the many. Yolanda's mother, for instance, had done the right thing, working, before her marriage, in the garment district of Manhattan to help put her three brothers through medical school.

But one family member, notable by her absence, was Cousin Marie, Yolanda's mother's first cousin, a woman who had been estranged from the family for as long as anyone could remember. Cousin Marie, it was conceded by all, was brilliant. Though a female, she had gone to college, and yes, she had even married. But then she had gone too far, both literally and figuratively. "She had worked for a year in Europe as a translator," says

Yolanda Mercutio, "so therefore she did not have a traditional ladylike occupation." To make matters worse, Cousin Marie did not want children. When her husband pressured her, she did the unthinkable and divorced him. Thus unencumbered, she joined an advertising agency known for its international accounts, and within a few years had become one of its vice presidents, traveling back and forth between New York and Europe.

Yolanda had never met her cousin, but even when she was a young child something about Marie captured her imagination. "As a child, I thought of her as being like one of the women that Katharine Hepburn played, like a lady lawyer, which is what I wanted to be at the time. I was always her defender. I thought she was wonderful, and I wanted to meet her."

So even as a child, Yolanda Mercutio had seized on Cousin Marie as a figure of some significance, despite the fact that she was construing a family story in a way it was never openly meant to be. Three factors, in addition to Yolanda's own embryonic ambitiousness, made this possible. "The first was that my mother would always say, 'You're like Cousin Marie. You're brilliant just like she is.' "

So with her mother's perhaps subversive encouragement, Yolanda was being invited to identify with her cousin. The second factor was that there was just enough pride in the family's accounting of Cousin Marie to make identification with her permissible. "I knew there was some danger in being like her, that being so ambitious was a bad thing somehow, but the family didn't completely condemn her, which I think was fortunate for me." And the third factor was that even as a child, Yolanda recognized that too much subordination of one's own self to the familial weal could backfire. She sensed that her mother resented the sacrifices she had been asked to make for Yolanda's uncles' advancement. "My mother had been told by my grandmother that her brothers would always watch out for her, and of course they didn't. They became Americanized, life changed. I understood that promises made at one point don't always get carried out."

With this perspective, Yolanda maintained her "awe" for Cousin Marie even when her cousin, during the 1950s, not only did the unthinkable but, to the family, the unforgivable. "Her mother died, and her father, my grandfather's brother, got older, and Cousin Marie put him in a nursing home. She was unattached at the time and yet she still wouldn't stay home and look after her father. This was when she was cut off from the relatives."

Many years later, somehow or another, Cousin Marie came back into the family picture, her years of banishment having resulted in more career success, a handsome new TV producer husband, and a home on the Upper East Side of Manhattan. "All these good things had happened to her," says Yolanda, "so I felt secure." But Yolanda, who was in her early twenties by then and in graduate school working on a Ph.D. in psychology rather than a law degree, still had never seen her. "Then," says Yolanda, "there was a family function to which she was invited. I was awed, I could barely talk to her, but I made sure to tell her I was in graduate school. I think what I wanted to say was 'You don't know it, but you are an extremely important person in my life.'

"Then we went to another family function and at that function, they announced people's birthdays. May eleventh is my birthday, and they announced that it was her birthday, too! I almost died! I had felt this kinship, too. When I got married, I invited her to my wedding, and she came. I don't think anybody's presence could have pleased me more."

Yolanda Mercutio is forty now, a practicing clinical psychologist, still married and the mother of two daughters. Obviously she has not duplicated Cousin Marie's life, though she certainly fueled her own dreams—for decades—with what she knew of that life. And yet the remarkable point is that the inspiration was not Cousin Marie herself—now, Yolanda thinks, a woman of about seventy—but the family stories she heard about Cousin Marie. "I don't even know her," says Yolanda. "I met her on only those two or three occasions. And yet the stories about her influenced me tremendously. I think we're all primarily shaped by the family, and extended family traditions are rich because they give a large pool from which to draw. Cousin Marie did seem more real to me, even though I didn't know her. Because she was a family member, what she did was something to aspire to, something attainable."

The family patron saints men feel drawn to are distinct from those chosen by women. Men are raised with more options and a greater sense of latitude, but they, too, need ancestral guides as they make their way forward in the world. It may be because all people, men and women alike, are uncomfortable with the prospect of being entirely *sui generis* and need to see familial sources for themselves.

Men characteristically are inspired by relatives who are male. But most men do not choose their fathers as role models as they move away from their families and into the world. The reason may be that the internal presence of one's own father tends to inhibit rather than encourage independence; the father's presence seems imposed rather than freely chosen, and keeps the younger man perpetually defined to himself as the son, and therefore the subordinate.

Danny Ballow, now thirty-two, was the only man I interviewed who actively embraced his father as a guide, and there were several factors that made this possible. First of all, his father died before Danny Ballow reached the age of thirty, and there was no urgent need to get away from a man who was already dead. Second, Danny's father was quite an old man as Danny knew him—he hadn't had Danny, his second child, until he was well over fifty. The power Danny attributed to his father was a power his father had through the family stories Danny had heard about him when he was much younger. The father in the stories was, therefore, already somewhat removed from the father Danny actually knew. But third and most significant, his father had had a severe handicap: he had been totally deaf from the time he was an infant. Therefore, there was a particularly unthreatening valorousness—the valor of the underdog, the runt— that Danny saw in his father. His father had never seemed titanic to Danny, just courageous in the face of enormous adversity, an adversity which Danny, as a hearing person, didn't share.

The central family story for Danny, told to him by his father, is one he calls "The Story of the Shriveled Testicle."

> It loomed large in our family. I was very young when I heard it—eight or nine. My mother was ironing and she had her back to me, so since she was deaf, too, she couldn't hear it.
>
> It began with him telling me about how he had mumps, and then leaps forward to my parents' courtship by mail when he was in America and she was still in London. He told me that during the course of their correspondence, he wrote, "I think I have to tell you something. I have a shriveled left testicle, and I can't marry you because I'm not able to have children."
>
> He sealed the letter and mailed it, and then he thought, "Oh no, what did I do?" He went to the mailbox but the postman had already come and taken the letter. So he went down to the central mail office in Brooklyn. Here's this deaf man pleading to get his letter back, and they said, "Well it's somewhere in all these sacks." My father said, "I've got to get it." And he went through the sacks. I have this image of my father going through millions of letters. And he found the letter! He tore it up, and he didn't send it.

It is a story that still impresses Danny Ballow. "The story represents my father ultimately: that he just would not accept that anything was impossible. Anybody else would just have said, "Well, what can you do?" But here's my father—he's deaf, and deaf people carry less authority in society—and yet he manages to do these things. He made me really feel like I could affect the world."

There was a second story which also impressed Danny Ballow.

> There was a transportation strike in England in 1920, when my father still lived there. He had to walk to work, and then he decided to make it sort of a game. So he would time himself, and then he would try to better his time. Finally he was walking *very* fast, and somebody said to him, "Why don't you go in a road race?"

So my father did, and the first road race, he didn't know how to do anything right. He didn't wear the right shoes, and he had all these blisters. But he got better and better, and finally he got good enough to join the London Poly-technic Harriers, which is really the top athletic club. He became a very great athlete. He went on to hold the American record for race-walking twenty-five miles, and there are boxes of clippings to prove it.

Danny Ballow, with his father as a model, has gone on to embrace his father's belief that he can do anything. Profession-ally, as a historian, he has done exceptionally well. While still in his middle twenties, he was offered a teaching position at an Ivy League university. His first book was published—and ex-tremely well received by a number of the most significant aca-demic patriarchs in his field—before Danny turned thirty. He has a second book published and a third book now under way, plus offers from both academic and commercial publishers for a variety of other undertakings. "I've gotten a tremendous amount from my father," he says. "I think I'm just beginning to realize that. Everything is influenced by him."

And yet this intense embrace of his father as a role model is perhaps possible because, in addition to the reasons already men-tioned, Danny Ballow has in some ways always defined himself in opposition to his father, thus enabling him to keep his father at a necessary distance. "My father thought goodness was as-sociated with how much money you had. I have the opposite view of money. I really deliberately never wanted to equate money with any kind of moral good, and I've chosen a profession where I earn very little money, a profession which my father could in no way understand. Also for a long time, I never did any sports, and I never wanted to. I had only contempt for it."

People's choice of a role model stems from what they already have, what they need, and what is available for them to choose from. Danny Ballow seems to have found a stance in relation to his father with just the right amount of productive dynamic tension. One suspects that had he needed more from his father, he would have had to reject more, or reject it more vehemently, just to keep the balance. But as these things go, his is a choice that works. He sees himself as an unimpaired man with a confident sense of his own ability to shape and affect the world.

Gerald O'Connor, a fifth-generation Irish-American, had also been strongly affected by his father, although more by his presence than by influential family stories about him. In fact he believed that throughout his growing-up years, his father had been his most powerful role model, and Gerald's source for his own wry humor and love of storytelling. Furthermore, like Danny Ballow's father, Gerald's father was dead by the time he reached adulthood. He died at forty-six when his son was not much more than twenty.

But there the similarities between the two younger men's experiences of their fathers end. Gerald O'Connor's father was, on the whole, a baleful role model, passing on to his son a legacy of doubt as well as a strong inclination toward alcoholism and suicidal self-destructiveness. Therefore, while Danny Ballow, at thirty-two, could keep his father to help him move on, Gerald O'Connor, also thirty-two, had to let his father go in order to move on. It was a more complicated and more painful undertaking than Danny Ballow had had to face.

But if Gerald O'Connor had simply let go—if such a thing were possible were at all—he would have been left empty-handed. At the time I met him, he was trying to find out more about his great-great-great-grandfather in the hopes that he could make him a potent enough role model to counteract his father's legacy. "I've been thinking a lot about him," mused Gerald, "because in the last year there have been a number of estates to settle, wills, contested trust funds. Mostly by way of documents from lawyers, I've become acquainted with uncles, great-uncles, and especially my great-great-great-grandfather, who I'm desperately trying to get information about. I'm soon going to go home to South Hadley, Massachusetts, to get references from the town records and newspapers."

The legal documents may have given Gerald O'Connor a focus for his concerns, but his passionate interest in trying to escape the legacy of his father, and several other O'Connor men, had to do with the fact that Gerald himself had entered what has traditionally been a dangerous decade for O'Connor men, a decade when they married, raised families, undertook conventional professions, and drank excessively. The self-destructiveness invariably accompanied their prosperousness.

It was an understanding of masculinity that Gerald had already embraced. Indeed to do other than what his father had done struck Gerald O'Connor as "traitorous," and therefore only another role model from among the O'Connor men seemed to offer Gerald an alternative that wouldn't make him feel that he was betraying his father. "What I want is at once to be a cultivated man whose pleasures are civilized. I want to be well read and well educated"—which he already was, having attended Amherst, like his father and grandfather before him—"and I want to take pleasure in all those things. But I also want to be remembered and known as a rough-and-ready guy who, if you pester him in the barroom, will punch you in the nose, and all that silly manly stuff. I'm never more comfortable than when I'm standing at a bar drinking and talking with a friend. It's wonderful because it's tradition, it's masculine behavior, and it's full of wonderful opportunity for talk."

So for Gerald O'Connor, masculinity was inextricably linked with drinking. No teetotaler, family member or otherwise, could possible serve him as a masculine ideal, but he had been combing through the generations of O'Connor men looking for an ancestor who had been "manly" without destroying his liver in the process. When I met him he had already rediscovered his great-great-great-grandfather, Anthony O'Connor, who had come to Massachusetts from Ireland more than a century earlier.

"He was called Red Anthony," says Gerald, "and as a kid I would hear about him. The mythology about Red Anthony was that he was the strongest man in Holyoke, Massachusetts. He was able to lift a keg of beer from the floor to the bar. I loved the notion of this brawling burly red-haired guy. It was his strength and vigor and burliness and irreverence."

As to the truth of the story, to Gerald it's a matter of indifference. "The whole story may be apocryphal. It doesn't matter,

either." Nonetheless, he feels, or has made, a connection with
this earliest O'Connor, which, when I met him, he was intent
on pursuing. When he had gone home the previous Christmas
he had "asked a lot of questions," and the day before I spoke
with him, he had been making phone inquiries trying to find
the location of Anthony O'Connor's grave.

He had already made two connections which were of value
to him. Gerald's middle name was Anthony and that pleased
him. Also, he knew that his great-great-great-grandfather had
had red hair. "I'm not red-haired," he said, "but when I grow
a beard, it's a red beard." So in a fashion, he saw himself as
being the recipient of at least a few of Anthony O'Connor's
genes, and that was an inheritance that, to Gerald, augured
well. "He embodied what I want," said Gerald, meaning a way
of reckoning with alcohol, thus preserving for himself a masculine attribute without being vanquished by it. The proof of
Red Anthony's success was that he hadn't died young of alcohol-
related disabilities. "I don't know what he did for a living, but
I know he had a fairly conventional life and death. He had a
wife named Barbara, and some sons—one who was a priest, one
who ran off and disappeared, and one who was my great-great-
grandfather Martin, a very bright, industrious guy, who by the
time he was in his twenties had made something of a fortune
for himself, making those great ledger books the railroad used
to use. He, too, was a great paternal father figure."

Perhaps because of his age and perhaps because of the complicated nature of his undertaking, rife with the danger of betraying his father, Gerald O'Connor is still very much in the
throes of sculpting a suitable and useful familial role model for
himself. There is, to his account, an experimental feel, a ten-
tativeness and a very rich disorder. But his reflections illuminate
how intricate a process creating an ideal is and how much fertile
imagination it takes to fully become oneself while simultaneously
maintaining loyalty to one's family.

One of the ironies of Gerald O'Connor's heritage is that it
presumes the innate familial ability to succeed at work and yet
simultaneously devalues it. This presumption may stem from the

fact that the O'Connors have been assimilated Americans for
so long that they take for granted their access to the most prestigious academic and corporate institutions. Those with newer
roots make no such presumptions. Indeed, if one has come from
a working-class background or an ethnic minority, even dream-
ing about certain professions may seem a form of hubris.

For both men and women, finding a suitable work identity
and integrating it within their overall sense of themselves is a
major undertaking. Because of the way things were, women don't
have as much ancestral help in this effort as they could use.

Men are luckier. In choosing familial role models they are
often able to find a male ancestor whose achievements in work
life seem analogous to their own dreams. Such ancestors seem
to provide a permission to proceed, leaving their heirs free of
the feeling they are moving too far away from the shade of the
family tree. In some cases, a man may be able to intensify his
commitment to a specific career or vocation because a male
lodestar relative had undertaken—and succeeded at—a related
calling. This was certainly the case with Carlos Morton, a playwright who grew up in Chicago. The ancestor who inspired him
was his grandfather Lopez, a man he'd never known and in fact
a man his own mother had barely known, since he died when
she was nine.

"I have pictures of my grandfather Lopez, and he's a very fair-
skinned man with a high collar and a tie and a suit. He was a
writer, a newspaper editor in Havana. Just recently, I found
copies of his articles. My aunt had them. I had always been told
he was a writer, and I believed it but I couldn't see the proof.
But seeing those articles—it was like finally discovering a part
of me that I never knew! I read what he'd written—he had a
column and wrote all kinds of things. He had his biases and
prejudices, but he was a very articulate man."

Now, Carlos Morton is a playwright and his grandfather Lopez
was a journalist, but for Carlos the difference in genres seems
to be irrelevant. In fact he recounts his own work history in a
way that emphasizes the similarities between the two. "I always
knew I wanted to be a writer. I wanted to be a newspaper writer,

and I used to work for the city news bureau in Chicago, as an editorial assistant and copywriter. Finding out about my grandfather's stuff sort of hit the nail on the head. God damn! I felt like it was in my blood. Or in my destiny or something. I felt I took the right vocation after all."

Carlos Morton's phrasing perhaps reveals the psychic undertaking involved in his resurrection of his grandfather Lopez, especially in his announcement that it was like discovering "part of me that I never knew." There are two ways of reckoning with what we might call the family oversoul. The first way involves feeling oneself absorbed by it, so that one doesn't feel like oneself but like a drop in the larger bucket, or a chip off the old block.

But Carlos Morton has taken the family oversoul—here represented by his grandfather Lopez—and defined it as an extension of himself: "the part of me that I never knew." The happy result is that his sense of self is enhanced while, simultaneously, he need not forgo his sense of affiliation with his family. If anything, his sense of his grandfather Lopez allows him to feel more, not less, affiliated with them. Carlos Morton knows himself to be middle class. But previously he had felt that this facet of his identity took him away from his family. "You see, I had always thought that we were very poor; you always get the impression of immigrants dressed in rags. My mother had only a sixth-grade education, and after my grandfather died, the family hit hard times."

But the more he discovered about Grandfather Lopez, the more he felt that the ground he walked on—economically as well as professionally—had already been cleared by his grandfather, a revision which gave him more room to move. "My mother's family was a hell of a lot better off earlier on than I had thought, until my grandfather died." And so Grandfather Lopez, whoever he actually was, helped do for Carlos Morton what Don Juan did for Carlos Castaneda—he became an aspect of Castaneda himself as he moved through uncharted territory on his way to somewhere new.

Though men often use their patron saints to help them navigate their way into their work, what the patron saints offer need not always relate to an heir's work. Sometimes the similarities are simply what allow the heir to make the special connection to a predecessor, just as Yolanda Mercutio saw special significance in the fact that she and Cousin Marie had the same birthday, or as Gerald O'Connor applied great meaning to the fact that when he grew his beard, it was red, just like Red Anthony's hair.

Ted Court, a carpenter and contractor, had already set up his business by the time his maternal great-grandfather Orville Oates began to matter deeply to him, but the handiness he shared with his antecedent seemed the first proof of their likeness. Says Ted Court, "The interesting part for me is at the time of his marriage"—Ted himself had been married just a year or two—"he was a carpenter contractor. He built houses all around New England and the South. Then, after he went through the Civil War, he settled in Olmsted County, Minnesota, just outside of Rochester."

Orville Oates was successful enough as a craftsman so that the local papers of his time carried occasional stories about him. "I was able to do research up there and found whole bunches of stories about him," says Ted Court. In the course of combing through old newspapers, Ted Court came across a photograph of his great-grandfather, and the fact that the two men, separated by almost a century, bore an uncanny resemblance to each other intensified Ted's sense of connection. "The fact that I look like Orville just blew me away. I was in the county historical museum at the time—I'd planned this trip there with my mother—and I showed the picture to the woman at the desk. She said, 'Whew, you sure are kin to him!' "

Orville Oates had not always been a figure of significance to his great-grandson. "As a kid, I'd hear the name Oates and maybe that he worked with wood. My earliest memories of him might have been that he was this old, slow-moving sodbuster, and I couldn't even figure out why anybody would want to know about him."

What changed for Ted Court seemed to be that he had recently entered into a new phase of his life—not just marriage, but the wish to create a family with his wife, Rowena—and felt that he had arrived inadequately equipped for family life. He was very much a Court man in his own mind, and what this meant was that he had an inclination toward angry violence. "I can just fly off the handle, and I allow myself to rant and rave. My grandfather, my father's father, according to stories I've heard, would come home from work highly mad, frustrated, pissed off, and upset. He would slap the kids around, push them around, and he would abuse my grandmother verbally." Ted's own father had behaved to his own family in somewhat the same manner. "My father used to come home drunk when I was a kid. He would say, 'Why aren't the goddamned potatoes ready?' And he would slap at us."

What Ted Court needed, then, was a new understanding of how to live comfortably in a family. He needed—and wanted—to learn a new style or stance because he now had a wife and hoped soon to have children. In the face of this rather urgent need, Orville Oates, as he existed in family stories that Ted's mother had long ago told him, became a figure of hope and significance.

> Orville Oates was a real unusual guy. He believed that it was important after every meal for the family to kind of sit down, not talk for a while, look each other in the face, and then, maybe after a half hour or an hour, they could talk and have pleasant conversation. The half hour or hour was supposed to help the digestion, help you relax and get hold of yourself. My mother told me how, after meals, they would talk about things—about the world and about society, trying to stimulate each other's thinking. He encouraged that: the intellectual side of the family. He was also encouraging the family members to relate together and to be close. What I also see in Orville is that he was the person who fed the family emotionally and physically. Life is more sacred to those people than to the Courts.
>
> For me, anybody who would take an hour or two hours to sit with his family in the drawing room when he's got a farm and a whole bunch of other things to do—it's worth something to be like that. I don't know whether you'd call

him my archetypal image of a nice way to be, or what, but Orville Oates is it. And Orville is the way I want to be— a little bit more in control of things and not having to run your life so ragged that you're always trying to catch up with it. Orville seemed in charge of what he wanted, where he was going. He was relaxed and I want to be like that— to develop that attitude and make that happen again.

Ted Court says that his mother would often refer to this story nostalgically. "Maybe it was when she or the family were going through something hard, and she would remember and say, 'This was good,' or 'Oh, if it could be like this again.' " In short, it was an idealized image of a family man and a family's life in the past. For Ted Court, the apparent idealization of his great-grandfather does not diminish the importance of the story, for what Ted Court is in search of is an ideal, which makes it all the better if Orville Oates is purified of imperfections or even spared too rich and distracting a characterization. Ted Court's primary male legacy consisted of an extreme of masculine behavior, and his need is to augment it or ameliorate it with something softer and more soothing.

As Ted Court talks, it becomes clear that his sense of Orville Oates consists of not one, but two traits, and the hint of the second trait pokes through even the first story in his characterization of the talk around the table as "intellectual." This is another part of his ideal, one that he felt was not fostered or promoted by his Court legacy.

"Being a Court, I had to live up to images I didn't agree with. From the Courts, I got a certain pushiness, a certain boasty attitude. But it's from my mother's side of the family that I developed a sincere interest in the arts, an interest in philosophy and literature. The Court side of the family does not resonate that interest at all." Ted himself has already found a way to support his own interest in the arts through his work. He says that when he does contracting work for artists who can't afford his fees, he works by barter, accepting a canvas in exchange for what he builds.

Ted also sees Orville Oates as the familial source of his intellectual interests. "Orville Oates was in the Civil War, in Andersonville, as a matter of fact. He wrote my great-grandmother letters during the war, and gave her a subscription for some magazine. From the trenches, he wrote to her saying, 'I don't want your mind to go stagnant. I want you to keep up with reading.' "

This is Ted Court's gloss on the story because it is his need to see his own intellectual interests rooted in his familial past, all the more so because it was an interest at odds with everything Ted Court knows about his father's family. "I don't know how things get transmitted, but I guess it's important for me to feel consistent through the years with that heritage. In terms of my interest in ancient history, or my art appreciation or my interest in letters, writing, I'm much more an Oates type than a Court type."

The need to feel affiliated with Orville Oates now runs deep for Ted Court, and he does everything he can to strengthen the link straight back to his great-grandfather. His trip to the county museum in Olmsted County, Minnesota, took place shortly before his own marriage. While there he came across a newspaper account of Orville Oates's wedding, which mentioned that the couple had married beneath a bower laced with flowers.

"We pretty much duplicated all those arrangements for our own wedding," says Ted. "I built an arch and decorated it with roses." And why not? Ted Court first felt his need of his great-grandfather on the brink of his own marriage, when he recognized that he didn't like how the Court men acted as husbands and fathers. Orville Oates, a contractor, had perhaps built his own bower of earthly delights, and Ted felt it would augur well for him if he were to do the same. "It's what I wanted to do," he says, "once I saw that I could have this connection."

Both men and women are most likely to search their ancestral past looking for a role model when they contemplate some arena of life for which they feel their family has left them unequipped or ill-equipped, or when they are actually on the verge of some major rite of passage, often relating to marriage or work. Among the people I interviewed, those most likely to be preoccupied with a family role model were men and women in their twenties or thirties.

Women and men with close ties to their appointed familial guides had much in common. Yet there was a distinction between them too. The men were not content with the stories alone. The stories were their starting point, and from there they went on to read old newspaper clippings, visit county museums, and call cemeteries. The obvious explanation for this is that what men do is more often acknowledged in the world beyond the family simply because, historically, men have lived more in the world than women have, or at least their doings have been of more interest to the world. Women, up till recently, have rarely been major athletes or professionals of any sort.

But the more subtle reason, as I suggested earlier, is that the family has not, characteristically, meant the same thing to men as it has to women. For women, the family has been their arena, and family culture has evolved, generation to generation, under their guardianship. Men, on the other hand, are always slightly less at home in the family. Therefore, although men too are profoundly shaped by the family, they also look to the world in order to find their place. For men, then, it is ideal—and an act of integration—to be able to find in the world references to and information about someone they first discovered at home.

CHAPTER 10

IN PURSUIT OF FREEDOM

M ariana Russo comes from a family that has always kept an attentive eye on their dead. Soon after her grandmother died, her grandfather put a glass of water and a piece of bread on the windowsill so that the spirit of her grandmother wouldn't go hungry. This Mariana knew from a story she had heard from her aunt. But her mother and aunt, teenagers at the time, hadn't understood the significance of the offering and had taken it away. "My grandfather scolded them for it, and he put it back again."

Mariana Russo hadn't quite known what to make of the story when she heard it. "It was just like a tradition, maybe a superstition, to me. I didn't really believe a spirit was going to come for the bread and water. But I was a lot younger then, and I think I almost pictured in my mind the scene of it all happening and even a spirit coming to get the bread and water."

Mariana Russo still remembers the day when her mother told her the story of how her grandmother had died, even where they were sitting when her mother told her.

I was about ten years old, and she was sitting in the chair in the kitchen when she told me. She said that when her mother died, everybody was getting ready for school. It was

early in the morning, and her mother was in the kitchen
fixing the breakfast. Suddenly, she just collapsed. She died
of a heart attack. My mother was the only one that wasn't
up. She was still in bed, lollygagging about, and they got
her up, and I believe they put her mother on her bed. I
believe my grandmother died before they could get the
doctor there. My mother was sixteen or seventeen at the
time, still in high school. She said she had had a premonition that her mother was going to die.

She didn't say a whole lot more, just what I told you,
and then she cried. For some reason I was shocked when
she cried. I thought that so much distance and time would
end those feelings.

The story might have been relegated to the attic were it not
for what happened in Mariana's own life. Ten years ago, when
Mariana herself was sixteen, her own mother died. It was a slow,
painful death, agonizing but certain. "My mother had cancer
and they knew she was going to die, but I wouldn't accept it. I
wasn't letting it sink in because I didn't want her to die." Mariana
remembers that the very night before her mother died, she went
out on a date. "A friend of mine said to me, 'How could you
have gone out when your mother was that sick?' I guess that
really got to me because by the next morning my mother was
gone."

The friend's reproach was incidental—Mariana Russo was already immobilized by her own sense of guilt. She felt guilty over
her denial of her mother's illness in the first place, guilty for
what she felt was her abandonment of her mother, and still
guiltier over her anger at her mother's helpless abandonment of
her. Mariana still remembers that on what turned out to be the
last afternoon of her mother's life, she was angry that her mother
was so sick that she couldn't even tell her what had happened
that day in school.

To an outsider, Mariana's reactions were understandable. She
was then in the throes of adolescence, needing both to cling to
her mother and to push her away. Given Mariana's own need,
her mother's unavailability was therefore more devastating than

it might have been had Mariana been more securely anchored in her own life. Her denial of what was happening, one of the more primitive human defense mechanisms, was the best she could manage in order to cope.

But none of this diminished Mariana's overwhelming sense of guilt. Was there anything that could? Even ten years after her mother's death, she had by no means mastered her own guilt, but she had found a way to at least nick, if not hack, away at it, and her efforts involved a new vision of the story about her grandmother's death that her mother had told her so many years before.

As Mariana now retold that story, she took care to underscore the parallels between her own experience and her mother's, and she did so with a satisfaction that verged on pleasure. She pointed out that she and her mother were both sixteen when their own mothers died, both still in high school. "Another connection I make with that story my mother told me is that when my grand-mother died, my mother was still asleep, and they had to wake her up, and when my mother died I was still asleep, and they had to wake me up. Also my mother said she had a premonition about her mother's death, and I did, too. One day in class, a terrible shiver just went through me, and I thought, 'She's going to die.' I knew she had cancer, but I didn't accept it, and so to me, it was like she died of a heart attack."

There is another parallel as well. "My mother died at three o'clock in the morning, and I was the only one who slept through it, just like she was the only one who slept through her mother's heart attack. Everyone else in my house was awake—there were relatives and the doctor, and then the coroner. It's strange that I slept through it," says Mariana, genuinely puzzled, "because I'm such a light sleeper. Any little noise wakes me up. And what's really strange was that her bedroom was right next to mine, and her bed was right up against my wall."

Though one might observe that Mariana was projecting her own experience onto her mother's story, the parallels she insisted on in her new understanding of the story not only reaffirmed her connection with her mother, but they transformed her mother back into the daughter she had been, back into the daughter that Mariana still was. Thus, in a sense, Mariana could see herself and her mother more as allies than adversaries.

And that perspective gave Mariana her first shot, through some rather intricate machinations, at lessening her own guilt. If her mother had had almost the identical experience, then wasn't there the hope that her mother could, in Mariana's mind, take Mariana's own point of view? And if Mariana could imagine her mother doing that—having also been a "lollygagger" in bed—then wouldn't her mother have understood Mariana's apparent abandonment of her? If Mariana could believe her mother would have understood, then she could also believe her mother would have forgiven her, and then—and here was the psychological destination Mariana hoped to arrive at—Mariana could forgive herself.

Mariana is by no means completely successful in this undertaking. For one thing, she is, at twenty-six, still learning her own ropes and still not all that far away from the devastating experience of her mother's death. It is an experience that still has not settled into its meaning for her. "It'll be ten years in October that my mother's dead," says Mariana. "One day I have fond memories of her, and the next day I hate her, and I still haven't gotten to the point where I can accept having both. And I always have sad feelings about her."

In addition, her efforts to come to terms with her relationship with her mother are, she feels, stymied by her aunt's view of her mother. "My aunt," she observes, "has made my mother into a saint." It is a vision of her mother to which Mariana herself is susceptible, and it is a damaging vision because it throws Mariana right back into her guiltiest sense of herself: to have abandoned and been angry at a "saint" is invariably unforgivable.

The freedom Mariana Russo pursues is freedom from guilt through forgiveness, and she seems implicitly to understand that she is still in the throes of her venture. Mariana Russo thinks that someday, she, too, would like to put out bread and water for the spirit of her mother. "I want to carry on the chain of tradition. I would like to keep that going as much as possible.

And when I have a child, if I ever tell my child about my mother dying, I'll probably cry, too."

Mariana Russo's efforts to use her mother's story to forgive herself can hardly, at this point, be called successful, but her undertaking points to a particularly valorous and creative use one can make of family stories. It is not only that we embrace them with their meanings intact when we need them—as those who searched through family stories for role models did—but that, in the pursuit of some particular freedom for ourselves, we refashion them, reinterpret them, and make them mean something they never meant at all when we first heard them. And yet the paradox of such efforts is that for all they potentially offer by way of emotional reward and for all the artistry at the heart of the effort, they can't be undertaken deliberately; they are essentially unintentional, a tropistic groping in the direction of the light. Still, to make one's family stories one's own in the truest sense is to achieve the greatest autonomy—the autonomy of one's own point of view—while keeping hold of the best of one's connection to family.

Today, at forty-five, Mimi Runkle is a Chicago radio producer, a workaholic with a perpetual worried furrow in her brow. She worries about work, but also other things: one winter day it is a construction worker she sees out of her office window who prances about on a girder hundreds of feet in the air; another day, it is about an active pregnant friend, now in her seventh month, who she fears will imminently give birth in a taxi, or worse. Her attentiveness to both work and friends is conscientious and unflagging. She is loved and respected for both, but somehow she's never very pleased with herself or what she's done, either as a friend or as a professional.

Given the opportunity, she will compare herself unfavorably with relatives as far back as she can go. "My own life, in my view, does not measure up to the achievements of my great-grandparents, or my grandparents." Yet there are no hidden millionaires in her lineage, only generations of small farmers and entrepreneurs, who, on her mother's side, were members of a strict religious Protestant sect.

"My father went to the fourth grade," she says, "and my mother went to the eighth. Given the departure point I had— all the education and advantages—I somehow have not made as much of my opportunity as they did of theirs. I don't feel I have to show for my life at forty-five what my father had to show for his at thirty-five. When he was thirty-five, he had a ten-year-old bakery business, a wife, and three children. He had a home that was paid for, a car that was paid for. He never bought anything on time, ever. Me, I'm struggling on the salary I make. I don't know if I make more than he did or not, but he handled it better." Her expression is serious, her furrow deep as she brushes back a hair that has escaped from the tight bun she wears on top of her head. She is neither kidding in her self-assessment nor digging for compliments.

The severe, almost Calvinistic perspective Mimi Runkle applies to her own life is, she knows, her legacy from her family and the legacy she has most needed to disavow. "The primary message I got from my family was to work hard. Being lazy is unforgivable. To improve yourself is essential. The legacy of all that authority made you feel you have to somehow work harder all the time.

"Then there's the whole issue of money. A question my father always asks me is 'Are you saving money? How much money have you saved?' And I'm not my father's daughter because I haven't really saved any money. Compared to my father, I haven't really saved anything. There's a Horatio Alger cast to a lot of my father's stories. He literally did come here from Germany with fifteen dollars in his pocket, and within a very short time, he was on his way to becoming a very successful businessman. He tells me that he did everything in the most honorable way possible, without cheating or lying or stepping on anyone."

In the Runkle canon, there were many instructions but few permissible pleasures. Even family meals were not meant to be pleasurable. Instead eating was a job, and it had to be done efficiently and without distractions, such as conversation. "Daddy tried hard to have the same rule at his dinner table that his father had had at his, which was that there was no talking while we were eating. He used to tell us about a switch that his father had that hung from the middle of the ceiling over the table. There were ten kids around that table and *Grossvater* would take the switch and hit whoever spoke during the meal. There's an incredible legacy of authority on both sides of the family that has been handed down to me, and I've been fighting it all my adult life. I see that it's shaped me in ways I don't want to be, but it's such an integral part of my perspective of life. It was really drummed into us that all the adults at that dinner table had had a hard, strict life and that strict obedience on every level of life was a virtue—whether it was child to parent, or citizen to state, or member to church. Obedience was the watchword."

In contrast to everything the Runkles valued stood the gypsies. "Both families—my mother's and my father's—were familiar with gypsies," said Mimi. "They were 'poachers' and of course the farmers hated the gypsies, *hated* them, and were afraid of them. These people were heathens roving the countryside, stealing. And so when the gypsies did come, everybody would shut their doors. The next morning chickens would be gone, grain and corn would be stolen. My mother told me this. Those were prominent family stories, always told in a very disapproving tone. Even in this country, they were afraid of gypsies taking the children away. I had learned about gypsies in school, and I understood that they had a very different perspective, a carefree life."

Mimi was ill-suited to be a severe and abstemious Runkle, but her efforts to fulfill her own sensuous needs were made even more difficult by the fact that, at the same time, she also had the need to be the "obedient" daughter they so clearly wanted. But even as a child, she was one of the gypsies' party, drawn toward what was "carefree" and pleasurable. And she knew it, although she didn't dare voice it. "I didn't understand why my family had to be so severe on the gypsies. I often wanted to go back and be another voice in the story, saying, 'Give the gypsies water! Give them a chicken tonight! Give them corn! You have abundance on this farm. It's not going to hurt you to give to them.' "

There was an idiosyncratic exception to the Runkles' intolerance of what was carefree and pleasurable—a small crack in their otherwise formidable armor—and Mimi Runkle, epicure at heart that she is, knew it and seized on it. Even in their stories, there was a small vein of sensuosity, an attention to the physicality of things. "There was talk about what things looked like, what they smelled like, pleasure in the physical abundance of their simple farming life."

The dichotomy seemed to be that one's physical surroundings—the rooms one lived in, the food on the table—could be assembled with care and could—and indeed *should*—look beautiful even though one dared not take obvious pleasure in the results. Nonetheless, it was a permission that Mimi Runkle has embraced. In her bathroom, there is a newly renovated little alcove. Amidst a collection of pink-and-silver-tinted seashells are her body oils and emollients, all artfully arranged. Nearby, a fresh bouquet of flowers. The meals she serves to guests are made with an eye to beauty: a deep green parsley sprig against a freshly cut lemon wedge.

And music permeates her life. Mimi Runkle majored in music at college, and her radio is always on, even when she's not at home, allowing her the pleasure of walking into an apartment filled with symphonic music. In her work as a radio producer, she is most often involved with symphonic broadcasts, live or recorded.

She has not escaped her family legacy of severity entirely, but she has succeeded in going slightly beyond it, given a headstart by the vein of physicality they permitted. In her efforts, a few slight family stories have been of use, both in giving her something to interpret by her own lights and also in reinforcing and broadening the point of view she has long been heading toward. One story is about her maternal grandfather, who, as he is customarily characterized, was a model of religiosity.

> Everybody talks about my grandfather as being this stern man whom they respected. That was a key word. But in one story, my aunt Judith remembers him as this handsome

young man who used to cavort in the snow to entertain them when they were inside, sick or whatever. He had two horses he loved which weren't workhorses, and that was suspect because, you know . . . pleasure. He didn't allow dance music, but sometimes he would sit at the radio and tap his feet, and someone would say, "Oh, Grandpa . . ." and he would stop.

There was a judgment to these stories as they were told, a judgment of his susceptibility to pleasure, but Mimi Runkle heard the story differently. "I always thought it was too bad that he couldn't enjoy life more." And perhaps because she too respected him, his inclinations toward the mildest of pleasures made her own more acceptable to herself.

But the story which she took to heart even more was, aptly, a story about the gypsies. It was told to her by her father, and it was meant to be a warning against the gypsies and their carefree life, but Mimi Runkle has ultimately reinterpreted both her father's motivation for telling her and the story itself in a way that gives her more epicurean leeway than she might otherwise have had.

My father said that one day he and Uncle Bill were gathering blueberries in the woods, and they had been taught to be careful because the gypsies were prevalent there. They had been taught never to speak to them.

Well that day, crossing the road—I don't know how, but somehow—they got to talking to some gypsies, or some gypsies cornered them. My father tells this story over and over again. He remembers being trapped between their wagon and their horse. He was right there, and he couldn't get out. He was a very little boy, and he is convinced to this day that they wanted to kidnap him because he says they kept enticing him with things. Now I don't know if this was fantasized or if this really happened. He was a handsome little boy with tow hair and blue eyes. He had been told the gypsies stole children. And Daddy considers it a great stroke of his assorted ingenuities that he managed to escape from the gypsies.

But he talked over and over about the painted wagon

and how beautiful it was and how beautiful the woman was who sat in the wagon. I think he had a sense of the differentness of their lives. He always had this little streak of pleasure in him.

Even as Mimi Runkle tells the story, there is little to suggest that her father meant it as other than the cautionary tale it seems to be, so repeatedly is the motif of the danger of the gypsies underscored. But what she has fastened onto is, first, the frequency with which he told it—perhaps because it dramatized his essential conflict about pleasure of the senses—and second, his attention to what was beautiful about the gypsies. With no other encouragement than that—and with just a hint of ironic disparagement of his "assorted ingenuities" in arranging his escape—she has refashioned it into her father's small but implied permission to pursue what is pleasurable. In doing so, she seems to have attributed to her father an interpretation that is more nearly her own, but has nonetheless reaped the benefits for herself of what she has attributed to him.

The first time I ever saw Linda Lefkowitz, it was dusk and we were both guests at a very large floating birthday party on a chartered Hudson River dayliner that was circling Manhattan. The band was playing loud rock, and Linda, dressed all in white, was dancing alone, sensually and ecstatically, thoroughly consumed by the music. There was a self-conscious element to her dancing, to be sure, but she was clearly getting great frenzied pleasure as well.

Pleasure and glamour turned out to be important elements in her life. Later, when I'd gotten to know her, I learned about the dramatic adventures facilitated by her life as a writer. There were romances with rich, powerful and, occasionally, famous men. There were trips that took her to the movie sets of well-known directors in exotic European locations, fashion pieces that brought her to the Far East, travel pieces that transported her to South America, and, as a result of several of these pieces, television appearances on nationally broadcast programs. All of

these adventures she undertook with great relish, insisting that
the world and its inhabitants look at her. For Linda Lefkowitz,
it was never tourist class on the red-eye flight, it was always first
class on the *QE 2*, eye-catchingly bedecked every inch of the
way.

None of this could have been predicted. She grew up in the
Bronx, the daughter of a candy store owner. The family stories
she had heard as a child—stories about the cossacks, her grandfather's gangrene, hurricanes, and "suffering women"—told her
over and over that the world was a dangerous place and that
the Lefkowitzes were "little people" in constant jeopardy. The
narrative atmosphere of "What if?" perpetually snuffed the life
out of "Why not?" "To be a Lefkowitz," she says, "means to
suffer endlessly in an alien and hostile world, to survive, but
not to be proud of that fact." And the key to survival, she had
learned from her family stories, was "vigilance," keeping an ever-
watchful eye on a dangerous world.

One of the most prominent stories was a cautionary tale about
her cousin Izzy, and the possible dangers he courted by dancing:

> My cousin Izzy was coming to America, and in prepa-
> ration for the boat journey here, he hollowed out the heels
> of his shoes, so that he could hide his diamonds in them
> and not have to clear them at customs. And on the ship,
> there was a card game. They were playing cards and then
> dancing.
>
> At any rate, Izzy got all involved in the dancing and
> took his shoes off so he could dance better. My mother was
> too young to have been the seeing-eye in this story, so it
> was probably my grandmother—Izzy was her brother. So
> my grandmother got worried that Izzy would forget the shoes
> and that the diamonds would get lost.

Oddly, to me at least, that's the end of the story. There is
no further anecdotal addition where it's made clear that Izzy *did*
have his diamonds stolen, or for that matter, that he didn't. But
the fate of the diamonds, says Linda Lefkowitz, is not the point.
"The real emotional center of the story," she says, "is that he

wasn't alert, he wasn't vigilant. He got seduced and betrayed by gambling and dancing. The story is about worrying, which is what they mostly do," an activity which must, to the Lefkowitzes, seem constructive in an otherwise unmanageable world. It is a story whose meaning is clear to those who understand the Lefkowitz worldview.

Had Linda Lefkowitz's legacy of family stories simply rolled off her back? "No," she says emphatically. "These stories my mother told me really taught me lessons. Bad lessons. I inherited so much of that stuff, and I can't wait to get rid of the last of it." And yet these stories had not been imposed on her. She asserts that she actively reached out for them. "I'm obsessed with these stories, and I made a very deliberate effort to find out about them because they're an important part of my life history."

The additional—and crucial—point is that Linda Lefkowitz did not hear only the straightforward relating of events but the subliminal message. "How did I take all these stories of failure and make life possible for myself? I know that I am the child of women who managed to save themselves. The women in my family took the children, trekked across Europe, and escaped. So all those horror stories are also stories about courage. They're never told to me that way. They're told to me as misery, but I hear the courage."

There are more layers to her answer as well. She learned early that women suffer, but unlike Mimi Runkle, she did not receive huge story instructions on the virtue of obedience. She never had much desire to be the obedient daughter.

Furthermore, amidst her story legacy were stories about family black sheep, outlaws, and the skeletons in the closet—all of whom made appearances in cautionary family stories about people who had broken the rules—and very early on she decided to cast her lot with them. "I'm a family skeleton," Linda announces evenly. "If you asked my mother to tell you family stories about the family skeletons, she would tell you about me." There was a cost to Linda's solution, to be sure, but it was also an ingenious solution since it allowed her to both cut loose and stay connected.

Paramount among the black sheep, for instance, was her grandmother Lefkowitz, her father's mother. "My grandmother was definitely a 'bad woman' because she broke the rules: she played cards and went to the theater—on Saturday afternoons she'd take me to shows at the Roxy—and she wore perfume and makeup. My mother was horrified. My grandmother had a lot of pleasure in life that was very much frowned upon. She was my link to being in the world and not being stuck at home.

"I think I'm like my father's mother," Linda continues. "And I look more like the Lefkowitzes than like my mother's side. The Lefkowitzes all have dark hair, dark eyes, and a facial structure like mine." So once again, like others who have an almost magical belief in what the genes can carry, Linda believes that her capacity for pleasure may have come straight from her grandmother Lefkowitz. But in this choice of a role model, she differs from the others who have appointed family sources for themselves in adult life because she has had to transform the stories about her grandmother she heard—turn bad into good—for her grandmother to be of use.

A second and perhaps more important black sheep is Linda Lefkowitz's cousin Melvin. Today, he too runs a candy store in the Bronx, but the inspiration he provided Linda with came from stories about him in his earlier life. "In family stories, Melvin is the bad guy, the black sheep. My cousin Melvin wanted to be a dancer as a professional, a ballroom dancer. In my family, there's no appreciation for being artistic. So his father prevented him from doing it." It's a story which doesn't offer much, but meager as it was, Linda Lefkowitz embraced it, inspired by the valor of his wish.

But Cousin Melvin features as a bit player in two other small stories important to Linda. One of them is about when Linda was born. "When I was born, my mother was very groggy from all the anesthesia. Cousin Melvin had come for a visit, and the first words out of my mother's mouth were 'Melvin, will you teach her to dance?' " The story ends without Melvin's answer, though one assumes he agreed.

Small though it is, it is a story with real possibilities. It is, for example, a story which might have pointed to a crack in the armor, a moment when Linda's mother seemed to reveal her deepest wishes that her daughter should be more free than she herself was. But Linda only laughs in response to this suggestion. "My mother changed her mind about it later." Instead, she says, perhaps ironically, all it demonstrates is how groggy her mother was.

But the story works for because of the transformation of the material she herself has made. In its likeness to the tale of Sleeping Beauty, it has become a story in which Melvin is endowed with the magical powers of a fairy godparent, the power to help Linda escape from a fate that seemed inevitable. The fact that he, a favorite relative and a fellow black sheep, is the first guest at her mother's bedside has an importance to Linda that it surely did not have to her mother. He is the responsible godfather attending to the needs of his spiritual ward.

Thus Linda has taken a family story and made it her own first story, an appropriation that requires imaginative transformation. This is because one's autobiography is made up not just of what happened but of a view of oneself from a certain perspective. Given the perspective, certain facts, though true, are irrelevant, while other facts are accorded importance because they seem to support the vision of oneself, stated or unstated, that governs the autobiography. But even the facts that do matter have to be presented so that their significance is clear. The story of what happened between Linda's mother and her cousin Melvin are facts that mean something to both Linda and her mother, but something different to each. Therefore the story, originally her mother's, had to be tailored to fit Linda's own sense of her self. And in the tailoring, in the developing of one's own story, lies the pursuit and attainment of freedom.

If Melvin is introduced so early in Linda's story, it may be because he is very soon alluded to again in a family story Linda was told about herself. "This is my favorite childhood story. When I was a little girl, I named my dolls after the people who gave them to me, which seemed perfectly sensible to me. And I remember standing there at five with this gorgeous golden-haired, blue-eyed doll dressed in a dress that my grandmother, my mother's mother, had made. And these grown-ups said to me, 'What is your doll's name?' And I said, 'Melvin.' And they laughed and they laughed, and I didn't know why they were laughing."

One can see why Linda Lefkowitz would find significance in this story and continue to feel affection for it. First, it casts her comfortably with her favorite fellow outlaw—the doll comes from Melvin. But second, the outlaw doll has been dressed by the grandmother whose viewpoint was much the same as her daughter's, as Linda's mother's, and herein lies the significance: "Somewhere in that, there was permission to be like Melvin, somewhere in their mind, they approved of what he offered," at least as Linda has reinterpreted the story. Third, she is voicing a "perfectly sensible" piece of information, which the others, of course, don't understand. What she relishes in this moment is the image of herself as a lawbreaker from the beginning, but a lawbreaker who means no harm, who is simply applying a different system. It is a lawlessness that is therefore free of defiance. But also, despite her lawlessness, it portrays a moment when she is embraced by familial laughter, a friendly and approving laughter. She is different from them, an astute child among the dimmer grown-ups, and her perspective is different from theirs, but she is accepted all the same. "Somewhere in all that, there was permission for me to be different," says Linda, fully aware that she has invented the meaning of their lines and hence, invented a permission they did not, in fact, give. In context, then, Linda's dancing is her defiance, or a symbol of her defiance, just as her family's warnings about dancing are symbolic of larger warnings about vigilance. They understand each other perfectly.

I spent one winter afternoon sipping margaritas in a Columbus Avenue bar with David Wills, a composer of classical music whose works have been performed in concert by the New York Philharmonic, conducted by Boulez and Ozawa. I would have anticipated that as a Black man not from a background of privilege, David would have had some trouble claiming the entitlement to do what he does.

But no, the soft-spoken, self-assured man sitting across from me felt the entire business of entitlement had been taken care of by his mother. "What is it Freud said? A first-born son who has the approval of his mother is a force that can move mountains, heaven and earth. Coming from my family, there's no question but that I had to command respect." His permission to enter music also came from his family, especially from his grandmother, who insisted on music lessons for her own children and some of their children. "She was a very powerful woman," says David, "and the inspirer of people to do good works. 'Make something of yourself' was ever on her lips. As a result, I always feel I'm on the path. I never feel lost."

David Wills also mentioned that in the past he'd had trouble claiming time to be alone, time to compose, time to have for himself and his work, which didn't always look like work. The issue wasn't selfishness; it was that the necessary gestation time for any of his musical compositions looked like unacceptable idleness, like wool-gathering, even to David himself.

But in the course of our conversation, it emerged—slowly—that David Wills had gotten permission to "wool-gather" through his refashioning of a somewhat equivocal family story that his grandmother had told him about her father, his great-grandfather. It wasn't clear for a while what the story meant to him, only that it was deep under his skin, insistently tickling him.

David Wills's great-grandfather was a full-blooded Creek Indian who was also part of the Black community in Burnt Corn, Alabama. He was a man at once familiar and alien to his daughter. "She always spoke of him with great affection, though I think she never knew quite what to make of him. He was Christian—I think anyone in the South in the nineteenth century had to decide they were Christian—and 'a pillar of the community.' " Clearly David Wills's grandmother approved of these aspects of her father.

But this wasn't the part of the story that riveted David Wills. Instead his gaze was fixed on the part of the history his grandmother judged most severely. "Every once in a while he would disappear," says David Wills, "sometimes for weeks on end. He would flee, go off into the woods, into the deep forest of his people." The family would know he was gone again only when there was an empty seat at the dinner table, or they failed to hear him in the morning, getting ready for the day. There was never warning. He often disappeared wearing the suit and tie he had put on that morning. "I never found out whether he took off his suit and tie when he left."

One time David's grandmother went with him, though whether she secretly followed him or begged to be taken David doesn't know. She told him that the Indians didn't talk much. "The thing she really remembered," he says, "is that they could sit on their hair."

The obvious appeal of such a story is that, like the tale of Robin Hood, *A Midsummer Night's Dream*, or *Huckleberry Finn*, it offers the freedom of the fresh green woods as an alternative to the suits and ties of civilization. If necessary, it is a freedom anyone can enjoy without even admitting to, since one doesn't have to decode the woods to feel the breeze. But this wasn't what the story meant to David Wills. In fact, he had never put into words, even to himself, why the story mattered to him.

It was only as we were winding up our conversation a few hours later that the power of the story became clear. It was in the context of David Wills's explaining why he had told that particular story to one of his own sons, a very talented artist in the fine arts, a medium different from his father's. "His mother is very upset that he hasn't had gangs of friends, and I try to assure her that he's highly talented according to everyone around him, and that he's happy."

Was it that it was important for his son to be able to claim space for himself, just as David Wills had, and just as his great-grandfather had? "Yes," said David. "I hadn't thought of that but that's the pattern, isn't it? I talk to my son a lot—these stories are important to him—and I felt that that story would be viable for him because it was viable for me."

Viable? "Yes, viable to me as a model. There are a lot of things about my great-grandfather that I like. I like that he was both a pillar of the community part of the time, but that he also disappeared into the woods, and answered the call of the wild part of the time. I like that.

"When I have a gang of people around, I get lost. I can't work. For me to look back for a male figure that I identify myself with—I think it would be my great-grandfather more so than my grandfather, who was an intellectual but very removed, or my father, who was accessible but not an intellectual. He was generous and hardworking, but he was a weekend alcoholic. And so I see this guy who looks like he's a synthesis of a lot of good stuff. I think I cling to that story a lot. My grandmother— I adore her, and I think she's the greatest thing in the world, but she still isn't a male. I can't fully identify with her."

In the course of this epiphany, David Wills never did say how the story of his great-grandfather related to him or his work as a composer. He never decoded his own metaphor, perhaps because, given his obvious admiration for his grandmother, he didn't want to acknowledge directly that the part of the story she had found troubling was the part that he loved, but it was clear that the charge for him had to do with answering "the call of the wild." As David Wills seemed to construe a story that was, for him, symbolic, his great-grandfather was not simply running *away*, he was running *to*, returning to people like himself. And in a way, to go just one step further on the same path, he was returning to himself, just as David Wills does when he is at work.

So David Wills was a tiny bit of an apostate. He knew what he needed—a retreat from suits and ties—but he had a hard time permitting himself his retreat, since it looked so much like idleness. But he hadn't known—perhaps out of courtesy to his grandmother, who believed that "her Indian half of her heritage would burn in hell"—that he had used her story, transformed it, to permit himself the psychic space in which he could sit around on his hair.

When Polly Gardner, a painter, visited Texas for the first time, she was startled by the vast blue open dome of the sky and the flatness of the land. There was so much room that anyone could stand up straight. She was tied to Hardburly, Kentucky, where she'd been born and had grown up; she loved its textures and its colors, and she depicted them again and again in her paintings, but she felt all the same that the craggy, gnarled Cumberland hills were fingers in a clenched fist, caging her, obscuring the sky.

Polly looks almost as if she had been fashioned from that unyielding soil. She is spare, even bony, or so I thought one day as she sat in my kitchen, not eating her soup, not finishing her sandwich, and not drinking her tea. Although she is only thirty or so, she already has a pinched quality, something that Walker Evans and James Agee would have seized on. And yet there is a generosity and a droll humor to her, and sometimes a lyricism that distracts one from her physical meagerness as she talks about her family and its stories.

There was nothing in either her family or the mining town where she'd grown up that seemed to promise much of a future for her, much less a future as an artist. Today she is a prize-winning painter with a strong regional reputation and the beginnings of a national one, having recently had a show in a New York gallery. Most of her ancestors, she says, were miners or alcoholics, or both. And as for the residents of Hardburly, "They graduate from high school and marry their prom dates. The guys go into the coal mines, they put a trailer in the backyard, and maybe they take over their mother's house, their father's house, when they die. Maybe they put aluminum siding on.

"You should see Hardburly. It's where CBS News comes and says, 'Here's a poor coal miner out of work,' one of the worst coal-mining areas in Kentucky. They all have these gaunt faces—you look at the children hiding behind the women, and the sparkle's gone out of their eyes. You've seen people who have no life? It's a whole town like that, and the children get crushed really early.

"From the beginning to where I am now," Polly continues, "it's been a long trip. I'm the only one in my family with a college degree. There were a hundred in my high school graduating class. There are only three of us with terminal degrees—two ministers and me with an MFA. And maybe there are a few more—seven to eight—who have gone to college so they could replace dead English teachers at the junior high. They're the ones who have put aluminum siding on their houses." She laughs wryly. "Even as a little kid, I knew I wanted out."

In short, there was little that had nourished her and nothing that had inspired her, with the exception of her mother and her grandmother, both of whom had raised her after her mother's divorce when Polly was six months old. "I had a lot of love from my mother and my grandmother. I really believed my grand- mother when she said, 'Believe in your dreams.' I don't know whether she meant it or not, but each time it was like a little cheer. 'Don't give up.' She was a harsh woman," Polly adds, "very religious and very right-and-wrong about things. There's very little gray in my grandmother's life. I'm about the only thing she's ever allowed to be gray. I was allowed to be different. I was allowed to be weird."

So as Polly Gardner experienced her grandmother, she re- ceived from her at least the seeds of entitlement, not to be an artist specifically, but to try whatever she needed to try. From her mother and her grandmother as well she heard one or two stories about herself, seeming dross which she has turned into gold. They are stories which she now tells about herself, part of her *Königsroman*, because they place her impulse to be an artist back in her childhood, giving her a sense of the depth and continuity of the urge.

"They tell me that I always wanted to be alone as a kid. I didn't want to be held. To keep me from crying, they would put me in my bed by the window, and I'd lie there all day looking out. If they tried to interact with me, I'd get upset. 'She's al- ways been weird. She wouldn't even let us hold her as a kid.' When I was a little older, I spent a lot of time in the woods by myself.

"Now I know I was telling stories in my head. I was the Lone Ranger in my head. My mother and I would go for walks in the woods. She offered me a sense of play and a real sense of fantasy. While I was the Lone Ranger, she was Betty Grable. My mother offered me a lot of freedoms, and that's where I think my art comes from now—that first period with the freedom and the visualness. I was allowed the freedom of going into the woods."

But what Polly Gardner relied on most heavily to give her a boost up and out of Hardburly, Kentucky, consisted of two family stories that had a powerful and sustained impact on her, stories that (once she'd transformed them) fed her for years. The first story, previously mentioned, was about a family black sheep—her paternal grandfather, a physics professor who impregnated his secretary, married her, and then, three days after the wedding, joined the merchant marines and "was never seen again."

It was, as it was told to Polly, one of several stories testifying to the unreliability of men. "I see the screwup of values in it—he abandoned a pregnant lady, which is not a good thing to do, but I've always thought it was a neat story." Ironically enough, Polly's father used to invoke the story, negatively, in order to underscore unflattering likenesses he saw in both his father and his daughter after she'd quit her teaching job because it interfered with her painting. "He used to say, 'You must be a vagabond just like your grandfather. It must be in your genes.' He didn't want me to be an artist. He tolerated my being an art major because he figured I might end up marrying an engineer."

But this unflattering story ultimately became a vehicle that allowed Polly Gardner to pursue her vocation because it allowed her to value and embrace a "selfishness" she saw as absolutely necessary to her art. "My grandfather didn't surrender. He could have surrendered and said to his wife, 'Oh, let's go back home.' But he knew he couldn't live that way.

"I like the story, and maybe I use the colorfulness of it to say, 'Oh, I can be colorful, too'—not eccentric—but it offered me more than I found in a lot of lifestyles I saw. I also learned from it to value things that other people will call selfish. I try hard not to hurt anyone, but I will incorporate selfishness to get what I want, to do what I want, to demand my own time and my own space."

In transforming a less than ideal family story so it permitted her detachment and retreat, she is similar to David Wills. But the likeness of their maneuvers is even more pronounced in relation to Polly Gardner's second story about an Indian ancestor. That story, even more than the first but very much like it, concerns Polly's grandmother's grandfather, her own great-great-grandfather, and, to the rest of the family, an irredeemable black sheep.

> His name was Caldwell—that was his first name. When he started having children, that became their last name. He was a real character—an Indian and a scout for the cavalry. I have a template of him, one of the first photographs on metal. It's sepia. He has long braids that reach over the front of his gold-buttoned cavalry uniform.
>
> He was an alcoholic [here Polly laughs uneasily] and he retired from the United States government with a small pension check. That's the way the story goes. I don't really know what changes it took in getting to me. He had a bunch of children, and his wife had died—probably from having to take care of eleven children by herself because he was no help. But she had everything under control.
>
> Then Caldwell married a much younger woman, and she wanted part of the pension check to run the household. That was his money, and he said no. He drank it all. He was the town drunk.
>
> Then I guess he pretty much flipped out. Or something happened. So she reported him to the law, the sheriff or the marshal. She was trying to have him arrested so she could take over the money. And Caldwell put on his cavalry outfit and went to the mountains.
>
> Now Hardburly sits like this [Polly indicates with her hands a valley between two mountains] and one of the mountains has a rock cliff on it. It's right outside my grandmother's house. They realized that he was there on this rock cliff, so they sent a little posse out to get him. They were saying, "Come down, come down," but [and here Polly laughs again] instead of coming down, instead of turning over his check to his wife and children, he just sort of jumped off the rock.

This is not a story which the rest of the Gardners rush to embrace. "All my cousins know it," says Polly, "but I'm the only one trying to bring it back. 'Aw,' they say, 'that dumb shit. He jumped off the cliff.' " But for Polly, in whose version the story ends with a soaring leap, it is not a story about defeat, alcoholism, and suicide. She does not say, 'He knew he would die, that the rocks below would batter and gore him.' Instead, like Milkman in search of the meaning of an ancestor's life in Toni Morrison's *Song of Solomon*, she understood that "if you surrendered to the air, you could *ride* it." That story allowed her to fly in a number of ways.

The second value of the story for Polly Gardner has to do with the fact that her great-great-grandfather Caldwell was an Indian. Her own painting, she had said, was very indebted to nature, to her own early experience of the natural world and its colors and textures. Caldwell was, to the white cavalry officers, a decoder of nature's signs, a follower of its portents. Caldwell knew nature and the officers did not. "Sometimes I've wondered," said Polly, "if that quiet way of looking at nature that I have is a little bit of Indian heritage in me." What the story offered Polly—as David Wills's had offered him and as such stories offer a good many others—was a diffuse belief in the mystical power of the Indians, and more particularly the Indian genes which were part of her birthright.

In a broader way, the story, as Polly Gardner hears it, gives her a substantiality and a feeling of "specialness" that she wouldn't otherwise have. "I grew up feeling that I was nonspecial in a nonspecial place. That story made me feel that maybe there was a little bit of something special going on, that maybe I did have a little something going for me—a little background, a little glitter, a little strength from the past, a little heritage. Everything else in my background I was kind of ashamed of. It was the only thing in that town or in my background where I thought, 'That's neat!'

"I'll always have trouble with my ego—there's a voice always saying, 'Why should I? . . . What makes me think I can do this? . . . I'm nobody, I'm nobody.' But these stories have little quirks that I think I've taken something from. They were saying, 'There are alternatives.' Without those stories, it probably would have been too late before I realized there were alternatives, ways to get out. Very few get out, but," she says, the sparkle in her eyes intact, "I got out."

Lucky for Polly Gardner that she got out; lucky, too, that she didn't leave empty-handed but took with her stories that could provide, even if she had to transform them herself. Perhaps making such personal meaning of our family stories is the ideal final destination for all of us.

But what has come before is not merely a means to this end. When I think now of my favorite family story as a child, about the night my great-grandmother ran off in her shift, I understand that it remained such a powerful story at very different periods of my life because of its versatility.

For a young child, it was a good love story with a dash of adventure; there was the thrill of seeing a defiant daughter triumph. But it was also an invitation into the community and culture of family, a culture built on the bedrock of language. Families have their heirlooms, of course—their bibles and photographs, their locks of hair and cameos, their dance cards and pocket watches. But without the attendant family stories, these are dead objects robbed of their mana and ready for the flea market. And so what family stories do, as mine did for me, is welcome the child into a context, into the realm of shared living meaning. The stories are the medium that keep all those heirlooms afloat with significance, the agent that thickens the air in our midst with meaning.

If our first effort is to enter into a group, and absorb without resisting, our next, some years later, is to distinguish ourselves in the family's midst, to reach independently for what's at hand. The stories are there and they mean something, but they acquire an additional charge once we've asked the questions to which we see these are the answers. Family stories, whatever else they are, can be little moments of history or slices of sociology. As to our personal questions about who we might become, family stories obligingly offer us our own talismans and mentors, whose chief virtue is that they willingly go back to being good old characters in a good old story once our need is past.

Eventually we come of age and tell the story of our own lives in which the past has become our prologue; we have our own family and invent an ethos for it. This is the stage of transformations, willed or unwilled, the point at which we make our own meanings. Our meanings are almost always inseparable from stories, in all realms of life. And once again family stories, invisible as air, weightless as dreams, are there for us. To make our own meanings out of our myriad stories is to achieve balance—at once a way to be part of and apart from our families, a way of holding on and letting go.

NOTES

INTRODUCTION

9   See Robert N. Bellah et al., *Habits of the Heart: Individualism and Commitment in American Life* (New York: Harper & Row, 1986), p. 154.

PART I • FAMILY STORIES AND THE FAMILY

CHAPTER 1 • FAMILY GROUND RULES

18   *There was once a study:* See Leonard Covello, *The Social Background of the Italo-American School Child: A Study of the Southern Italian Family Mores and Their Effect on the School Situation in Italy and America,* ed. and with an introduction by Francesco Cordasco (Totowa, N.J.: Rowman and Littlefield, 1972), pp. 376–381. See also Nathan Glazer and Daniel Moynihan, *Beyond the Melting Pot,* 2nd edition (Cambridge, Mass.: MIT Press, 1970), pp. 194–202.

19   *On a statistical level:* These are figures from the 1983 Census, cited by Alex Shoumatoff, *The Mountain of Names* (New York: Simon & Schuster, 1985), p. 172.

   But it seems to me that men's hold on the family: Lawrence Stone makes the point that the "affective" family—a family which perceives itself as owing *emotional* fealty to its members—is a relatively new development, no older than seventeenth-century England. Earlier, "one wife or one child could substitute for another, like soldiers in an army. The purpose in life was to assure the continuity of the family, the clan, the village or the state, not to maximize the well-

being of the individual." Stone does not, however, distinguish between men's and women's emotional roles. See his book, *The Family,
Sex and Marriage: In England 1500–1800*, abridged edition (New
York: Harper Colophon Books, 1979), esp. pp. 149–180, 254–299.
See also Robert N. Bellah et al., *Habits of the Heart: Individualism
and Commitment in American Life* (New York: Harper & Row, 1986),
pp. 85–90.

21   *Family stories such as this:* All the data in this paragraph appear in
      "Who's Taking Care of Our Parents?" *Newsweek*, May 6, 1985, p.
      61.

22   . . . *the emotional responsibility continues to fall on the women in the
      family:* See also Glenn Collins, "Many in the Work Force Care for
      Elderly Kin," *The New York Times*, January 6, 1986, p. B5; and
      Nadine Brozan, "Infirm Relatives' Care: A New Women's Issue,"
      The New York Times, November 13, 1986, pp. C1, C6.

      Anthropologist Robin Fox believes: Cited in Shoumatoff, *Mountain of
      Names*, p. 27. From Fox's *Kinship and Marriage: An Anthropological
      Perspective* (New York: Cambridge University Press, 1984).

23   *If the mutual bonds between mothers and children:* As Alex Shoumatoff
      demonstrates, historically the family bond between brothers, at least
      in many European countries, has been fraught with resentment as a
      result of primogeniture. See Shoumatoff, *Mountain of Names*, pp.
      98–99 and ff.

24   *Erik Erikson, in* Childhood and Society: See Erikson's chapter "Re-
      flections on the American Identity," especially pp. 288–305, 2nd
      edition (New York: W. W. Norton & Company, 1963).

30   *In* Habits of the Heart: Bellah et al., p. 154.

CHAPTER 2 • FAMILY DEFINITIONS

34–35 *The late David Kennedy:* See Peter Collier and David Horowitz, *The
       Kennedys: An American Drama* (New York: Simon & Schuster, 1984).
       Collier and Horowitz write of the Kennedy family definition in terms
       of "the Kennedy Legacy." For Robert F. Kennedy, it meant: "No
       longer was it enough to be personally ambitious, as Joseph Kennedy
       and Jack had been; now a Kennedy must prove his right to lead by
       accepting responsibility for a whole liberal philosophy and social
       tradition" (p. 365). An offshoot of the Kennedy myth involved
       tenets such as "Kennedys don't cry" (p. 383).
            From early childhood David Kennedy was perceived as having un-
       Kennedylike "weaknesses," including a "fondness for wildflowers,"
       and "a tendency to cry" (p. 343). The implication is that one of
       the ways the Kennedys could continue to subscribe to their myth

was by defining David Kennedy as something less than a true Kennedy, despite the fact that his father, Robert F. Kennedy, identified with him as the "runt" (p. 343), and was genuinely tender with him.

35 *The breadth of definition:* While family therapists often define family "myths" in a negative fashion because of the distortion they inevitably involve, there are some practitioners who see the family myth as something benign which provides coherence and unity. See Edward M. Scott and Kathy L. Scott, "Healthy Families," *International Journal of Offender Therapy and Comparative Criminology*, Vol. 27, No. 1, 1983, pp. 71–78. Scott and Scott hold the conviction that family myths exist in healthy families and are in fact necessary.

40 *To put it another way, as writer Alex Shoumatoff has:* See Shoumatoff, *The Mountain of Names* (New York: Simon & Schuster, 1985), pp. 79–80.

44 *. . . families . . . claim as their own . . . exactly those traits which . . . might be used to stereotype them:* For a discussion of how ethnicity correlates with belief systems, see Monica McGoldrick, John K. Pearce, and Joseph Giordano, eds., *Ethnicity and Family Therapy* (New York and London: The Guilford Press, 1982). In the volume see, especially, Monica McGoldrick, "Ethnicity and Family Therapy: An Overview," pp. 3–30; and John Spiegel, "An Ecological Model of Ethnic Families," pp. 31–51.

    Meanwhile both the Holmeses and the Terrells: See McGoldrick et. al., *Ethnicity and Family Therapy*, especially David McGill and John K. Pearce, "British Families," pp. 457–479. "British Americans are taught that the meaningful issues and struggles of life all lie within the self and that there are few external constraints that cannot be overcome by individual effort" (p. 458). See also G. Gorer, *The American People: A Study in National Character* (New York: W. W. Norton & Company, 1964).

CHAPTER 3 • FAMILY MONUMENTS

62 *But there are regrets, dissatisfactions, and reluctances that inevitably attend even the most deeply welcomed marriage:* For a discussion of this, see Monica McGoldrick, "The Joining of Families Through Marriage: The New Couple," in *The Family Life Cycle*, ed. Elizabeth A. Carter and Monica McGoldrick (New York: Gardner Press, Inc., 1980), pp. 93–94.

63 *The central paradox and challenge of marriage is that we have to make family out of someone we're not related to:* Peter Berger and Hansfried Kellner do not pick up the issue of spouses' becoming family, but they discuss at length the process whereby "two strangers come to-

gether and redefine themselves." See Berger and Kellner, "Marriage and the Construction of Reality: An Exercise in the Microsociology of Knowledge," in *The Psychosocial Interior of the Family*, 3rd edition, ed. Gerald Handel (New York: Aldine Publishing Company, 1985), pp. 3–20.

64   *As folklorists have observed, the courtship story tends to be a staple:* See Steven J. Zeitlin, Amy J. Kotkin, and Holly Cutting-Baker, eds., *A Celebration of American Family Folklore: Tales and Traditions from the Smithsonian Family Folklore Collection* (New York: Pantheon Books, 1982), pp. 82–92. Especially informative is an article by Steven J. Zeitlin, which argues that family courtship stories "typically transfigure reality" in three ways: by establishing the motif of love at first sight, by suggesting that destiny has played a part in the match, and by including in the story fictional correspondences. "As the narrative is told across generations," Zeitlin writes, "it becomes progressively less bound by historical reality and approximates still more closely an informal tradition of family courtship stories." My discussion of family love stories has been enriched by Zeitlin's observations. See Steven J. Zeitlin, " 'An Alchemy of Mind': The Family Courtship Story," *Western Folklore*, Vol. 39, No. 1, 1980, pp. 17–33.

 It is the first collective memory of the new family, paradoxically shared in even by children who were unborn at the time: In literature as well as autobiography, how the protagonist's parents met is often, by convention, perceived as part of the protagonist's own story, from Dickens's *David Copperfield* to Russell Baker's *Growing Up*.

70   *Anthropologist Robin Fox speculates:* In Alex Shoumatoff, *The Mountain of Names* (New York: Simon & Schuster, 1985), p. 231.

 Alex Shoumatoff writes that intermarriage also occurs in nonrural populations: Ibid., p. 232.

73   *A story she would never have told:* Our sense of our own autobiographies is always in flux, always in revision. For more on the fluid nature of our stories about ourselves see the writings of Roy Schafer, especially "The Psychoanalytic Life History," in *Language and Insight: The Sigmund Freud Memorial Lectures 1975–76, University College, London* (New Haven and London: Yale University Press, 1978), pp. 3–27; and *The Analytic Attitude* (New York: Basic Books, 1983).

CHAPTER 4 • UNDERGROUND RULES

76   *. . . what social scientists have to say about the varying ethnic groups:* See note for Chapter 2, page 44.

80   The section entitled "Illness and Injury" is based on the assumption, widely held in the literature of family relations, that individual mem-

bers of a family have implicitly designated roles to play in the family—
e.g., the sick one, the smart one, the lazy one, the stupid one, and
so on. The "healthier" the family, the more flexible the roles; the
"sicker" the family, the more rigid and narrow the roles. In the most
distressed families, there is usually a member designated as the emotionally "sick" one. Family therapists say this "scapegoat" is the
symptom bearer for the entire family.

See Murray Bowen, *Family Therapy in Clinical Practice* (New York:
Jason Aronson, 1978); Salvatore Minuchin, *Families and Family Therapy*
(Cambridge, Mass.: Harvard University Press, 1974); Mara Selvini
Palazzoli, Luigi Bosco, Gian Franco Cecchici, Giuliana Prata, "Fam-
ily Rituals: A Powerful Tool in Family Therapy," *Family Process*,
Vol. 16, No. 4, 1977, pp. 445–453; and Ezra F. Vogel and Norman
W. Bell, "The Emotionally Disturbed Child as the Family Scape-
goat," in *The Psychosocial Interior of the Family*, 3rd edition, ed.
Gerald Handel (New York: Aldine Publishing Company, 1985), pp.
401–419.

86   *"An individual relates to members of his or her nuclear family"*: Norman
Ackerman, Introduction to "The Family with Adolescents," in *The
Family Life Cycle: A Framework for Family Therapy*, eds. Elizabeth
A. Carter and Monica McGoldrick (New York: Gardner Press, Inc.,
1983), p. 150.

93   *As A. Alvarez pointed out:* See A. Alvarez, *The Savage God: A Study
of Suicide* (New York: Bantam Books, 1973), p. 106.

94   *This is how theoreticians:* See Ivan Boszormenyi-Nagy and Geraldine
M. Spark, *Invisible Loyalties: Reciprocity in Intergenerational Family
Therapy* (Hagerstown, Md.: Harper & Row, 1973).

CHAPTER 5 • FAMILY MYTHS

98   *. . . shared blood means shared susceptibilities:* There is ample evidence
from psychiatrists and psychologists that mental illness *does* run in
families and that it is silently and secretly transmitted from one
generation to another through a process that is still imperfectly
understood. See R. D. Scott and P. L. Ashworth, "The Shadow of
the Ancestor: A Historical Factor in the Transmission of Schizo-
phrenia," *The British Journal of Medical Psychology*, No. 42, 1969,
pp. 13–32. Particularly susceptible to such "transmission" are "those
patients with a parent who has been exposed in the first five years
of life to illness in a close relative," such as a parent or sibling (p.
31). Scott and Ashworth believe "the affected parent was led to
form a particular relationship with a child who was born quiet and
undemanding—a relationship which forced that child into an identification with the 'image' of the ill relative" (p. 31). What is in-

novative in Scott and Ashworth's analysis is that they believe the transmission of mental illness has to do with "social influence"—or family culture—rather than genetic factors.

Family therapist Murray Bowen also believes mental illness can be transmitted through the generations through the family culture and "years of nagging pronouncements." See Bowen, "The Use of Family Theory in Clinical Practice," in *Family Therapy in Clinical Practice* (New York: Jason Aronson, 1978), pp. 152–155.

99   *As Bruno Bettelheim explained:* See Bettelheim, *The Uses of Enchantment: The Meaning and Importance of Fairy Tales* (New York: Alfred A. Knopf, 1976), pp. 5–6.

102   *In every family, say family theorists, individual members have their assigned roles:* See Scott and Ashworth, "Shadow of the Ancestor," p. 27; Dennis A. Bargarozzi and Steven Anderson, "The Evolution of Family Mythological Systems: Considerations for Meaning, Clinical Assessment, and Treatment," *The Journal of Psychoanalytic Anthropology*, Vol. 5, No. 1, Winter 1982, p. 72; Bowen, "Use of Family Theory," pp. 154–155; John Byng-Hall, "Family Myths Used as Defence in Conjoint Family Therapy," in *Developments in Family Therapy: Theories and Applications Since 1948*, ed. Sue Walrond-Skinner (London and Boston: Routledge & Kegan Paul Ltd., 1981), pp. 105–120; John Byng-Hall, "Re-Editing Family Myths During Family Therapy," *Journal of Family Therapy*, Vol. 1, 1979, pp. 103–116; and H. Stierlin, "Group Fantasies and Family Myths," *Family Process*, Vol. 12, 1973, p. 120.

The first to elaborate on the notion was psychiatrist Antonio Ferreira: See his article "Family Myth and Homeostasis," *Archives of General Psychiatry*, Vol. 9, 1963, pp. 457–463.

He asserted that these beliefs go unchallenged: Ibid., p. 457.

103   *The individual family member may know:* Ibid., p. 458.

. . . *those who do therapy . . . make the assumption:* See note for page 80 on the work of Mara Selvini Palazzoli et al.

104   *If enough people think someone is incompetent:* See Lily Pincus and Christopher Dare, *Secrets in the Family* (New York: Pantheon Books, 1978), p. 38.

106   *"The myth, like the defense":* See Ferreira, "Family Myth," p. 462.

PART II • FAMILY STORIES AND THE WORLD

CHAPTER 6 • THE PECKING ORDER AND HOW TO SURVIVE IT

115   . . . *59,000 free Blacks:* Lerone Bennett, Jr., *A History of the Negro in America: 1619–1965*, revised edition (New York: Penguin Books, 1980), p. 62.

. . . *half a million free Blacks:* Geraldyn Hodges Major with Doris E. Saunders, *Black Society* (Chicago: Johnson Publishing Company, 1976), p. 4.

. . . *slaves of their own:* Bennett, *History of the Negro,* p. 72. See also Michael P. Johnson and James L. Roark, *Black Masters: A Free Family of Color in the Old South* (New York: W. W. Norton & Company, 1984), and Michael P. Johnson and James L. Roark, eds., *No Chariot Let Down: Charleston's Free People of Color on the Eve of the Civil War* (Chapel Hill: University of North Carolina Press, 1984).

116   *Folklorists have said:* William H. Jansen, "The Esoteric-Exoteric Factor in Folklore," in *The Study of Folklore,* ed. Alan Dundes (Englewood Cliffs, N.J.: Prentice-Hall, Inc., 1965), pp. 47 and ff.

117   . . . *two million Italians arrived here: Harvard Encyclopedia of American Ethnic Groups,* ed. Stephan Thernstrom (Cambridge, Mass., and London: The Belknap Press of Harvard University Press, 1980), p. 547.

         They seem to be characters in ethnic jokes: Ethnic jokes seem to have existed for at least the last century. See Stephanie Bernardo, *The Ethnic Almanac* (Garden City, N.Y.: Dolphin Books, 1981), p. 360.

119   . . . *they are split, as folklorists have observed:* See Wilcomb E. Washburn, "The Noble and the Ignoble Savage," in *Handbook of American Folklore,* ed. Richard M. Dorson (Bloomington: Indiana University Press, 1983), pp. 60–66. See also Robert F. Berkhofer, Jr., *The White Man's Indian: Images of the American Indian from Columbus to the Present* (New York: Alfred A. Knopf, 1978).

123   *Those who feel themselves to be insufficiently welcome:* See, for example, Clayton Faris Naff, "At Home in the Smithsonian," in the "My Turn" section of *Newsweek,* September 10, 1984, p. 10. He writes, "Our only wealth was a treasure of immigrant stories saved up by my aunts and uncles."

125   *"There is hardly an American":* The quote of Alexis de Tocqueville is cited by Milton Singer, "On the Symbolic and Historic Structure of an American Identity," *Ethos,* Winter 1977, p. 433. Singer argues that in American culture there are "sudden swings" between desire for the future and nostalgia for the past (p. 432).

132   . . . *a zealous amateur genealogist:* All references to Stanley Perin's account may be found in his article "A Tradition in Search of Its Origin," *New England Historical and Genealogical Register,* Vol. 121, 1967, pp. 29–36.

133   *As one Black folklorist put it:* See Kathryn Morgan's *Children of Strangers: The Stories of a Black Family* (Philadelphia: Temple University Press, 1980), p. xiii.

145   *"Every real story . . . contains":* See "The Storyteller" in Walter

Benjamin's *Illuminations*, ed. and with an introduction by Hannah Arendt, translated by Harry Zohn (New York: Schocken Books, 1969), p. 86.

CHAPTER 7 • OF MONEY, SELF-WORTH, AND LOST FORTUNES

147   *Money is such a powerful symbol:* See Robert H. Walker, "Rags to Riches," in *Handbook of American Folklore*, ed. Richard M. Dorson (Bloomington: Indiana University Press, 1983), pp. 67–72.

150   . . . *at the heart of the American experience:* For an insight into several specific unspoken assumptions of American culture, see Alan Dundes, "Folk Ideas as Units of World View," in *Toward New Perspectives in Folklore*, ed. Americo Paredes and Richard Bauman (Austin and London: University of Texas Press, 1972), pp. 93–103. For a discussion of the myths that underlie our culture, see "American Cultural Myths," in *Handbook of American Folklore*, pp. 56–59.

        Also see Richard Sennett and Jonathan Cobb, *The Hidden Injuries of Class* (New York: Vintage Books, 1973), pp. 20 and ff; on the subject of American assumptions see Ronald Segal, *The Americans: A Conflict of Creed and Reality* (New York: The Viking Press, 1968), pp. 22–30 and ff.

151   *Anthropologist Margaret Mead had an explanation:* Margaret Mead, *And Keep Your Powder Dry*, revised edition (New York: William Morrow & Company, 1965), pp. 43–45 and ff.

        Among the Puritans: See Harvey Wish, *Society and Thought in Early America* (New York: David McKay Company, Inc., 1950), pp. 29–30.

        This analysis of the symbolic importance of money: For more on the idea of plenty, see Dundes, "Folk Ideas as Units," pp. 93–103.

152   Alexis de Tocqueville, *Democracy in America*, ed. J. P. Mayer, trans. George Lawrence (Garden City, N.Y.: Anchor Books, 1969), pp. 281–283.

        When they fail to make money: See Sennett and Cobb, *Hidden Injuries*, p. 97. For an insight into how "luck" and "initiative" prove difficult to reconcile for a young man in a well-to-do Black family, see Robert Coles, *Privileged Ones: The Well Off and the Rich in America*, Vol. V of *Children of Crisis* (Boston: Atlantic Monthly Press, 1977), pp. 335–337.

156   *A much more serviceable variety of family story:* See Mody Boatright, "The Family Saga as a Form of Folklore," *The Family Saga and Other Phases of American Folklore* (Urbana: University of Illinois Press, 1959), pp. 1–19; Stanley Brandes, "Family Misfortune Stories in American Folklore," *Journal of the Folklore Institute*, Vol. 12, 1975, pp. 5–17; and Steven J. Zeitlin, Amy J. Kotkin, and Holly Cutting-

Baker, eds, *A Celebration of American Family Folklore: Tales and Traditions from the Smithsonian Family Folklore Collection* (New York: Pantheon Books, 1982), chapter on "Lost Fortunes."

160 Studs Terkel, *Hard Times* (New York: Avon Books, 1971), pp. 19–21.
Folkorists have observed: Brandes, "Family Misfortune Stories," p. 7.

PART III • FAMILY STORIES AND THE INDIVIDUAL

CHAPTER 8 • Legacies

166 *As family therapists:* See Lily Pincus and Christopher Dare, *Secrets in the Family* (New York: Pantheon Books, 1978), p. 38.
. . . *design coherent, if changing, narratives about our lives:* See Roy Schafer, *The Analytic Attitude* (New York: Basic Books, 1983). Schafer writes: "In psychoanalysis, the versions of significant events change as the work progresses, and with these changes go changes in what is called the experience of these events, for the narrative accounts and the experiences are inseparable" (p. 186). Thus "there is no single all-purpose psychoanalytic life history to be told, for the account of that life keeps changing . . ." (p. 204). These ideas are developed at length in Chapters 11–15 of Schafer's book.

167 *In Jean-Paul Sartre's biography of French playwright Jean Genet:* See Jean-Paul Sartre, *Saint Genet: Actor and Martyr* (New York: George Braziller, 1963), p. 17.

184 *As Margaret Mead demonstrated throughout her books:* See especially Margaret Mead's *Sex and Temperament in Three Primitive Societies*, 2nd edition (New York: William Morrow & Company, 1963); and *Male and Female: A Study of the Sexes in a Changing World*, Apollo Edition (New York: William Morrow & Company, 1967).

185 *According to Eleanor Maccoby and Carol Jacklin's study:* *The Psychology of Sex Differences* (Palo Alto, Calif.: Stanford University Press, 1974).

187 Susan Brownmiller, *Femininity* (New York: Simon & Schuster, 1984), p. 213.

CHAPTER 9 • FAIRY GODMOTHERS AND PATRON SAINTS

199   *Whether we call them role models:* See Gail Sheehy, *Passages: Predictable Crises of Adult Life* (New York: E. P. Dutton & Company,
1974), pp. 27, 51–52, 131–132.

202   *It was only as an adult:* Sheehy observes that women, who often give
over their twenties and even their thirties to nurturing, may find
themselves in the throes of an identity crisis, and in need of a mentor,
in their thirties or forties, later than men do. Ibid., especially pp.
108–109.

207   . . . *the internal presence of one's own father:* Sheehy, *Passages,* pp.
37–43.

CHAPTER 10 • IN PURSUIT OF FREEDOM

224   . . . *in the pursuit of some particular freedom for ourselves:* Throughout
this section, "autonomy" is synonymous not with achievement or
absence of impediment but with a feeling of self-centeredness in the
most benign sense. It is what Dickens may have had in mind for
David Copperfield, who begins to tell his own life story with the
story of his birth, a story surely told to him by someone else. Copperfield's very first words, which open the book, are "Whether I
shall turn out to be the hero of my own life, or whether that station
will be held by anybody else, these pages must show." His effort is
to transform stories he heard about himself into the stories he tells
about his own life, to be "the hero of my own life."

ABOUT THE AUTHOR

Elizabeth Stone's articles have appeared in many national publications, including *The New York Times Magazine*, *Psychology Today*, and *The Village Voice*. She is an associate professor of English and media studies at Fordham University's College at Lincoln Center and lives with her husband and two sons in Manhattan.